Only Imagine

Only Imagine offers a theory of fictional content or, as it is sometimes known, 'fictional truth'.

The theory of fictional content Kathleen Stock argues for is known as 'extreme intentionalism'; the idea that the fictional content of a particular work is equivalent to exactly what the author of the work intended the reader to imagine. Historically, this sort of view has been highly unpopular. Literary theorists and philosophers alike have poured scorn upon it. The first half of this book attempts to argue that it should in fact be taken very seriously as an adequate account of fictional truth: better, in fact, than many of its more popular rivals. The second half explores various explanatory benefits of extreme intentionalism for other issues in the philosophy of fiction and imagination. Namely, can fiction give us reliable knowledge? Why do we 'resist' imagining certain fictions? What, in fact, is a fiction? And, how should the imagination be characterised?

Kathleen Stock is a Professor of Philosophy at the University of Sussex. She works in the philosophy of fiction, art, and imagination; and on philosophical issues around sex, gender, and sexual orientation.

Only Imagine

Fiction, Interpretation, and Imagination

Kathleen Stock

OXFORD
UNIVERSITY PRESS

Great Clarendon Street, Oxford, OX2 6DP,
United Kingdom

Oxford University Press is a department of the University of Oxford.
It furthers the University's objective of excellence in research, scholarship,
and education by publishing worldwide. Oxford is a registered trade mark of
Oxford University Press in the UK and in certain other countries

© Kathleen Stock 2017

The moral rights of the author have been asserted

First Edition published in 2017
First published in paperback 2019

All rights reserved. No part of this publication may be reproduced, stored in
a retrieval system, or transmitted, in any form or by any means, without the
prior permission in writing of Oxford University Press, or as expressly permitted
by law, by licence or under terms agreed with the appropriate reprographics
rights organization. Enquiries concerning reproduction outside the scope of the
above should be sent to the Rights Department, Oxford University Press, at the
address above

You must not circulate this work in any other form
and you must impose this same condition on any acquirer

Published in the United States of America by Oxford University Press
198 Madison Avenue, New York, NY 10016, United States of America

British Library Cataloguing in Publication Data

Data available

Library of Congress Cataloging in Publication Data

Data available

ISBN 978–0–19–879834–7 (Hbk.)
ISBN 978–0–19–884976–6 (Pbk.)

Links to third party websites are provided by Oxford in good faith and
for information only. Oxford disclaims any responsibility for the materials
contained in any third party website referenced in this work.

To my parents, Guy and Jane Stock

Contents

Acknowledgements ix

Introduction 1
1. Extreme Intentionalism about Fictional Content 13
2. Intentionalist Strategies of Interpretation 45
3. Extreme Intentionalism and its Rivals 82
4. Fiction, Belief, and 'Imaginative Resistance' 114
5. The Nature of Fiction 145
6. Back to the Imagination 175
Conclusion 208

Bibliography 211
Index 221

Acknowledgements

This book was generously funded by an AHRC Research Leave Grant in 2010–11, and a year of research leave from the School of History, Art History and Philosophy at the University of Sussex in 2014–15. Versions of its contents have been aired at the Universities of: Barcelona, Birkbeck, Bucharest, Cardiff, Essex, Fribourg, Geneva, Hamburg, Hertfordshire, Konstanz, Lisbon, Manchester, Nottingham, Oxford, Padua, Sussex, Tampere, Tilburg, Tuebingen, Uppsala; and the Institut Jean Nicod, the Institute of Philosophy, the London Aesthetics Forum, the Open University, and NYU.

I'm extremely grateful to the following people for helping me along the way, in terms of written comments, conference organization, and/ or stimulating discussions: Catharine Abell; Lucy Allais; Hanne Appelqvist; Margarita Arcangeli; Magdalena Balcerak Jackson; Olle Blomberg; Ben Blumson; Michael Braddick; Emily Brady; Anne-Sophie Brüggen; Elisa Calderola; Ezra Cohen; Brandon Cooke; Diarmuid Costello; Gregory Currie; Eva Dadlez; Richard Dammann; David Davies; Alison Denham; Harry Deutsch; Julian Dodd; Jerome Dokic; Anthony Everett; Marcello Fiocco; Stacie Friend; Amanda Garcia; Manuel Garcia-Carpintero; Louise Hanson; Robert Hopkins; Anna Ichino; Matthew Kieran; Amy Kind; Tilmann Koeppe; Denise Kong; Norman Kreitman; Peter Lamarque; Joshua Landy; Julia Langkau; Sandra Lapointe; Jessica Leech; Jerrold Levinson; Derek Matravers; Patrick Maynard; Andrew McGonigal; Seiriol Morgan; Adam Morton; Henry Pratt; Murali Ramachandran; Francois Recanati; Debbie Roberts; Fiora Salis; Elisabeth Schellekens; Roger Scruton; Robert Stecker; Guy Stock; Dustin Stokes; Daniele Tagliafico; Alan Thomas; Robert Thomas; Katherine Thomson-Jones; Cain Todd; David Turner; Neil Van Leeuwen; Kendall Walton; Edward Winters; Richard Woodward; and two anonymous referees. Thanks too to Peter Momtchiloff and Louise Larchbourne.

A great debt is owed to colleagues at the Department of Philosophy at Sussex for their help and support, especially Tony Booth, Paul Davies, Katerina Deligiorgi, and Sarah Sawyer; and most especially, Michael Morris, for being so generous with his time and stimulating in discussion. I'm very grateful to successive years of undergraduates in my Aesthetics and Language, Truth and Literature classes for discussing my ideas with me and making them better; and to Manuel Garcia-Carpintero and the graduate community at the University of Barcelona Department of Philosophy for discussing my book with me over the course of a highly rewarding week. Thanks are also due to Dr James Hiddleston for teaching me properly about literature in the first place; and to the late, much-missed, Peter Goldie for being so supportive and inspiring. Fabian Dorsch is another person to whom I owe much professionally and whose absence is a huge loss to the community of philosophers of imagination.

Finally, I'd like to thank the following dear people for the love and support which has kept me, and so this book, going: my partner Laura Gibbon; my sons Magnus and Alec and their dad Gregor Beedie; my parents Guy and Jane Stock; and my sister Sarah Stock and family.

Introduction

> The legend that characters run away from their authors—taking up drugs, having sex operations, and becoming president—implies that the writer is a fool with no knowledge or mastery of his craft. This is absurd. Of course, any estimable exercise of the imagination draws upon such a complex richness of memory that it truly enjoys the expansiveness—the surprising turns, the response to light and darkness—of any living thing. But the idea of authors running around helplessly behind their cretinous inventions is contemptible.
>
> (John Cheever, quoted in Grant 1976)

> Bert and Ernie are best friends. They are not gay, they are not straight, they are puppets. They do not exist below the waist.
>
> (Statement from Gary Knell, Sesame Workshop, 1994)

In the first half of this book, I offer a theory of fictional content or, as it is sometimes known, 'fictional truth'. It is *fictionally true* in *The Girls of Slender Means* by Muriel Spark that Joanna Childe is the daughter of a country rector. It is *fictionally false* in E.M. Forster's *Howards End* that Henry Wilcox meets Jacky Bast for the first time at Evie's wedding party (in fact, it is fictionally true that they were lovers long before the party). It is *fictionally indeterminate* in *Harry Potter and the Philosopher's Stone* (at least, according to its author)[1] what skin colour Hermione has. The theory I offer attempts to explain these facts—to explain what makes them true.

The theory of fictional content I argue for is 'extreme intentionalism'. The basic idea—very roughly, in ways which will be made more precise in the chapters to come—is that the fictional content of a particular text is equivalent to exactly what the author of the text *intended the reader to imagine*. Historically, this sort of view has been very unpopular. Literary theorists and philosophers alike have poured scorn upon it. This book is partly an attempt to argue that extreme intentionalism should be taken seriously as an adequate account of fictional truth; more seriously, in fact, than its more popular rivals.

The bad reputation of extreme intentionalism has several sources. In literature departments, relevant influences include: New Critics, including Wimsatt and Beardsley on 'The Intentional Fallacy' (1946); reader-response theorists, who see literary meaning

---

[1] See Crompton (2016).

as significantly produced by the reader and not just the author; and work on textual meaning grounded in post-structuralist and deconstructionist theories of language. In analytic philosophy departments too, Beardsley has had an influence, as has the sustained joint attack on extreme intentionalism offered in recent years by philosophers such as Noel Carroll, Gregory Currie, Stephen Davies, Jerrold Levinson, and Robert Stecker. In the work of these philosophers and others, a core set of objections to extreme intentionalism tends to get rehearsed, presented as if they ruled it out as a non-starter, obviously and definitively.

The first half of this book argues directly for extreme intentionalism, defending it against these oft-repeated and usually unchallenged objections, and showing how the theory generally explains practices concerning fictional content very well. I will seek to ground my views in a background Gricean theory of ordinary conversational communication which many have found independently plausible. Space restrictions as well as intellectual limitations preclude me from defending this Gricean picture more generally against alternative pictures of language, such as those endorsed by post-structuralists and deconstructionists. Hence I will not be speaking directly to those anti-intentionalists whose position depends on such pictures. My aim rather will be to show that if one grants a Gricean intentionalist view of the content of ordinary conversation, or something like it, there is no good reason not to extend this view, with certain adjustments, to fictional content as well.

The second half of the book is concerned with reaping further explanatory benefits of my position, by showing how extreme intentionalism and the lessons learnt from it can illuminate cognate questions in the philosophy of fiction and imagination. For instance, I will argue, my position helps us to explain how fiction can provide us with reliable testimony (Chapters 3 and 4); it helps explain the phenomenon of imaginative resistance (Chapter 4); and it fits with, and so supports, a persuasive theory of the nature of fiction itself (Chapter 5). In my final chapter (Chapter 6), I show how attending to intentionalist practices of interpreting fictional content can illuminate the nature of propositional imagining. Based on my discussion of imagining in relation to fiction, I argue both against a view of imagining as constrained in a 'belief-like' way; and against a view of imagining as wholly unconstrained and stipulative. In doing the latter, I defend the claim that the imagination can play a significant role in acquiring counterfactual and modal knowledge. I also discuss the relations between imagining, belief, and supposition.

I move to three important preliminaries. First, in order to avoid misunderstanding, it will be helpful to point out some matters which I am emphatically *not* addressing, in constructing a theory of fictional content or truth.

Sometimes, intentionalism of some kind is defended with respect to the meaning of *art generally* (e.g. Livingston 2005). This is not my position; not least because at least one artistic medium, film, usually involves hundreds of agents in the creative process, each with their own intentions with respect to the work. It is true, of course, that there is an obvious sense in which fiction films have 'fictional content'—what is true in the story of the film. But given the multiple agents involved, it looks as though a rather complicated story will have to be told about how such content is generated. I prefer to start with a more simple case. So, to be clear, my view concerns only fictional texts (or orally delivered stories, though mostly I will focus on texts as my examples). That is, I am concerned with *fictions made out of words*. Moreover, for the most part, I shall be talking about *single-authored* fictional texts or oral stories.

Even where it is exclusively addressing fictions made out of words, and not art generally, intentionalism, extreme or not, is often presented as a theory of 'literary meaning'. Yet talk of 'literary meaning' can be loose and cover a variety of sorts of case. So to be clear, I will not be claiming that *all* aspects of 'meaning' of a fiction are determined by what the author intends. For instance, if the value of a fiction is counted as part of its meaning, then I deny that authorial intention determines meaning in that sense. Obviously, a work does not count as *good* or *valuable* or *successful* simply because the author intends it to be. Equally, those aesthetic or expressive properties that a text has—its counting as *beautiful*, or *haunting*, or *sad*, or *funny*, for instance—are not directly determined by the author's intentions. Works intended to be these things can fail to count as such.[2]

Equally, in talking about fictional content, I am not talking about poetics, or the poetic meaning of a text—that is, any figurative, allusive, connotative, or other poetic effects the words of a fiction might have, *apart from where these influence what should be said about fictional content*. Insofar as my interest is fictional content, I am unconcerned with any implicit 'real-world' comment a fiction may be making or implying about the nature of art, narrative, or fiction itself.[3] And yet another kind of meaning which can accrue to a fiction, and which I will not be discussing, is, for instance, what it (consciously or unconsciously) reveals to us about the zeitgeist at the time of writing, or about the social psyche, or economic circumstances, or about political attitudes, and by extension, what has changed since then or what has stayed the same. That is, a fiction can be a source of material for historical insight. (Equally, a fiction written in the past can cast light on fictions written more recently.) My view does not rule out such possibilities, since it does not concern them.

I am also uninterested in what fictional characters, or texts, *remind us of*, collectively or individually—Jungian archetypes, cultural or literary stereotypes, historical figures, or whatever—except, again, where these connections plausibly relate to fictional content or truth. And quite obviously, a fictional text can have personal meaning for a reader: it can remind her of a happy time in her life, or can be a source of solace in a bad one, for instance. Characters can be ones particular readers especially like, or hate. My variety of intentionalism has nothing to say about any of this, one way or the other. To reiterate: it is purely concerned with what is fictionally true.

---

[2] These and other aspects of literary meaning are illuminatingly discussed by Taylor (2014) under the heading of Gricean 'natural meaning'.

[3] However, as noted, in Chapters 3 and 4 I discuss the relation of fiction to the promulgation of belief.

Often, literary criticism and literary theory are concerned with 'meaning' in one or more of the senses just listed. It will be no objection to my view that such meanings are not produced as a result of authorial intention, because (depending on the case, of course) I am likely to agree. In my view, construing extreme intentionalism as a theory of literary meaning generally (and a fortiori, 'artistic' meaning) has meant that it was bound to fail. Much better to confine it to fictional truth, and see what can be done with it under this heading.

A second important preliminary is to situate my project methodologically. In various places, I will be offering claims about the natures of fictional content, fiction, and imagination respectively. One traditional approach to describing the nature of things has been what is known as conceptual analysis, but this is not the approach I will be adopting (or not uncritically).

In the field of philosophy of mind, conceptual analysis has often taken the form of 'analytical functionalism': a theory which tries to define mental states by looking at their associated folk-psychological concepts (what ordinary people, at least implicitly, take those entities to be). The basic thought is that we can identify the nature of a mental state x by attending to the 'platitudes', or other-things-being-equal generalizations, implicit in the folk-psychological concept x. These supposedly will link x to various characteristic causal 'inputs' (e.g. perceptions, beliefs, desires, feelings) and/or 'outputs' (e.g. beliefs, desires, feelings, behaviour). In this way, it is hoped, a characteristic functional role will be discerned, with which the mental entity in question can be identified (Lewis 1972; Goldman 2000).

A problem with this approach, as putatively applied to the concept of *imagination* (italics are used here to denote a concept), is that there are barely any platitudes about the causal role of the imagination, implicit in ordinary language or the usage of the associated folk concept. Perhaps unlike other mental entities such as belief and desire, the functional role of imagining is relatively unclear. For instance, imagining has few regularly associated behavioural manifestations. There is little distinctive behaviour associated with either imaginings with particular contents, or imaginings generally. Say, for instance, that a person imagines herself riding a unicycle. She might do this whilst physically pretending to ride a unicycle (making physical movements roughly consonant with this activity), but equally she might imagine this whilst sitting doing absolutely nothing, or whilst walking along the street. The point generalizes for every kind of imaginative content: no distinctive behaviour is associated.

Equally, there seem to be few predictable generalizations connecting imagining to other mental states or events. It is true that imagining is usually deliberately initiated, via an intention—indeed, this will be important in what follows—but equally it can in exceptional cases be non-voluntarily initiated; as in recurrent images or morbid daydreaming (Scruton 1974: 109). Nor is it distinctively connected to desire, either as a companion or as an effect of it. If you imagine something, you do not have to have any particular desire directed towards the state of affairs you are imagining: you might desire that state of affairs, or you might strongly desire its non-occurrence, or be neutral. It apparently bears no distinctive causal relation to belief either. Sometimes it has belief as a causal outcome—as in the imaginative consideration of counterfactuals, where we work out what else would be true, given some imagined scenario—but equally, sometimes it does not (as in fantasizing). Some have argued that imagining importantly *resembles* belief (e.g. Currie and Ravenscroft 2002; Nichols 2004). The extent to which this is so will be examined in Chapter 6 of this book. But either way, this is not the same as saying it is distinctively causally related to any particular sort of belief.

This lack of available data about imagining, relatively speaking, makes it a candidate for philosophical controversy. Questions include: whether imagining must be accompanied by mental imagery (Kind 2001; Chalmers 2002: 151; Gaut 2003: 153); what the relation between imagination and behaviour is (Velleman 2000; O'Brien 2005); whether one can imagine something and believe it at the same time (Nichols 2004: 129; Gibson 2007: 166); whether some kinds of imagining are inevitably *de se* or self-involving (Peacocke 1985; Noordhof 2002); whether we can imagine what is blatantly impossible (Kripke 1980: 114; Gendler 2000: 67); and whether *imagination* is a unified concept or not (Strawson 1970: 31; O'Shaughnessy 2003: 339–70; Dorsch 2012). Some of these questions will be illuminated over the course of this book.

So: conceptual analysis looks of limited value for characterizing *imagining*. A putative conceptual analysis of *fictional truth* or *fiction* also looks unsatisfactory, though for different reasons. Take the concept of *fiction*. If the search is for—as is traditional in conceptual analysis—a limited set of necessary and sufficient conditions governing ordinary usage of the folk concept, it seems unlikely we will find one. Ordinary language categorizations of non-natural kinds generally tend to be deficient in various ways. They can be messy and obfuscatory, reflecting varying contexts of application as usage expands, and glossing over potentially interesting differences between those contexts. There is little reason to think *fiction* will be different.

Indeed, when we look, we find folk usages of 'fiction' which apply, apparently variously, to deliberate lies, inadvertent falsehoods about real existents, invented claims about non-existents, accidentally true claims, and stories based on largely true events. Meanwhile, amongst philosophers, fiction has been variously characterized as essentially related to pretence (Searle 1975); falsehood (Goodman 1982); invention (Deutsch 2000); imagining (Walton 1990; Currie 1990; Lamarque and Olsen 1994; Davies 2007); or none of these (Friend 2011, 2012; Matravers 2014). It might be suggested, as it sometimes is in the context of an enquiry into the nature of *art*, that we should offer a 'cluster account' of fiction, i.e. a disjunctive list of sufficient conditions (e.g. Gaut 2000). However, it is not clear how this would help. An exhaustive list of the relatively diverse conditions sufficient for application of the concept *fiction* according to ordinary usage is not of obvious explanatory value. Similar points apply, with adjustment, to the possibility of successfully conceptually analysing the folk concept of *fictional truth*, especially since here the concept looks even less securely established in public consciousness.

What might we do instead? One attractive thought, which I shall pursue in this book, is that we might try to *clean up* or even *develop* ordinary usage and the folk concepts associated with it. After all, even defenders of analytic functionalism allow that a folk concept may be incoherent or wrong in certain respects (Jackson and Pettit 1993: 302). The most basic approach would be reflectively to correct aspects of the concept that look blatantly inconsistent, or mask some fairly obvious deeper distinction. Alternatively, a folk concept might be more thoroughly reformulated so as to provide a category or categories with *more explanatory value* than the existing one.

Often, what counts as having 'explanatory value' includes explanations of potential worth to scientific understanding. To take just a couple of examples: with respect to mental states, it has been argued that the folk concept of *desire* should be replaced with the economist's concept of *subjective value* to better accommodate neuroscientific findings (Hartner 2014). Also on the basis of input from the sciences, the folk concept of memory has been putatively segmented into categories such as *implicit, explicit, semantic, autobiographical*, and *procedural* memory (Hartner 2013: 925).[4] Equally though, proposed improvements to folk categories may explain aspects we care about from perspectives *other* than science. For instance, 'dual process' theories of emotion have been criticized because they appear to characterize emotion as something for which one could not have moral responsibility, where this is seen as an important commitment (Roeser 2012: 106). Equally, proposed changes to ordinary usage are sometimes defended in terms of the contribution they would make to explaining philosophical puzzles. For instance, Tamar Gendler (2008) introduces the concept of a wholly new, hitherto unrecognized, mental entity called an 'alief', partly as a response to the philosophical puzzle of how to characterize emotional responses to fictional situations.

Let's call the sort of theory we are looking for an 'explanatory theory', rather than one of straightforward conceptual analysis: one that attempts to specify the natures of, respectively, fictional content, fiction, and (to some extent, though not exhaustively) imagination, in a way that offers explanatory value in some respect.[5] An explanatory theory of x is not aimed simply at recovery of the conditions governing the folk concept of x, but aims informatively to supplement or even in some cases transform our current understanding of x. Ideally a theory of x will at least fit with uncontroversial cases of the folk concept, in order to avoid the impression of talking past the original topic. However, the account may also include items not ordinarily classified as 'x', or exclude others ordinarily so classified. It also may permissibly redraw the boundaries of the concept. In contrast, whilst conceptual analysis permits occasional rejection of

---

[4] Generally, amending folk concepts in order to better accommodate the aims of science is the approach of what is known in philosophy of mind as 'psychofunctionalism' (Levin 2013). Mental states are treated as identical to the functional roles initially identified by folk psychology but then legitimated, made more precise, or perhaps even radically altered by scientific psychology and neurology.

[5] In discussions of imagination, offering an explanatory theory is what many philosophers of the imagination take themselves to be doing (e.g. Currie 1995b: 160; Kind 2013: 149).

at least some ordinary intuitions about particular cases, it remains largely deferential to ordinary language usage (Jackson 2000: 35).

Baldly put, the mark of a good explanatory theory of x is that it should explain something we care about. More specifically, explanatory value might include: accounting for relations between entities in a way which solves existing puzzles about them; complementing and providing elucidation of existing theoretical commitments in related areas; or showing the point of some aspect(s) of our current practice. Ideally, the theory should also aim to display traditional theoretical virtues: for instance, to cover a wide range of interesting cases, though not so wide as to obscure important-looking distinctions where they emerge; and to be simple and elegant, relative to rivals. My aim in this book will be to construct three explanatory theories simultaneously, which complement and support one another: a theory of fictional content, a theory of fiction, and at least a partial theory of (propositional) imagination too.

A note is required on the latter. In attempting to construct a (partial) explanatory theory of propositional imagination, as I do in the final chapter of this book, supposedly neutral pre-theoretical intuitions are not the best place to start. Too often, what seems 'obvious' or 'natural' to a philosopher will be the result of prior allegiance to a theory which readers may not share. Instead, I propose, we look in some detail at a particular context in which, according to almost everyone, the imagination gets *used*: fiction. A fiction, I will argue, is best understood as a set of instructions to imagine things. That is (roughly): in constructing a fiction, an author makes certain utterances, intending that the reader or hearer imaginatively engage with them. The fictional content of a fiction is what the author intends readers to imagine. If these things are right, then we can legitimately inspect in detail what the sort of imagining called for by fiction actually looks like. Inspecting the sort of mental events made appropriate by fiction will be a way of getting information about how the imagination works in practice.

Proceeding in this way has several advantages. The main one will be the explanatory pay-off: as we will see, we will get some surprising insights. But there are further methodological advantages. First, by considering imagining in detail in a real-world context, any substantive claims made about imagination are less likely to count as ad hoc. The philosophy of imagination is littered with claims offered only on the most cursory of intuition pumps. Think, for instance, of Gendler's claim that we can imagine the blatantly impossible, on the basis of one rather brief thought experiment (2000: 67); or the widely endorsed claim that imagining exhibits 'inferential orderliness' in a way which mimics belief with the same content, usually presented on the basis of only a couple of quick examples (e.g. Nichols 2004: 129).[6] In looking closely at the way fiction actually works, with many examples, and scrutinizing what kind of mental events is called for on the part of the reader in order to facilitate its understanding and appreciation, I hope to give my substantive claims deeper roots than is often the case. Also to this end, since they too risk being ad hoc in their formulation, I will avoid, wherever

---

[6] I will discuss these claims in Chapters 4 and 5 respectively.

possible, the common practice of making up one's own fictional cases—describing 'fictional fictions', if you like—in order to illustrate particular points about fiction or imagination. Instead, I shall focus on cases of published or other established fictions, sometimes quoting at some length in order to get a full sense of the relevant case.

A second advantage of approaching the nature of imagining via detailed scrutiny of fiction is that it reduces a potential problem with introspection about mental events generally, and in particular about imagining, given its apparent lack of distinctive functional role relative to other mental events and behaviour. Namely, it alleviates the apparent difficulty of ensuring that two thinkers comparing introspective claims about the nature of some imagining are having the same thought in the first place. In an experimental context this worry also occurs: experiments need to ensure that they are reproducing 'the same thoughts' across multiple experimental subjects, given the lack of external, more objective markers. To control variability and make it more likely that the same type of thought token reoccurs, where they can, experimenters use 'external' publicly observable prompts (Ericsson 2003: 6). Effectively, I propose to do something similar, except that I shall be calling upon both general facts about the nature of fiction, and particular published examples of it, to focus minds and constrain discussion.

The third advantage of my approach pertains to a common worry: that the concept of *imagining* may well be a loose umbrella concept for a range of subconcepts, which have little or nothing in common. Apparently related concepts include *visualizing, fantasizing, daydreaming, pretending, supposing, conceiving, entertaining a thought, conjecturing, dreaming,* and *falsely believing*. Psychology casts the net yet wider, including under the rubric of *imagination creativity, lying, 'future thinking',* and *'magical thinking'* (Taylor 2013). Strawson sums up the worry in an oft-quoted passage:

The uses, and applications, of the terms 'image', 'imagine', 'imagination', and so forth make up a very diverse and scattered family. Even this image of a family seems too definite. It would be a matter of more than difficulty to identify and list the family's members, let alone their relations of parenthood and cousinhood.   (1970: 31)

To make things worse, it has recently been argued that invocations of the imagination in particular explanatory contexts collectively presuppose inconsistent commitments about the nature of the imagination, so that no single theory of the imagination could do all of the explanatory work being claimed on its behalf (Kind 2013).

Now, if all this were right, then there would be little mileage in looking for a theory which covered all or most significant contexts in which the term 'imagining' was invoked. Better then to focus at a more fine-grained level on a *particular kind* of imagining, as I will be doing. And even if the assumption of a lack of unity turns out eventually to be wrong (a matter on which I will not be commenting),[7] looking at the use of imagination in detail, in a very familiar context, will presumably help us understand more about what the general features of imagining might be.

---

[7] See Dorsch (2012).

Some might worry that there is something illegitimately circular in, for instance, simultaneously characterizing fiction as (roughly) 'the sort of thing that is intended to prompt a certain sort of imagining' whilst simultaneously characterizing that sort of imagining as (again, roughly) 'the sort of thing that is intended to be prompted by fiction'. There is no need for alarm, however. For one thing, many of the claims I make about fiction, which in turn then give rise to claims about the sort of imagining appropriate in response to fiction, do not themselves depend on any particular story about the imagination. Thus an impression of circularity is limited. But secondly, when constructing explanatory theories, to make one's claims about a particular kind of entity cohere with claims about importantly related entities is a virtue, not a vice. Often, in philosophy, theories about separate entities adjust their respective claims until they cohere with one another. 'Reflective equilibrium'—i.e. the practice of mutually adjusting general principles and particular judgements until they cohere—is predicated on the permissibility of doing so (Daniels 2013). Or look again at analytical functionalism: there, philosophers simultaneously look *both* for a functional role distinctive of a particular mental state, *and* for a 'realizer' of that role: the states or entities (physical or otherwise) that contingently happen to fulfil those roles, in human beings. Any realizer found will most likely be 'imperfect'—it will not exactly fit a given functional role (Nolan 2009; Braddon-Mitchell and Nola 2009). In that case, there will be room for philosophers to legitimately adjust details of the functional role to fit the physical story (Braddon-Mitchell and Nola 2009: 9). In short: that I am simultaneously offering accounts of fiction, fictional content, and the sort of imagining which fiction makes appropriate, strengthens, rather than weakens my view, since it extends its explanatory reach.

A final important preliminary is explicitly to identify a methodological principle that will also apply to what follows, and which is often ignored by analytic philosophers working on fiction, in particular. Namely: what we say about fictional content should be responsive to the facts about how readers tend to engage with real novels and short stories, and in particular, the facts about how competent readers do so, including critics. Given that our target is fiction, our exegesis should focus upon the most centrally important forms of it in human life, and the way that users interact with it in those contexts. Of course there are local debates amongst readers of novels and short stories about particular matters of interpretation or approach; in those cases it is best for a philosopher not to take sides. However, at least, her theories of fiction should either i) be consistent with broad trends in the practices of competent readers of novels and short stories or ii) explain why those practices are misguided in some sense. A theory of fiction cannot afford simply to ignore critical practice, at the risk of talking past what fiction is for those who enjoy it and know how to use it.[8]

This is not to say that we should attempt to develop a theory that fits with the pronouncements of every literary critic, for instance. For one thing, since critics tend to disagree amongst themselves, this would be impossible. For another, it is possible that

[8] For a comparison, see D. Davies 2004: 16–24.

some literary critics are in the grip of implausible theories about the nature of textual meaning, including fictional content, and that their practice has become overly influenced by such theories. However, away from the margins of overtly theory-driven critical practice, it seems to me that there is still a core of interpretative techniques and strategies, inherited from previous generations of scholars rather than consciously adopted in response to new philosophical trends, which a theory of fictional content should aim to accommodate and, if possible, justify.

I conclude with a brief summary of the following chapters.

In Chapter 1, I begin my defence of extreme intentionalism. I introduce the notion of an intention in some detail, as well as some skeletal presuppositions about the sort of imagining called for by fiction (which I stipulatively call 'F-imagining'). I then introduce Grice's theory of the meaning of conversational utterance and outline how it might be extended to fictional content, with certain important adjustments. On the view I favour, the content of fiction is what a reader is reflexively intended by the author to F-imagine, rather than what she is intended to believe. I finish by introducing four common objections to extreme intentionalism, and reject the first of these: namely, that extreme intentionalism entails that individual speakers can arbitrarily change or elude the conventionally given, rule-bound meanings of sentences; so that miswriting is ruled out as impossible.

In Chapter 2, I address the popular complaint that extreme intentionalism standardly forces the reader who engages in interpretation to posit private, or hidden, authorial intentions, for which she has little or no evidence. I first argue, at some length, that there are no automatic strategies of interpretation of fictional content: at every stage, that a given interpretative strategy is appropriate is subject to the presence of relevant authorial intention as a sanction. The fact that there are no automatically-applied interpretative strategies itself is taken to provide evidence that extreme intentionalism is true. This section includes a discussion, and rejection, of the views of David Lewis and Gregory Currie about fictional truth, and an examination of certain of the consequences of this rejection. It also includes a discussion of the relevance of genre to fictional content, and considers the issue of unreliable narration for an intentionalist view.

I then emphasize how, in interpretation, a reader may legitimately bring to bear her knowledge of factors such as conventional sentence meaning, conversational implicature, fictional genres, stereotypes, stock characters, and culturally popular symbolic associations (among other things) upon the evidence provided by a text, in order to work out reasonable hypotheses about what the author intended her to imagine by their use in that text. Equally, she may legitimately make reference to extra-textual evidence about authorial purposes concerning the text, since such purposes are bound to be pursued via the fictional content of the text itself. Given the wide range of evidence available in principle, it is therefore false to think of the extreme intentionalist as being committed to 'hidden' or 'secret' meanings in the ordinary case.

In Chapter 3, I conclude my defence of extreme intentionalism, by attacking its main rivals in the analytic tradition: 'modest' intentionalism, hypothetical intentionalism, and value-maximizing theory. I first address a source of apparent support for all three, and in particular a central motive for modest intentionalism: the thought that extreme intentionalism takes an implausible stance towards unsuccessful authorial intentions that a fiction should have a certain content. I argue that in fact, extreme intentionalism is in a better position to accommodate unsuccessful intentions than its rivals. I then move on to general criticisms of hypothetical intentionalism and value-maximizing theory. In particular, I focus on the extent to which each can accommodate the plausible thought that fictions often contain reliable testimony, and can act as a respectable source of belief. I argue that in this respect too, extreme intentionalism is in a stronger position than its opposition. Also in this chapter, I discuss the issue of post hoc meanings; and show how extreme intentionalism, though a monistic position, is compatible with many of the critical judgements which have tempted some towards critical pluralism.

In Chapter 4, I start by focusing on the possible relation between fiction and the inculcation of justified belief via testimony. I defend the claim, relied upon in Chapter 3, that fictions can be sources of testimony and so justified belief. I then implicate the fact that fictive utterances can, effectively, instruct readers to have beliefs, in a new explanation of 'imaginative resistance': that is, an explanation of those cases where, it is alleged, a reader experiences difficulty in imagining something an author has instructed her to imagine. The right account of this phenomenon, I suggest, should cite the reader's perception of an authorial intention that she believe a counterfactual, which in fact she cannot believe. I defend this view against several rivals, and distinguish it from certain other views, including the influential view of Tamar Gendler. I finish with a consideration of whether one can propositionally imagine what one believes to be conceptually impossible, looking at a range of fictional cases which apparently ask us to do this. I conclude that one can.

In Chapter 5, I draw upon extreme intentionalism to build a theory of fiction, arguing that a fiction is a set of instructions to a reader, instructing her to F-imagine various things. Call this 'the basic claim'. I defend my view from those, such as Gregory Currie, Peter Lamarque and Stein Olsen, and David Davies, who would agree with the basic claim as *one* condition of fiction, but who would argue that a theory of fiction also needs additional conditions. I also defend my view against those, such as Stacie Friend and Derek Matravers, who would reject even that basic claim. I finish by considering what to say about less straightforward cases, such as split narrative, 'ambiguous fictions', 'fictions within fictions', unreliable narration, and those cases where a fictional character appears as such in a fiction.

Finally, in Chapter 6, I return to the propositional imagination, examining it in the light of the conclusions reached thus far about the nature of fiction and what it calls for, properly understood. In particular I reject two dominant tendencies in treatment of the propositional imagination: on the one hand, to treat it as significantly 'belief-like' in a certain sense, and on the other, to treat it as radically unconstrained and stipulative. I argue that, though propositional imagining *can be* either significantly belief-like in the sense indicated, or radically unconstrained, depending on the purposes to which it is being put, neither of these characterizations is good as a general description. Room is therefore left for an account of imagination as integral to the provision of counterfactual and modal knowledge. I explore further differences between imagining and belief; and conclude with a discussion of the nature of supposition and its relation to propositional imagining. I conclude, perhaps somewhat surprisingly, that fictions tend to call extensively for supposition on the part of the reader.

1

Extreme Intentionalism about Fictional Content

1.1 Introduction

My topic for this and the next few chapters is fictional content, also referred to as 'fictional truth'. It is fictionally true in *The Prime of Miss Jean Brodie* that Jean Brodie is a Scottish spinster schoolteacher who admires Mussolini; and fictionally true in Toni Morrison's *Beloved* that Sethe is haunted by the ghost of her baby. It is not fictionally true in Nabokov's *Lolita* that Humbert Humbert is a kind and selfless man. My question is: what constrains the correct attribution of fictional content in this way? What makes it right to say that Jean Brodie is a schoolteacher, but wrong to say that Humbert Humbert is kind? Obviously, this is not a matter of corresponding directly with what is true in our actual world: Jean Brodie and Humbert Humbert do not exist. These are fictional 'truths', not truths. So what has to be the case for their correct attribution?

In this chapter, I shall introduce and start to defend a position sometimes called 'extreme intentionalism'. Extreme intentionalism is supposed to be an explanatorily useful view. It says that if we treat fictional content as (only) generated by authorial intentions, then this a) fits with a lot of what competent readers actually do and say about fiction; b) is consistent with many aspects of fiction, which readers tend to find valuable; c) helps us explain various other things about fiction and our relation to it, to be explored at various points in this book; and d) is a better theory of fictional truth in these respects than are its main rivals.

Both philosophers and literary critics have tended to find extreme intentionalism hopeless.[1] Its bad reputation has been built on a series of misunderstandings and uncharitable criticisms, I shall argue. Actually, the position can accommodate most, if not all, of the important things we want to say about fictional content. Moreover, I shall later show, the most popular rivals to extreme intentionalism within analytic philosophy—'modest' intentionalism, hypothetical intentionalism, and value-maximizing theory, as well as a kind of anti-intentionalism effectively argued for by the philosopher David Lewis—fail to accommodate many important features of fictional content in their own right.

---

[1] Recent exceptions are Irwin 2015 and Taylor 2014.

1.2 Extreme Intentionalism Introduced

For nearly a century, it has been a truism in some literature departments that any kind of intentionalism about fictional content is misguided. Originally fuelled by the New Criticism, including an influential paper by Wimsatt and Beardsley on 'The Intentional Fallacy' (1946), Western academics have, at least in theory if not in practice, eschewed the idea of reconstructing authorial intention as a guide to fictional content. The favoured alternative approach, influenced by reader-response theories, or by post-structuralist and deconstructionist philosophies of language, has often been to move away from intentionalism altogether as a sanctioned means of determining content. Within philosophy departments in the analytic tradition, meanwhile, though anti-intentionalism on those grounds has never been in vogue, there has still been a tendency in some quarters to its adoption on other grounds. Amongst those working in philosophy of language and metaphysics, one such ground has been an approach to fictional truth which resembles that taken to counterfactuals (this will be discussed in Chapter 2). Amongst those working in aesthetics, another has been an attraction to what is known as value-maximizing theory (this will be described fully in Chapter 3). Meanwhile, those deterred by some of the consequences of anti-intentionalism have opted either for 'modest' (or 'moderate' or 'partial') intentionalism, or 'hypothetical intentionalism' (both also to be discussed in Chapter 3). Where literary theorists and philosophers have tended to agree, however, is that the position of 'extreme intentionalism' is untenable.

Extreme intentionalism is a variety of what is often called 'actual author intentionalism'. This characterizes fictional content in terms of what the actual author intended, in producing that fiction.[2] Extreme (actual author) intentionalism says that authorial intention of a certain sort is both necessary (*has to be* present) for fictional content of a given kind *and* sufficient (its presence is *enough*) for fictional content of that kind.

Despite near-universal opposition to it, at first sight, at least, extreme intentionalism has several things going for it. It is more streamlined and less ad hoc-looking than 'modest' versions of intentionalism. On these latter sorts of view, an author's intentions are determinative of fictional content *only in certain circumstances*, but not always (Carroll 1992, 2000; Stecker 2006; Livingston 2005). For instance, they are determinative where they do not violate conventional sentence meaning (Irvin 2006: 119), or where they do not otherwise fail. Where they do these things, some other feature determines meaning. Extreme intentionalism eschews such inelegant caveats.

Equally, extreme intentionalism also apparently fits nicely with a fact upon which nearly everyone agrees: namely, that necessarily, to write a fiction is to engage in an intentional action. Indeed, many think, as I do and will argue in Chapter 5, that to produce a fiction is, necessarily, to *intend some readers or auditors to imagine something*.

---

[2] 'Actual author' may seem superfluous to the uninitiated, but is needed to distinguish it from a different view, hypothetical intentionalism, which I shall discuss in Chapter 3.

People who think this include some vocal critics of actual author intentionalism as a theory of fictional content: for instance, Currie (1993, 2004) and D. Davies (2007: Ch. 5). There is therefore an odd mismatch, on these last authors' views, between what a fiction is and how it should be interpreted.³ Relatedly, extreme intentionalism also fits well with prevalent practices of valuation in relation to fictions. Authors tend to be praised or criticized, rewarded, or sometimes even sued, for the content of their works. My position can easily account for this, since fictional content is something the author intentionally brings about and is responsible for.

I shall now formulate the central tenet of extreme intentionalism in more detail. The following claim will require certain modifications, but the main idea is that:

> An author *Au*'s utterance *x* (or set of utterances *S*) has fictional content that *p*, if and only if: *Au* utters *x* (or *S*) intending that i) *x* (or *S*) should cause F-imagining that *p* in her intended readership *R*; ii) *R* should recognize this intention; and iii) *R*'s recognition of this intention should function as part of *R*'s reason to F-imagine that *p*.

In §§1.3–1.9, I shall explain this further. (What 'F-imagining' refers to will be explained in due course; until then, there is no harm in the reader's thinking of this as simply referring to imagining generally).

I shall start with some points about the nature of intention. The main purpose of this is to bring the reader to a more sophisticated understanding of intentions than is often revealed in philosophers' objections to extreme intentionalism. It is my general hunch that the knee-jerk reactions to extreme intentionalism have tended to depend on various misunderstandings of the nature of the view, including some about the nature of intention. Clearing up these misconceptions should go a long way towards reducing the attraction of the rivals of extreme intentionalism.⁴

1.3 What is an Intention?

Here my aim is to stay as general as possible, avoiding allegiance to particular substantive theories of intention in case their eventual failure threatens my view. This makes the description of an intention tricky, since there is so much controversy in the area (notably, about whether intentions are mental states or not). However, there are still some informative and relatively non-controversial things we can say.

The first thing to say is that I am concerned with what is sometimes called 'an intention with which': i.e. the intention that animates a given action at the time of acting (Setiya 2014). Some bits of behaviour or causal outcomes of behaviour are not intentional at all—spasms, sneezes, accidental effects of one's actions, etc. But writing a

---

³ In fact, I'll argue in Chapter 5, a fiction is constituted *necessarily and sufficiently* by utterances that, their author intends, the reader is to imagine: so the fit with intentionalism about fictional content is even closer than one might think.

⁴ Additional objections to those rivals will be offered in Chapter 3.

fiction is not like this: it is deliberately done in the light of certain intentions, which, moreover, can be offered as part of the reason why the text was written in the first place (Anscombe 1957). My claim is that the fictional content of a text is determined by certain of the intentions with which the text is written.

It should be noted that these may be different from the intentions the author had before starting to write at all (sometimes called 'intentions for the future'—Setiya 2014), and even perhaps from those she had as she began it. Intentions can change between conceiving of a future action and starting to execute it, or even during the execution of it: just as one can start to make a cake and end up making scones instead, one can start to write a text with one set of intentions, and finish writing it with a different set. So my claim is that the fictional content of a text is determined by certain of the intentions the author has with respect to the final version of her copy.

The attribution of intentions to an agent is supposed to at least partly explain particular actions of hers: what she was aiming at in behaving in a certain way. That is, there is a special relationship between a person's goals and her intentions. Human agents have ultimate goals or purposes: things they want or at least judge as desirable for their own sakes. These may produce subsidiary, instrumental goals: goals adopted in order to achieve further goals. Very often, agents intend to pursue their goals, both ultimate and instrumental. So: just as practical reasons may nest—an agent may do C in order to bring about B, and B in order to bring about A (and so on)—so too intentions may nest. An agent may intend to C in order to B in order to A (and so on).

Say, for instance, that my goal is to get fit by the summer. Normally, in virtue of that goal, I will intend to get fit by the summer. And because of this ultimate goal, it is likely I will also have instrumental intentions: e.g. I will intend to go running every day, to go to the gym twice a week, and to eat healthily. I will intend to do these things in order to achieve the further intention of getting fit.

On some accounts, to have a goal just *is* to have an intention, or very close to it. For instance, an intention has been characterized as 'an all-out unconditional judgement that the action is desirable' (Davidson 1980: 99) or as 'a conclusion of practical reasoning' (Harman 1976: 168). However, this is controversial, and in order to avoid the conflict, my claim is only the more innocuous one that *very often*, when one has a goal A, one intends to A. Thus, minimally: *evidence of a person's goals is often good evidence of the likelihood of their having certain relevant intentions*. This will be relevant to discussion later. Additionally, where we have a reason to impute to an agent the intention to A, and we have reason to believe that she thinks that B is a good means of A-ing, this may count as partial, defeasible evidence that she intends to B as well.

We can also say that intending to pursue something entails, at least, *being committed to trying to get or achieve it*, for at least as long as one's intentions have not changed (Bratman 1987: 20). This is true even where one's intention is that *someone else* does something: as where one instructs someone else to do something, intending they will do it. Here too one is committed to trying to get the other person to do what one intends them to. So, where an author Au intends to get a reader R to imagine such-and-such, they must be committed to bringing this state of affairs about. *Evidence, via an agent's behaviour, of a total lack of commitment to procuring A is evidence that an intention to A is lacking.*

This fact that intending to A entails being committed to trying to get or achieve A arguably gives rise to a particular constraint upon intention. Namely, to intend to A entails (at least) that one does not believe that one cannot or could not A. This is arguably because one cannot rationally be committed to trying to get or achieve A where one also believes that getting or achieving A is ruled out as impossible. (Unlike desires, intentions are often thought of as subject to norms of rationality—see, for instance, Bratman 1987—and I shall make this assumption too.)

Several variations of this constraint are described in the literature, some of which are stronger than others. Some hold that to intend to A entails believing positively that one can or could do A (e.g. Davidson 1980). Others hold, more strongly, that one must not believe that one will not A (e.g. McCann 1987); or that one must believe that one's action makes A more likely (Sinhababu 2013: 681). And others go further still: to intend to A involves believing that one *will* A (Audi 1973). But again, to steer clear of controversy, I endorse only the more limited claim that intending to A requires not believing that A is impossible (see also Irwin 2015: 144-5).[5] This condition has a corollary where one's intention is that *someone else* does A, which is particularly salient to future discussion. This is that one cannot intend someone else to A where one believes that that person cannot or could not A.

Just now, I suggested that evidence, via an agent's behaviour, of a total lack of commitment to procuring A is evidence that an intention to A is lacking. It is important to note that this is possible, *even where the agent says that they fully intend to A.* Though normally we grant a degree of first-personal authority to an agent, with respect to their mental states, there are circumstances in which an 'external' interpreter should ignore the agent's own pronouncements. It is true that much of the time, an agent introspectively scrutinizing her own mental states, including intentions, has some degree of enhanced first-personal authority with respect to their nature (see Moran 2001: Ch. 1 for discussion). However, this authority can lapse in certain circumstances.

At least for rational agents, one such circumstance, as we have just seen, is where the agent says that she intends to A but there is good evidence that she believes that A is impossible; or where she makes no effort at all to A, even with no apparent obstacles. Another is where the agent has reason to repress knowledge of her intentions. We are familiar with the idea of repressed desires. Given that intentions are so close to desires, it seems plausible that there could be repressed intentions too (Taylor 1981). In an obvious case, a person might say something intending to hurt another person, but sublimate this unpleasant knowledge, explaining away her utterance to herself simply as the result of a virtuous desire to be honest. In the context of writing fiction, an author might repress knowledge of painful intentions too, in certain circumstances.

---

[5] Someone who demurs is Ludwig (1992).

A further case where an agent's descriptions of her own intentions reasonably may be discounted is where the agent lies about them. We sometimes have prudential reason to lie to others about what our intentions really are or were: to cast ourselves in a light incompatible with their revelation. We might disavow intentions suggestive of unethical motives; or claim intentions we did not actually have in order to take credit for what was in fact luck. The same goes for authors (see also Irwin 2015: 142). In these sorts of case, proper scrutiny of the context might well present evidence which conflicts with the agent's self-assessment.

Given that an intention need not be consciously present to an agent, as she acts, it follows pretty swiftly that it may not be consciously present to an agent afterwards either; or at least, not without more or less sustained reflection. Moreover, even where there is no particular reason for repression, an agent may simply be inattentive to her reasons for acting, and their relations to one another, and so of her intentions too. That is, an agent may not know or have any conscious view at all, without reflection, about the intention with which she acts on a given occasion. She may not know immediately what she is or was trying to do, exactly, in acting in a certain way. Some people know themselves less well than others do.

A further point is that, where an action is in the past, the agent may not be able to call upon any first-hand recollection of any 'interior' feelings or cognitive processes at the time of acting; she may not even clearly recall her ultimate goals with respect to the action, or may misremember what they were (that is, she might give an account of them which differs from the one she would have more authoritatively given at the time). In other words, she may be in the same boat as the external interpreter. In interpreting what she intended in a given case from the past, she may have to look at, among other things, the evidence of what happened as a consequence of a given action, as well as evidence about what her goals *likely* were or *might have been* in so acting, and her *likely* beliefs at the time about how those goals could be achieved.

In sum: there are circumstances where an agent may not have an authoritative grip on her own intentions. But at the same time, this fact alone does not make the intentions which explain actions occult or hidden in some pernicious way. I have stressed that there is evidence for our intentions in our surrounding behaviour, much of which is accessible to 'external' interpreters just as for the agent herself. Chapter 2 will focus on the sorts of evidence an interpreter of fiction legitimately and standardly may call upon to uncover the authorial intentions which, I claim, determine fictional content.

1.4 What is a Reflexive Intention?

I claimed just now that for an author's utterance to have fictional content that p, the author must not only intend readers to imagine that p, but she must also intend that readers recognize this intention, and also intend that the reader's recognition of this intention function as part of their reason to imagine that p. In other words, the intention in question has a relatively complex 'reflexive' structure. The notion of a reflexive intention famously comes from Grice (1957). I'll introduce it in context, because understanding Grice's position more generally will help us understand some other things of importance for my view too.

For Grice, to communicate something to someone, generally, is for an agent to do something (to ϕ) with a particular complex intention. Let's call the person communicating, S, and the person S is communicating to, T. For communication to occur, S must i) intend her ϕ-ing to produce a certain response in T; ii) intend that her intention as described in i) be recognized by T; and iii) intend that T's recognition of S's intention as described in i) be a reason for T to ϕ. Grice's central example, at least in his early writing (1957), is the communicating of belief via speech. This involves, according to him, S's intending that her speaking produce in T the response of belief that p, whilst also intending that T's recognition of that intention count as a reason for T to believe that p.

The relevant intention is specified in this complex way to exclude the following sort of case from true communication. Say I eat a lot of chocolate in front of my son and then groan, clutching my stomach. I intend that he believe, as a result of my action, that eating too many sweets is unhealthy, so that he is put off from doing this in future. Call this my primary intention. I do not intend that he *recognize* my primary intention (I want him to think I am genuinely ill, with the belief that eating too many sweets is unhealthy as a consequence); nor do I intend that his recognition of my primary intention should function as part of his reason to have the belief in question. I intend him to think that my groaning and stomach-clutching are inadvertent, brought on by the chocolate binge, and nothing to do with him. In this case, my groans do not have the meaning, in the relevant sense, that eating too many sweets is bad, even though they are intended to cause my son to believe something (see also Grice 1957: 384). In contrast, in communication, according to Grice, the intention that auditors believe that p should also be intended to be *a reason* for them to believe that p. A complex intention structured in this way is called a 'reflexive intention'.

My claim about fictional content is Gricean in this respect. I claim that the author of a fiction does not just intend that her readers imagine certain things, but also that her intention that they imagine those things be recognized, and that the recognition function as a reason for their so imagining.[6] Insisting upon this point offers certain theoretical advantages, which will be explored in Chapter 5.[7]

I return now to intentionalism. In §1.7, I shall come back to Grice's view, extending the comparison with my view about fictional content and thereby filling in more detail about the latter. In the meantime, some information about imagining is needed, since

---

[6] For a response to worries about possible circularity in the idea of a reflexive intention, see Bach 2012.
[7] In Chapter 5, I will argue that it also allows us to mark an important distinction between, on the one hand, fictions (including illustrations accompanying stories), and on the other, many pictures, maps, and other representations which may be intended to prompt imagining but not in any reflexive, communicative sense, and which are not happily classed as 'fictions', though they form a theoretically interesting class of their own.

I am claiming that inducing imagining in others is the goal of the author who produces a fictional text.

1.5 What is F-imagining?

A. F-imagining is propositional

As explained in the introduction, my aim in this book is not just to give an account of fictional content and fiction, but also to develop some interesting observations about the kind of imagining called for by fictions. The idea is that we will motivate an account of the nature of (one kind of) imagining more securely if we look seriously at a context in which it gets used.

So for the moment, let's stipulate that 'F-imagining' is whatever kind of imagining is appropriate, at a minimum, as a response to fictional content.[8] My claim is that there is a certain sort of imagining which readers appropriately extend to the contents of fiction, and the contents of fiction are determined by an author's intention that they have particular imaginings of this sort. In this section I shall say some very minimal and basic things about F-imagining, the better to explain its role in extreme intentionalism.

The first thing to say is that F-imagining is—obviously—a species of imagining, and that imagining is different from belief. Believing something is functionally tied to perceptual inputs, other mental states, and behavioural outputs, in a way that merely imagining it is not, I will assume. If I believe something, normally I do so on the basis of having taken in some evidence or reasons for it, or having been told it by someone I take to be reasonably authoritative on the matter. If I believe something, I am also disposed to feed the belief in a potentially unrestricted way into inferences with other beliefs. For instance, if I come to believe that *Lake Konstanz is on the Swiss-German border*, and I already believe that *water contains oxygen* and that *lakes contain water* then (typically) I will be believing that *there is a lake on the Swiss-German border that contains oxygen* (which is not to say that I need be aware of this belief until I have reason to access it, in a given circumstance). Additionally, if I believe something, I shall be disposed to act upon that belief, in relevant contexts, no matter how remote. For instance, to continue the example, in the light of a belief that *Lake Konstanz is on the Swiss-German border* and (among others) an additional belief that *I'm going to Konstanz*, I might well order euros as well as Swiss francs in preparation.

None of these things are true of imagining something. In that case, often I will not have seen any evidence for what I imagine, nor have been authoritatively told it: I might easily just 'come up with it' myself. Nor, when I imagine something, am I disposed to feed it into inferences with other beliefs in a potentially unrestricted way: if I imagine

---

[8] In Chapter 6, I shall return to the nature of F-imagining, arguing that we can discern several further interesting features of it given my arguments to come about fictional content. At that point, I shall also further discuss the relation of imagining to belief.

that *Lake Konstanz is in Scotland*, and I already believe that *Scotland's national dish is haggis*, I need not be disposed to infer, under some circumstance, that *Lake Konstanz is in a country where the national dish is haggis*.[9] Nor, obviously, need I be disposed to act upon my imagining in a given set of circumstances: I simply imagine it, without its issuing in any directly related action as a belief with the same content would.[10] In brief, I am not committed to its truth in the way I would be, were I to believe it.

Now, to F-imagining. The first thing to say is that F-imagining is a species of imagining that takes propositions as its content. That is, it is a variety of 'propositional imagining'. To be clear: in talking of 'propositional imagining' I do not necessarily take on all of the commitments of other philosophers who have talked about something under that heading.[11] What I mean at this stage is simply 'imagining which is propositional in content': no more, no less.

What are propositions? Philosophers often focus on 'categorical propositions': those that relate some object (the subject term) to some class of objects (the predicate term): e.g. *a badger is a mammal*; or *Kate is not a playwright*. But more loosely, for our purposes we can think of propositions as the contents of declarative sentences, i.e. sentences that declare that some state of affairs is (or was, or will be, etc.) the case. As the parenthesis suggests, propositions can be tensed in all the familiar ways. As such, propositions are the bearers of truth values: true or false. It will be part of my view that one can F-imagine something true, or F-imagine something false.

Fictions, I take it, are propositional. Let's look at a straightforward case. The opening lines of Alice Munro's short story 'Half a Grapefruit' tell us that:

Rose wrote the Entrance, she went across the bridge, she went to high school.   (Munro 1991: 41)

This consists of a complex sentence that explicitly contains three propositions: that *Rose wrote the Entrance*, that *she went across the bridge*, that *she went to high school*.

Not all sentences in fictions express complete propositions, however. Some passages of direct speech, exclamations, and rhetorical questions do not. Or take the following opener from a different Munro story, 'Royal Beatings':

Royal Beating. That was Flo's promise. You are going to get one Royal Beating.   (Munro 1991: 3)

The first sentence here does not express a complete proposition. However, it does *imply* one. A full grasp of context tells us that it is fictionally true that Rose, remembering Flo's promise, is mentally rehearsing the words Flo used to make it. It tells us, roughly, that 'Rose mentally rehearses the phrase 'Royal Beating'. Generally, where no

---

[9] In fact this is controversial: I shall defend it in Chapter 6.
[10] This is consistent with saying that some imagining apparently can issue in *pretence* behaviour, in conjunction with certain other mental states (for discussion see O'Brien 2005).
[11] This will be made clear in Chapter 6 where I disagree with other philosophers about aspects of propositional imagining.

proposition is directly expressed by a sentence in a fiction, nonetheless one or more is normally implied indirectly, in conjunction with other sentences accompanying it.

Fictions, then, are propositional: they either directly express or imply propositions. (The question of how exactly they imply propositions will be part of the subject of Chapter 2.) When we read or otherwise discern a set of propositions in a fiction, I suggest, we implicitly are instructed to imagine their truth. What is it to imagine that p, with respect to proposition 'p'? My aim is not to give a complete account but only to indicate some basics. One such basic is that imagining that p must at least involve understanding the proposition 'p', rather than, say, simply let the words flow through one's mind in an uncomprehending fashion. But it also seems to involve more than this: namely, in some sense, *thinking that p* (see also Scruton 1974: 89).

This is *not* to say that imagining that p is simply *equivalent to* thinking that p. My claim is that imagining that p is an instance of thinking that p, but there are other instances of thinking that p which are not forms of imagining (or not obviously). Other mental activities which involve thinking that p involve, I assume, *considering that p, entertaining that p*, and *accepting that p for the sake of argument*. Nor am I saying that imagining that p is equivalent to *believing* that p (that is, I am not using 'thinking that p' and 'believing that p' as synonymous, as discussion just indicated). Actually, if thinking is a conscious act, and (as our earlier example involving Lake Konstanz indicated) believing can be unconscious, then not all believing is thinking. *Consciously reflecting upon one's belief that p* looks like a kind of thinking that p, however.

So, a very minimal claim is that, as one reads propositions 'p', 'q', and 'r' in a fiction, normally, one thinks that p and that q and that r in response. Let us stipulate that propositionally imagining that p is 'quasi-factual', by which we mean: it involves thinking that p.

An instructive contrast can be made with desiring that p. Though it is not uncontroversial to do so (see e.g. Thagard 2006), desiring is usually also thought of as propositional: one desires *that* a certain state of affairs is the case. Let's accept this for the sake of argument. Even so, desiring that p need not involve thinking that p, or even being disposed to think this. In desiring that p, instead one may be relevantly disposed to think *only* that p is *not* the case.

To take a basic example: say that my fridge is actually empty, but I desire that *my fridge is filled with delicious cakes*. In desiring this, my desire-related thoughts may represent only the fact that *my fridge is empty*. I need not think, or be disposed to think, that *my fridge is filled with delicious cakes*, even if this is what I desire.[12] (Moreover, given that my fridge is actually empty, and I believe this, then were my desire-related thoughts to involve the thought that *my fridge is filled with delicious cakes*, it would be natural enough to describe this as a case where I was *imagining* that this is so.)

In contrast to desiring that p, I suggest, imagining that p necessarily involves thinking of p as being the case. It has this in common with consciously reflecting upon a

---

[12] Of course, one must in some capacity be thinking of cakes; my claim is only that one need not think that one's fridge is filled with them.

belief that *p*, although imagining and believing differ in many other ways (I shall further explore the differences between imagining and belief in Chapter 6).

Putting things in this relatively simple way is, I think, preferable to David Velleman's attempt to distinguish, on the one hand, imagining and believing, and on the other, desiring.[13] He argues that imagining, in common with beliefs but unlike desires, involves the attitude of 'regarding-as-true'. So far his claim and mine look similar, but he cashes his out in a particular way; namely, beliefs and imaginings present events to a thinker as *already made the case*, rather than 'to be made the case', as desire does. They

> treat their...objects as being already true of some completed, though unreal state of affairs, rather than to be made true by the completion of such states.   (2000: 111)

There are a couple of worries here. The first pertains to future-directed propositions which take the form '*such-and-such will be the case*'. Velleman looks committed to saying that where 'p' is this sort of proposition, in regarding-*p*-as-true effectively a thinker must be treating it as already a completed state of affairs that *such-and-such will be the case*. When applied to imagining, it looks as if it follows from this that imagining about an open future is ruled out: wherever one imagines that *such-and-such will be the case*, effectively it is as if *it is already a completed state of affairs that such-and-such will be the case*. Perhaps this is right—after all, some have argued that all fictions have closed futures (Le Poidevin 2001)—but the matter presumably should be discussed. A more troubling implication of Velleman's view, though, is that apparently *beliefs* about the future also inevitably commit one to a closed future. For it seems to follow from his characterization of regarding-as-true that in believing that *such-and-such will be the case*, effectively for the thinker it is also as if *it is already a completed state of affairs that such-and-such will be the case*. This looks quite problematic.

A second worry about Velleman's view is that *desiring* that *p* be the case often seems to involve thinking of whatever 'p' describes as a completed state of affairs. Put simply, in desiring something, I *can* picture or otherwise entertain the thought of what I desire as already completed or achieved. This is allowed for on my view. My claim is only that, unlike believing that *p* or imagining that *p,* desiring that *p need not* involve this. Of course, Velleman could modify his claim accordingly, but it still would not solve the first problem. I conclude that it is safer for current purposes to venture only the more minimal claim that unlike desiring that *p*, both consciously believing and imagining that *p* involve thinking that *p*.[14] They are both quasi-factual, in this sense.

Moving on: F-imagining, qua propositional imagining, can also be informatively contrasted with two other kinds of imagining. The first is 'sensory' imagining (sometimes also called 'experiential imagining'). This is imagining which involves the having

---

[13] Notwithstanding that in the past I have made use of this distinction: e.g. Stock 2008: 371.

[14] Note however that my more minimal claim is not intended as any kind of response to the larger and more complex question of 'direction of fit', which Velleman's discussion is partly designed to address.

of mental imagery: imagining whose contents structurally resemble perceptual experiences. Where, for instance, I sensorily imagine an apple, my experience is structured in a way that noticeably resembles the way that perceptual experience of an apple is structured.

A second kind of imagining from which F-imagining, qua propositional imagining, should be distinguished is 'phenomenal' (or 'perspectival') imagining: imagining seeing, or hearing, or smelling, or touching, or feeling something. This sort of imagining involves imagining a perspective, with a distinctive phenomenology, and is expressed grammatically by attaching the verb 'imagine' to a gerund. If I imagine seeing Rome burning, or imagine tasting Marmite-dipped chocolate, or imagine feeling angry, then I am phenomenally imagining. Now, phenomenal imagining very often involves sensory imagining: in imagining seeing an apple, I sensorily imagine an apple. But arguably, not all phenomenal imagining involves sensory imagining: imagining feeling angry might not. Equally, arguably, sensory imagining need not be phenomenal: I can have an image of an apple without imagining seeing it (for discussion see Peacocke 1985; Noordhof 2002).

Both sensory and phenomenal imagining fall into the category of what Stephen Yablo has called 'objectual imagining': imagining which takes the grammatical form 'imagining an *O*' (1993: 27; see also Gaut 2003 for discussion). Obviously, sensorily imagining an *O* is objectual. Meanwhile, insofar as phenomenal imagining involves imagining a perspective, it too looks objectual (the object being—at least—the perspective in question). An objectual imagining of some object *O* can be more or less accurate about that sort of object. For instance, I might objectually imagine a tiger prowling through a jungle. If I objectually imagine a tiger with pink spots, for instance, then (presumably) no tiger in the world corresponds to this imagining exactly, and to that extent my imagining is inaccurate. However, objectual imagining cannot be true or false: its kind of content cannot bear truth-values. In contrast, as we've seen, propositional imagining can be true or false. It has a content that fits, or fails to fit, what is true.

I will assume that wherever there is objectual imagining of an *O*, there is also propositional imagining that *there is an O*. If, for instance, I imagine an apple, I imagine that there is an apple (which, of course, is not to believe that there is an apple). However, propositional imagining can take place without objectual imagining.[15] One can imagine that *there is an O* without objectually imagining the *O* in question. For instance, one can (propositionally) imagine that *there is a woman* without imagining some woman, with some determinate properties. In contrast, by definition, one cannot objectually imagine a woman without imagining some woman, with some determinate properties.[16] Though objectual imagining of an object *O* can be somewhat

---

[15] Some would classify propositional imagining without sensory imagining as 'supposing'. I do not: see Chapter 6.

[16] This is not to say that in actuality, there must be some particular woman who is the object of one's thought, of course.

indeterminate (Yablo 1993: 28), it also must attribute at least *some* determinate properties to O, over and above membership of the category 'O'.

Objectual imagining is not always a required, nor even an appropriate response to a fiction. Many a fictional passage seems to call for imagining, yet one does not need to sensorily or phenomenally imagine anything in particular in order to properly engage with the passage in question.[17] This is often so with passages describing a character's inner thoughts, where the thought content refers to states of affairs with no characteristic visible manifestation. The following examples are from *The Secret Agent*, *Mrs Dalloway*, and *American Psycho*, respectively:

The echo of the words 'Person unknown' repeating itself in his inner consciousness bothered the Chief Inspector considerably. He would have liked to trace this affair back to its mysterious origin for his own information. He was professionally curious. Before the public he would have liked to vindicate the efficiency of his department by establishing the identity of that man. He was a loyal servant. That, however, appeared impossible.
(Conrad 1961: 89)

Love destroyed too. Everything that was fine, everything that was true went. (Woolf 1964: 140)

On weekends or before a date I prefer to use the Greune Natural Revitalizing Shampoo, the conditioner and the Nutrient Complex. These are formulas that contain Dpanthenol, a vitamin B-complex factor: polysorbate 80, a cleansing agent for the scalp, and natural herbs.
(Easton Ellis 2015: 26)

In such cases, the most we could do, perhaps, is objectually imagine the relevant character having such thoughts (assuming we had information about their physical particulars, which we may not); or phenomenally imagine having such thoughts oneself. But this seems unnecessary for each fictional passage to function well. We can respond simply by propositionally imagining that the character had these thoughts, and also, where appropriate, that the thoughts are or were true.

Even more significantly, some fictional passages describe wholly abstract and non-experienceable states of affairs, which therefore could not be sensorily or phenomenally imagined; for instance:

The geometry of Tlön comprises two somewhat different disciplines: the visual and the tactile. The latter corresponds to our geometry and is subordinated to the first. The basis of visual geometry is the surface, not the point. This geometry disregards parallel lines and declares that man in his movement modifies the forms which surround him. The basis of its arithmetic is the notion of indefinite numbers. They emphasise the importance of the concepts of greater and lesser. (Borges 1970: 37)[18]

There seems to be nothing sensory or phenomenological for our imagination to capture here.

---

[17] Someone apparently indirectly committed to denying this is Kind (2001).

[18] Assuming that one can imagine this, I take this to be a counterexample to the view of Kind (2001) that all imagining is sensory imagining.

Of course, authors very often *do* signal that sensory and/or phenomenal imagining is appropriate for certain fictional passages: most obviously, by giving detailed descriptions of the perceptible properties of people and things. But even here, propositional imagining is clearly appropriate *as well*. Consider, for instance, the following famous passage from *Jane Eyre*:

> The red room was a spare chamber, very seldom slept in…A bed supported on massive pillars of mahogany, hung with curtains of deep red damask, stood out like a tabernacle in the centre, the two large windows, with their blinds always drawn down, were half shrouded in festoons and falls of similar drapery; the carpet was red; the table at the foot of the bed was covered with a crimson cloth; the walls were a soft fawn colour, with a blush of pink in it; the wardrobe, the toilet-table, the chairs, were of a darkly-polished old mahogany.   (Brontë 1966: 45)

The reader obviously is intended by Brontë to form a mental image corresponding to this passage. But equally, she is supposed to propositionally imagine that the things the passage describes are true (or at least, that Jane takes them to be). Additionally in this case, given the context of the wider novel, the informed and competent reader is also supposed imaginatively to describe this room for herself on a number of different levels, whose total content exceeds anything conveyable in a mental image alone. At a superficial level, this is the description of a rather grand and showy Victorian bedroom, over which someone has taken trouble in choosing the decorative features; but on another level, it is a womblike, claustrophobic, sensual environment towards which motherless Jane has ambivalent feelings; and on yet another, it is a temple-like space redolent of pagan rite and blood sacrifice, with the bed as 'tabernacle' and its 'deep red' curtains, and the windows 'shrouded'. At possibly the most dramatic level, it is a Hell-like enclosure, in which her uncle previously has died, and in which eventually she will be locked by her aunt and have a terrifying, possibly supernatural experience. All of this arguably implied content looks more adequately captured by propositional rather than objectual imagining.

Fictions, whatever other kind of imagining they call for, always call for propositional imagining. This, then, is the kind of imagining I will focus on in my account of fictional content. The fictional content of a text (or other set of utterances) is those propositions which one is reflexively intended to F-imagine, where F-imagining is propositional in content.[19]

If all this is right, then we should not expect F-imagining to have a rich or substantial phenomenology. Sometimes it is implied that fictions do not typically invite

---

[19] A further reason to exclude any reflexively intended sensory or phenomenal imaginings from fictional content is that, assuming the reader forms, and is intended to form, a relatively determinate image in response to a given descriptive passage, the precise determinate aspects of her image will nonetheless not correspond exactly to anything she is intended to imagine. In response to the passage above, for instance, the precise shade of crimson, the size of the windows, and the precise spatial relations of the furniture, as represented in one's image, are not dictated by the fiction but decided by the reader.

imagining, because the mental states of readers in relation to fiction need not be particularly phenomenologically rich or vivid (this line is detectable in Matravers 2014). But a lack of rich phenomenology is perfectly consistent with imagining being present, once we distinguish it from sensory or phenomenal imagining. F-imagining involves, minimally, taking a certain attitude of 'thinking that' to a given content that one reads, without a commitment to its truth, any automatic integration with one's belief set, or any automatic relevance to one's behaviour. It may not involve a substantial phenomenological aspect. It can be largely passive and involve little deliberate activity on part of the reader other than reading and processing of lines of text.[20]

B. F-imagining is potentially conjunctive

Turning now to a new point, we should also note that, a lot of the time, the propositions in a fiction are (normally) not presented merely consecutively but also *conjunctively*. If a fiction F says 'p; q; r' where p, q, and r are three different propositions, then (leaving aside for now worries about split narratives, unreliable narrations, and other tricky cases, which will be dealt with in Chapter 5) effectively F normally also implies that '*p and q and r*'. In the first Munro fragment presented just now, it was fictionally true that Rose wrote the Entrance *and* went across the bridge *and* went to high school. In this sense, fiction is normally *conjunctive*.

It follows that, assuming that we accept that fictions call for imagining at all, the sort of imagining called for by fictions is often also conjunctive. In reading 'p', 'q', and 'r', one does not just imagine that *p*, imagine that *q*, and imagine that *r*. One appropriately imagines that *p and q and r*. That is—again for the moment leaving aside the issues of unreliable narration, split narratives, and 'fictions within fictions'—one thinks that the events or situations that *p* and *q* and *r* denote co-occur *with respect to the same scenario*.[21]

Now, typically, a fiction is composed of many propositions, not just a few, and it would be far too demanding, given the normal limits on human memory, to expect a reader actually occurrently (that is, consciously) to enumerate each of them, conjoining them all in thought as she reads. So a better way of characterizing the point

---

[20] Around this point, or later, various commentators have tended to urge: 'yes, but what *is* imagining? What distinguishes it from belief?' Perhaps they are looking for some account citing necessary and sufficient conditions. Recall however that my strategy is not to make ad hoc pronouncements out of thin air, but to enumerate only basic and (I hope) relatively uncontroversial features of imagining at this stage. More will be said about propositional imagining in Chapter 6 after we have thoroughly examined a context in which it gets used; though even there my aim will not be to give a complete account. Something is better than nothing, however.

[21] Often, philosophers refer to the fictional 'world' described or made true by a fiction—e.g. Walton (1990: 57–61)—but there are worries about the baggage this terminology inherits from possible world semantics—see Sainsbury (2014). Indeed, to talk of fictional worlds may well be to prejudice the case in advance against intentionalism (see Lorand 2001 for an insightful discussion of the commitments of talking of 'fictional worlds'). To avoid any potentially problematic associations, I'll refer to a 'scenario' instead.

is that in F-imagining, the reader is at least *disposed to* conjoin in thought any propositions of which she is currently aware, as part of the fiction. Undoubtedly the presence of a physical text, which a reader can review and check whenever she likes, helps in this regard.

We can illustrate this by picking two sentences from Greene's *The Heart of the Matter*, the opening line and one much later:

Wilson sat on the balcony of the Bedford Hotel, his bald pink knees thrust against the ironwork. (1974: 11)

Scobie was left alone with the captain. (1974: 48)

At distinct points in her reading of the work, the competent reader occurrently imagines, among other things, that *Wilson sat on the balcony of the Bedford Hotel, his bald pink knees thrust against the ironwork* and (at some later point in her reading) *Scobie was left alone with the captain*. But additionally she thinks, or is disposed to think, of these things, as well as other things described in the fiction, as occurring at different times with respect to the same scenario. As this indicates, the 'scenario' in question can be thought of as temporally prolonged: a portion of time during which various things are happening, these among them.

What would it be to *exclude* two imaginings from conjunction with one another? If I picked up a book, read, and so imagined that

Wilson sat on the balcony of the Bedford Hotel, his bald pink knees thrust against the ironwork. (Greene 1974: 11)

and then knowingly picked up a different book and read and so imagined that

Martin Martinich's tobacco shop is located in a corner building. (Nabokov 2001: 6)

normally, it would not follow that I imagined that *Wilson sat on the balcony of the Bedford Hotel, his bald pink knees thrust against the ironwork and Martin Martinich's tobacco shop is located in a corner building*, even if I thought these thoughts consecutively. I would not imagine that both of these occur with respect to the same scenario. That is, I would exclude these two imaginings from conjunction with each other.[22] In contrast—to repeat—in imaginatively engaging with a single fiction, a reader (with certain exceptions already noted) typically does not exclude any particular proposition from conjunction in thought with any other in the fiction. Rather she is disposed to conjoin any she is aware of with all others she is aware of.

---

[22] There is a limited analogy here to desire: I can desire that *p* and *q* and *r* with respect to the same scenario, but equally, I might instead desire each of these only relative to some distinct scenario (if it rains, I want to stay in and read; if it is sunny, I want to go for a walk; I do not both want to stay in and read and go for a walk).

In this section I have laid out some basic features of F-imagining, though of course much remains to be said.[23] I turn now to a different and equally basic issue.

1.6 Extreme Intentionalism and Intended Readership

My claim, roughly, is that fictional content is determined by what an author reflexively intends her readership to F-imagine. Who, one might well ask, is her readership? Usually it is specified very broadly: anyone of relevant linguistic competency who comes to read this text. Sometimes it can be more narrowly specified to a particular group: children; 'intelligent, adult men and women, wherever they live'[24] or perhaps even 'a young boy in a small Midwestern town finding one of...[the author's]...books on a library shelf'.[25]

It is possible for a fiction to have two distinct intended audiences: for instance, one for whom certain fictional truths are intended to be more apparent than for another. This is, allegedly, what Charles Dickens did in making certain of his characters 'queer' in a way intentionally hidden from most but still (arguably) apparent to a few (Furneaux 2009). It is also what the cartoon *The Simpsons* does, in addressing one set of fictional truths to children and another more knowing set to adults. An author may make use of knowledge about her intended readership's special competences, common reference points, and other information she can use, in order to signal to them, but not more widely, that certain things are to be imagined.

But for the most part, the intention of an author will be directed relatively generally, drawing on assumed general competences. It will also be *conditional*: not that a particular group of people imagine certain things as a result of reading the work, but rather that, should anyone (perhaps, within a very widely specified group) read the work, they imagine certain things as a result. That is, the readership is those people, whoever they are, that read the work. Just as I can leave out some food in my garden for those birds, whichever they are, that arrive and find it; or a newspaper journalist can write a story, intending whoever reads it to believe it; so too coherently can I intend those people who read my work, whoever they are, to imagine certain things as a result.

The conditional nature of this intention provides an answer to an otherwise tempting objection to intentionalism: what about those authors who intend that no one read their work? Famously, Kafka asked his friend Max Brod to burn his work upon his death, and one can perhaps imagine a case where an author writes some fiction intending no one ever to read it at all.

A first thing to say is that we need not necessarily take the appearances here at face value, for it is perfectly possible for an author to write, intending that a future version of *herself* act as reader and imagine certain things as a result of reading. (Analogously,

---

[23] See Chapter 6.   [24] Raymond Carver, quoting John Cheever, in Simpson and Buzbee 1983.
[25] Raymond Carver, quoting John Updike, *ibid*. Carver is sceptical that this could have been Updike's genuine intention.

I might write a diary, intending a later and forgetful version of myself to believe certain things when I read it.) But say that this sort of interpretation is somehow ruled out. No matter: for intending that no one actually reads one's fiction in future (not even oneself) is compatible with intending that *should anyone read it*, they imagine certain things as a result. One can have several concurrent intentions with respect to alternative possibilities, recognizing that there is often a gap between intending something and achieving it. Even if I write a work genuinely intending no one to read it once I have finished, nonetheless I also might intend that *if anyone were to eventually read it, they would imagine certain things as a result*. This is not incoherent, because one can reasonably recognize that the former intention may, despite one's best efforts, somehow be thwarted in the future.

So much for background preliminaries. I return now to my basic claim about fictional content, which is (I remind the reader):

> An author Au's utterance x (or set of utterances S) has fictional content that p, if and only if: Au utters x (or S) intending that i) x (or S) should cause F-imagining that p in her intended readership R; ii) R should recognize this intention; and iii) R's recognition of this intention should function as part of R's reason to F-imagine that p.

To better understand this claim in detail, we now need to look more closely at Grice's theory of conversational utterance meaning, from which I have adopted many features of my view.

1.7 Grice on Conversational Utterance

As already noted, Grice thinks of communication generally as a deliberate action aimed at the intentional production of certain states of mind in another hearer, in order to procure some further goal of the agent's. His focus in most of his writing is on *conversation*, the primary goal of which, he assumes, is the passing on of information, in the form of beliefs, to others. (Of course, this is unlikely to be an end in itself, but only an instrumental goal of the speaker's, as a means to some further end of hers.)

On Grice's view: in conversation an utterer U means that p by utterance x if and only if U utters x intending that a) the utterance of x should produce a belief that p in an audience A; b) A should recognize this intention; c) A's recognition of this intention should function as part of A's reason to believe that p (Grice 1957). The structural similarity to my view should be obvious.

Grice thinks that in the central case of conversation aimed at information sharing, the meaning (or 'speaker meaning') of an utterance is determined in relation to the content of the beliefs the utterer reflexively intends to produce in the hearer, by producing that utterance. The hearer recovers that meaning in virtue of several factors.

First, she can appeal to conventional sentence meaning. Sentence meaning is determined by rule-bound conventions associating words with things. However, this cannot be the only resource appealed to, for speaker meaning tends to go beyond conventional sentence meaning, into territory traditionally characterized as 'pragmatics'. Very often, for instance, the truth-value of a speaker's use of a sentence (speaker meaning) differs from the truth-value of the sentence on its own (sentence meaning). We can see this by looking at just a few examples (for more, see Bach 1994).

'I haven't had breakfast' may be false for a person, strictly speaking, in that they have had at least one breakfast at some point in their life, but still truthfully may be used by that person on a given occasion, because the sentence is being used in that case to indicate that the person has not had breakfast *that day* (Recanati 2003: 8). Equally, 'you are not going to die' when said to a child who is panicking about a minor cut, is intended to convey that the child will not die from *that cut*, but says something strictly false, according to sentence meaning (Bach 1994: 134). Another famous example is Grice's own description of a teacher who is asked to comment on a student's academic ability, and replies only that he has excellent handwriting and is punctual. In that case, the teacher implies, though she does not state explicitly, that the student is not particularly able (1975). Conveying this, and grasping it as a hearer, depend on more than understanding conventional rules. They depend also on grasping what the speaker intends to communicate.

Grasping what the speaker intends to communicate depends upon, not just the hearer's knowledge of conventional sentence meanings, but a number of other factors too. First, the hearer must apply knowledge of the speaker's likely goals in speaking. Earlier I made it clear that an agent's intentions are closely related to her goals: where she has the ultimate goal *A*, and the instrumental goal of *B*-ing to achieve *A*, very often she will also intend (at least, be committed to trying) to *A*, and intend to *A* by *B*-ing. Relatedly, then, recovering a person's probable intentions with respect to a particular bit of behaviour, including speech, is usefully informed by a consideration of what goals they are likely to have had in speaking, and what beliefs about how such goals interrelate.

We can see these assumptions at work in the Gricean picture. The hearer, interpreting a given piece of conversation, assumes that the speaker has a certain goal in speaking—at least, to communicate informative beliefs to the hearer efficiently, but probably also some further goal as well. Given a grasp on those goals, the interpreter attributes to the speaker the use of certain techniques or strategies for achieving her communicative goal. For instance, according to Grice, assuming that the purpose of a conversation is 'a maximally effective exchange of information' (Grice 1975: 47) it will likely be governed by 'maxims' such as: make your contribution as informative as required (for the current purposes of the exchange); do not make your contribution more informative than is required; try to make your contribution one that is true; do not say what you believe to be false; and others too (*ibid.*). What is meant is worked out by the hearer against a shared understanding of the conversational goal, as well as a related assumption that the maxims listed, or others, are amongst the speaker's strategies at this moment.

For instance, in Grice's example of the teacher commenting on the student, hearers presumably have knowledge of conventional sentence meaning, but this will not be enough to get them to the implication that the student's ability is limited. To get this, it needs to be understood by hearers that the goal of the conversation is to convey information about the student's ability, and not to convey information about punctuality or handwriting. Speaking more generally, Grice writes:

[I]n cases where there is doubt, say, about which of two or more things an utterer intends to convey, we tend to refer to the context (linguistic or otherwise) of the utterance and ask which of the alternatives would be relevant to other things he is saying or doing, or which intention in a particular situation would fit in with some purpose he obviously has...Non-linguistic parallels are obvious: context is a criterion in settling the question of why a man who has just put a cigarette in his mouth has put his hand into his pocket; relevance to an obvious end is a criterion in settling why a man is running away from a bull.

(Grice 1957: 387)

Of course, Grice's view is not uncontroversial. One area of controversy is whether the main purpose of communication really is the conveying of beliefs about the world, rather than, say, about the speaker. It is objected: there are cases of what look like ordinary communication, but which cannot reasonably be analysed in terms of an intention to produce the response of belief about the world, and instead should be analysed in terms of an intention to produce a belief about the speaker. For instance, when one insults someone, the aim of saying that *p* is not to get the hearer to believe that *p*, but rather to get the hearer to believe that the speaker believes that *p* (Vlach 1981: 363). Equally, one might say something out of a feeling of duty 'without caring whether... [the]...audience believes it or not' (Searle 1969: 46); or where one is reminding someone else of something (Vlach 1981: 363-4). In response to these worries, Grice eventually retreated from his initial position to claim that what is essential to communication is rather the intention via one's utterance *x* that *p*, the audience should believe that the speaker believes or thinks that *p* (1969: 171). Others follow him in making meaning a matter of intending to produce beliefs about oneself, the speaker, rather than about the world (e.g. Bach 2012; Davis 1992: 247).

This dispute does not affect my view, however. If anything, it helps my cause, insofar as it makes clear that, since not all conversation is guided by the purpose of conveying information maximally effectively, a fortiori not all utterances are so guided. Other purposes might be implicit in a type of discourse instead. I will emphasize this point when discussing fiction, where, I take it, the purposes of writing, and the techniques used to convey fictional content, are often very different from those present in conversation (see Chapter 2).

In any case, there is no analogous worry with fiction. The objections we have just seen target Grice's conception of conversation as rather narrowly guided by one kind of purpose. Critics note that certain sub-kinds of conversational speech act, such as reminding and insulting, are motivated by particular purposes, where these purposes *are not compatible with* (in the case of reminding) or otherwise *instrumentally do not require* (in the case of insulting), the speaker's intention to induce some new belief about the world in an auditor, in the reflexive way indicated. However, there is no obvious analogous move to be made in the case of fiction. There are not obvious sub-kinds of utterance, akin to insulting or reminding, that have purposes either incompatible with the intention to produce imagining in the way indicated, or which do not require it. Obviously, that it is fictionally true that someone is insulted or reminded does not negate the thought that readers are intended to imagine this. Utterances in fiction look much more homogenous than ordinary utterances in this respect.

A further point of controversy surrounding the Gricean picture is whether Grice is right about the maxims which, he says, govern the interpretation of conversation. For instance, Wilson and Sperber (2004) have argued that we need only to observe that human cognition is geared towards maximizing 'relevance': 'connecting with background information [one]…has in order to yield conclusions that matter to [one]' (2004: 608). In conversation, they argue, hearers are entitled to expect speakers to offer an utterance (or another 'ostensive stimulus') which is a) 'relevant enough to be worth the audience's processing effort' and b) 'the most relevant one compatible with communicator's [SIC] abilities and preferences' (2004: 612). In turn, in the interpretation of utterances, hearers will 'follow a path of least effort' in interpreting meaning, and 'stop when [their]…expectations of relevance are satisfied' (2004: 613). In this way they will achieve hypotheses about both explicit content and implicatures, without adverting to individual Gricean maxims.

I do not need to pick a side in this disagreement. A couple of things can be said in response. The first is that, *whatever* interpretative strategies tend to be used in conversation (few or many), they will also often be used in the interpretation of much fictional content. This is because of at least two factors. The first is that authors of fictions often intentionally and knowingly represent conversations: either two-way conversations between characters, or one-sided conversations between a fictional narrator and the reader or other party (I will return to this point in Chapter 2). Authors have an implicit grasp of the strategies ordinarily used to interpret conversation, and they expect their readers to understand these too. With this expectation in the background, they can represent conversations intentionally in fictional passages, intending readers to use conversation-relevant interpretative strategies to work out the fictional content of those passages. The second fact is that sometimes authors use fictions as a vehicle for the conveying of information and belief to readers, in a way which resembles the way many conversations convey information and belief to hearers. These sorts of case will be discussed in Chapters 3 and 4. In this sort of case, where it is recognized as such, competent readers' strategies of interpretation are likely to resemble those they would employ in interpreting conversation (or at least, information-bearing discourse).

The second point to make in response to the disagreement about Gricean maxims is that again, whatever interpretative strategies tend to be used in conversation, some interpretative strategies apply *only to fiction*, and not to conversation, so that this dispute does not affect them. Fictional texts are aimed at the production of F-imagining in the reader. This is obviously a different communicative purpose from ordinary conversation (typically, anyway). Therefore, although as acknowledged there will be some overlap, the strategies of interpretation of fictional texts will differ significantly from those principles governing the interpreting of ordinary conversation. In Chapter 2, I will describe some of these strategies in more detail.

Summing up: there are several important things for us to notice in Grice's account. First, he thinks of communication as the intentional production of states of mind, or other responses, in another hearer, in order to procure some further instrumental or ultimate goal. Secondly, he thinks of the meaning of a conversational utterance as determined in relation to the content of the states of mind the utterer reflexively intends to produce in the hearer, by producing that utterance. Thirdly, he thinks of there normally being evidence available for the meaning of an utterance, in terms of not just a) conventional sentence meanings of the words used; but also b) evidence about the speaker's goals in speaking, both instrumental and ultimate; and c) knowledge of the strategies of interpretation which tend to be used to achieve those goals, and of which, one assumes, the speaker has at least implicit knowledge, expecting hearers to have the same.

According to my version of extreme intentionalism, the production of a fictional text is a communicative act, in the broad Gricean sense. What is communicated, normally, is determined by an author's reflexive intentions to produce certain imaginings in her audience or readership. The precise nature of those intentions can be discerned partly by considering conventional sentence meaning, but also by considering what goals, both ultimate and instrumental, the author has in producing her utterances, and her likely beliefs about how best to achieve those goals. Uncovering these intentions is a way of uncovering what she meant.

1.8 Fiction Versus Conversation

At this point, it is useful to address a possible misunderstanding. This emerges in a common criticism of the intentionalist position of Noel Carroll. Like me, Carroll is an 'actual author intentionalist' about fictional content.[26] One obvious difference between us is that he is a 'modest' intentionalist, whilst my intentionalism is extreme. However, a similarity between our views is that Carroll is also working in a Gricean tradition. He argues that an authorial intention that a text mean something is a Gricean-style reflexive one:

the meaning of an utterance is explicated in terms of the speaker's intention to reveal to an auditor that the speaker intends the auditor to respond in a certain way.   (1992: 97)

---

[26] In fact, he takes this position with respect to art meaning generally, as I do not (see my Introduction).

Carroll defends his intentionalism by arguing that interpreting meaning in art generally, and so a fortiori fictional content, involves entering 'a relationship roughly analogous to a conversation' (1992: 117). Just as successful conversation is a form of communication, and communication relies on the possibility of understanding one another's utterances via understanding their reflexive intentions, so too should we think of fiction as a would-be communicative act, interpretation of which depends on understanding the author's reflexive intentions.

Yet Carroll's view is sometimes criticized on the grounds that art generally is unlike conversation in certain ways. Recently, Huddleston (2012) has posed Carroll a dilemma: either art is unlike conversation in that it is one-sided, whereas conversation involves participants both speaking and listening; or art is like conversation, but only in the respect that readers as well as authors make a significant contribution to the meaning of works (thereby falsifying intentionalism).

This misses the point somewhat. The important point for Carroll is that art (or in my case, fiction) is a form of Gricean communication, not that it is a (two-way) conversation. Grice, the originator of the view of communication to which Carroll is committed, could perfectly well allow that communication is one-sided; indeed it actually follows from his account of communication that it *is* one-sided! To recap: communication occurs where (roughly) a hearer understands what mental states or other responses she has been intended to acquire by a speaker. This is a one-way relation. Conversation, insofar as it is a species of communication and replicates this structure with respect to the mental state of belief, is a one-way relation too, on Grice's view. So there is no problem with art, or fiction, being both like conversation and one-sided. This being so, the first horn of Huddleston's dilemma can be easily grasped: fiction is unlike *many conversations as commonly conceived*, perhaps, in that it is one-sided, but that does not mean it is not communicative, which is the required feature for Carroll's argument to work. Indeed, since on Grice's view, conversation is essentially one-sided, this fact would not even rule out fiction's being a form of conversation, though of course it is not, being governed by different purposes. In any case, that it is one-sided is consistent with the content of fiction being (wholly) determined by the author's intentions.

1.9 What Is the Relation Between Understanding Fictional Content and Imagining?

Another point to clear up before we go further is this. According to me, fictional cognition involves understanding what one is reflexively intended to F-imagine, as one reads a text. But then, one might wonder: if this is fictional cognition, what role does *actually F-imagining* play in it? The worry is that it starts to look superfluous. Yet this would be strange, since the starting point of my enquiry was that fictions and imagining are closely intertwined.

Here again, we need to compare the comprehension of conversation. To understand the meaning of conversation, a hearer simply needs to understand what she is reflexively intended to believe; she need not actually believe it. However, as a matter of fact, very often the hearer *will* immediately believe what she is intended to. That is, in many cases understanding what one is supposed to believe and believing it co-occur. In many cases of testimony, for instance, there is an imperceptible distance between grasping what one is intended to believe and believing it. A hearer's believing it immediately, where she does, is a source of evidence that (among other things) she has (quickly, automatically, sub-personally) applied mechanisms of comprehension and an appreciation of speaker purpose (etc.) and arrived at an understanding of what she was to believe. In other cases, though, the hearer merely understands what she is to believe, but does not believe it (say, where she mistrusts the speaker). Or else, in unusual cases (as when, perhaps, the speaker is using a code), she does not understand what she is to believe immediately, and has to work it out with reference to surrounding clues about the speaker's speech and behaviour.

Equally then: for fictional cognition, all the reader needs to do is understand what she is intended to F-imagine, not F-imagine it, though most of the time she will immediately F-imagine it as well. (Remember too that F-imagining need not involve a substantial phenomenology.) That is, in most cases understanding what one is reflexively intended to F-imagine and F-imagining that thing will co-occur.[27] Where this is the case, that one F-imagines something is a source of evidence that one has (quickly, automatically, sub-personally) applied mechanisms of comprehension and an understanding of authorial purpose (etc.) and arrived at an understanding that one is intended to imagine that thing. In other cases, however, the reader merely understands what she is to imagine, but does not imagine it. Relevant cases will be discussed in Chapter 4. And in yet another sort of case, the reader fails immediately to understand what she is to imagine, and instead has to work it out by reference to surrounding context. This sort of case will be discussed in Chapter 2.

Noting that for much of the time the reader immediately understands what she is intended to imagine wards off yet another familiar objection to intentionalism: that much of the time, the reader *does not feel as if she is working out an author's intentions, as she reads*. This is not a good objection to my view, just as it would not be a good objection to the claim that in interpreting action generally one is interpreting an agent's intention, to point out that most of the time it does not feel as if one is. Much interpretation of other people's actions and speech is effortless, because the strategies of interpretation one uses in the process are so well-embedded and familiar. But this does not mean that we are not interpreting intentions when we interpret action: we are simply doing so effortlessly and immediately. When the process breaks down—as when the

---

[27] In fact, presumably, it will happen even more readily than in the case of belief-acquisition following testimony, since, in contrast to that case, there is no requirement that the hearer take the speaker to be trustworthy, for instance. For more on the conditions governing belief-acquisition in relation to testimony, see Chapter 4.

reader is not sure what she is intended to imagine—a sense of effort and of deliberate thought about the author's purposes and context becomes apparent, but nonetheless, what one is doing there is continuous with what one was doing before, effortlessly.

1.10 Four Challenges to Extreme Intentionalism

I turn now to objections to my position, which will be discussed over chapters to come. As I have noted, extreme intentionalism about fictional content (or art more generally) is often presented at the beginning of philosophical discussions of interpretation as a daft view, to be avoided. Even fellow supporters of intentionalism reject it outright (Carroll 2000: 76). Four objections to it are offered standardly by analytic philosophers of art and fiction, and are taken to be decisive. Dealing with these challenges will bring out further important features of the position.

The challenges are as follows:

1. Extreme intentionalism entails that individual speakers can arbitrarily change or elude the conventionally given, rule-bound meanings of sentences; and that hence, miswriting (or misspeaking) is implausibly ruled out as impossible.
2. Extreme intentionalism entails that the fictional content of a text is hidden perniciously from readers, either generally or in particular cases.
3. Extreme intentionalism implausibly entails that there are no genuinely unsuccessful intentions that a text mean something.
4. Extreme intentionalism potentially 'decentralizes' the fictional text as a source of its own content, by potentially making other accompanying pieces of evidence more important in interpretation than the text is.

In the rest of this chapter, I shall deal with the first of these. A large part of Chapter 2 will be devoted to discussing the kinds of strategies, generally, that an interpreter reasonably may employ, in assessing fictional content; it therefore goes some way to addressing the second challenge. Chapter 3 will contain responses to the third and fourth challenges, in the course of discussing rivals to extreme intentionalism, who tend to try to make a lot of capital from these challenges in particular.

1.11 Speaker Meaning and Sentence Meaning

The first challenge as just outlined underlies several rejections of extreme intentionalism. For instance, (where 'linguistic meaning' stands for 'sentence meaning') Dickie and Wilson address an interpretation of Grice's view, according to which:

[I]n order to know the linguistic meaning of a sentence, one must know the speaker's intention in uttering the sentence…This interpretation…claims that knowledge of speaker's communicative intention suffices for linguistic meaning…[Yet this]…is readily disposed of. As we walk along a street in Chinatown, a merchant engages us. Understanding no Cantonese, we are not able to understand the sentences she utters. We might, however, recognize her communicative intention: she wishes us to buy the unfamiliar wrinkled pale green squash-looking vegetable she is waving in our faces. We recognize her intention, but that is not sufficient for us to understand in full specificity the sentences she utters. (Dickie and Wilson 1995: 241)

We find here the apparent assumption that it might be a commitment of extreme intentionalism that *sentence meaning is determined by individual speaker meaning*. This is assumed to be true by both defenders of extreme intentionalism (e.g. Knapp and Michaels 1987); and some of its critics. The latter worry that, if (extreme) intentionalism were true, we would have a parlous state of affairs where sentences meant just what speakers intended them to. Presumably for similar reasons, the complaint is made that if (extreme) intentionalism were true, *words* would mean whatever their utterers intended (e.g. Carroll 2000: 76). Hence, it is then assumed to follow also, for as long as an author intended that word 'x' mean 'y', she could never misspeak or use 'x' incorrectly.

Yet any assumption that according to extreme intentionalism, sentence meaning is to be determined by speaker meaning, is based on a misunderstanding of the intentionalist view. This can be shown easily by reverting to the comparative discussion about the meaning of conversational utterance.

It is true that, relatively unusually amongst intentionalists about conversation, Grice claims that in conversation, sentence meaning is ultimately determined by speaker meaning (1957: 385). However, he does not claim that sentence meaning is determined by an *individual* speaker's intentions, a position which seems to be the favourite stalking horse of the critics of extreme intentionalism. His claim is rather that sentence meaning is determined by *collective* speaker meaning (1957: 385). In any case, most philosophers of language would *reject* this part of Grice's view, instead holding that sentences get their meanings by virtue of public conventions associating them with certain referents. Nonetheless, most remain intentionalist about speaker meaning in conversation without any fear of inconsistency (Recanati 1986: 213).

On a plausible account of speaker meaning in conversation, the relation between speaker meaning and conventional sentence meaning is as follows. Speaker meaning normally (and intentionally) makes use of conventional sentence meaning. However, speaker meaning is not wholly determined by those meanings: it may deviate from them.

Speaker meaning is not wholly determined by conventional sentence meaning for two reasons. First, it may exceed it, since, as already noted, there is a wide number of ways in which meaning can be conveyed pragmatically (remember our examples earlier). Secondly, there are cases where some of those conventions are violated deliberately and systematically, in order to produce some further nonconventional implicature. Take some instances of irony, for instance. Say that K tells J, who has just crashed into K's car, 'Clearly, you are a brilliant driver'. Here K's meaning is the opposite of sentence meaning; K intends J (let's say) to believe that she is a terrible driver.

Most think that speaker meaning is usually at least partly determined by (conventional) sentence meaning. But this is only because using conventional sentence meaning is normally a good way of getting your communicative intentions across, as a speaker. The speaker knowingly calls upon her understanding of conventions governing sentence meaning, and employs sentences presuming her audience will share this understanding. Hence, for this reason, it is appropriate to infer, from the use of a word with a conventionally associated meaning, that the speaker intended to convey that meaning, unless we have good reason to do otherwise (Grice 1957: 387). Appealing to the conventional meanings of a sentence when uttered by a particular speaker *is a way of* recovering the speaker's speaker meaning (her intentions). However, as with irony, it is *not the only way*:

> Of course I would not want to deny that when the vehicle of meaning is a sentence...the speaker's intentions are to be recognised, in the normal case, by virtue of a knowledge of the conventional use of the sentence. But...I would like, if I can...to treat a conventional correlation between a sentence and a specific response as providing only one of the ways in which an utterance may be correlated with a response.   (Grice 1969: 160–1)

Does it follow that speakers may 'arbitrarily' make words mean whatever they intend them to mean? No! This is because of a constraint on the having of an intention, already noted in earlier discussion of intention generally: where a person *K* intends someone else to do something, *K* must at least not believe that the other person cannot or could not do what she intends them to do. Or as Grice himself puts it:

> [O]ne cannot in general intend that some result should be achieved, if one knows there is no likelihood it will be achieved.   (1969: 161)

It follows that, where *K* has a reflexive intention to produce a belief that *p* in her hearer via a certain utterance *x*, this requires, at least, *K*'s not believing that it is impossible that the hearer recognize that she is intended to believe that *p* on hearing *x*. (If she does not recognize this she will not acquire the relevant belief in the right way.) Let '*M*-intending' be the kind of Gricean reflexive intention that a certain response be provoked in a hearer. Stephen Neale writes, reconstructing Grice:

> What *U* meant by uttering *X* is determined solely by *U*'s communicative intentions; but of course the formation of genuine communicative intentions by *U* is constrained by *U*'s expectations: *U* cannot be said to utter *X M*-intending *A* to Ø if *U* thinks that there is very little or no hope that *U*'s production of *X* will result in *A* Ø-ing.   (Neale 1992: 552–3)

In other words, I cannot just mean my hearer to believe that *grass is green* arbitrarily by an utterance of 'it's ten past two'; for, normally at least, I would have no positive belief that my hearer could successfully grasp my intention for her to believe this by means of such an utterance.[28]

---

[28] See also Donnellan (1968: 213); Davidson (2006: 258); Carroll (1992: 99).

However, this is not to say that speaker meaning may not deviate and conflict with conventional sentence meaning at all. It may do so, *as long as the speaker believes that nonetheless the speaker meaning will be apparent to the hearer.* This is how private, playful codes get going: the speaker judges that the hearer will understand her, even given her disruption of conventional sentence norms.

So far I have talked only of conversation. But similar points can be made with respect to fictional content.[29] Like the intentionalist about conversation, the extreme intentionalist does not need to assume that in the production of fiction, conventional sentence meaning is determined by (individual) speaker meaning. She too can say simply and coherently: sentence meaning is determined conventionally. Authors writing fictional texts intentionally make use of sentence meanings. Much of the time, their intentions are straightforward, and so fictional content is at least consistent with the conventional meaning of the sentences they use. However, in many cases, in terms of implied fictional content, fictional content goes beyond conventional sentence meaning. Moreover, in some cases, fictional content intentionally *deviates from* conventional sentence meaning. However, this does not open up the possibility of arbitrary and random word meaning: for here too, the author cannot seriously intend a sentence to mean something which, she judges, her readers could not possibly recognize.

In many straightforward cases, fictional content makes use of conventionally-bestowed sentence and word meanings. Just as it is in conversation, employing conventional public meanings is one obvious way of ensuring that one's readership recognize one's intentions as to what they are to imagine (Stecker 2006 is clear on this point). This in turn means that, unless there is evidence otherwise, the interpreting reader is entitled to take speaker meaning to utilize the conventional meanings of words and sentences. Earlier I quoted Grice on this matter, on speaker meaning in general; here, for a change, is Strawson, talking about ordinary utterance but making a point easily applied to fiction too:

> The speaker has a motive, inseparable from the nature of his act, for making [his complex] intention clear. For he will not...have performed the act of communication he sets out to perform, unless his complex intention is grasped. Now clearly, for the enterprise to be possible at all, there must exist, or he must find, means of making the intention clear. If there exist any conventional linguistic means of doing so, the speaker has both a right to use, and a motive for using, those means. (1964: 450–1)

However, intentional use of convention is not the end of the story. Just as with ordinary speaker meaning in conversation, there is so much, potentially, to speaker meaning in fiction that could not be determined by convention alone (Stecker 2006: 431). In Chapter 2 we will look at examples where what is conveyed goes well beyond the

---

[29] S. Davies (2006: 228) is one of the few critics of intentionalism who recognize that if fictional interpretation were properly like the interpretation of ordinary conversation, we should be extreme intentionalists after all.

application of conventional rules, but for the moment a few relatively banal examples will suffice.

The Nabokov story 'Revenge' starts:

Ostend, the stone wharf, the gray strand, the distant row of hotels, were all slowly rotating as they receded into the turquoise haze of an autumn day.   (Nabokov 2001: 67)

It turns out that it is not fictionally true that Ostend is *literally rotating*; rather it is fictionally true that the onlooking professor is on a boat which is turning away from it. Discerning this is not a matter of grasping some convention: the very same sentence, in a different fiction, could mean that Ostend was literally rotating. Equally, in Jean Rhys's *Wide Sargasso Sea*, when Antoinette recounts:

These were all the people in my life—my mother and Pierre, Christophine, Godfrey, and Sass who had left us.   (Rhys 2001: 7)

it is not fictionally true that she means literally 'all the people', but rather 'all the significant people' (yet in an apocalyptic fiction, the sentence might have been intended to quantify literally).[30]

Equally, meanwhile, an author can coherently intend a content for a sentence or word in a way that deviates even more strongly from conventional use. Irony occurs in fiction just as in ordinary conversation, if not more often; but for a particularly interesting example, take the opening pages of Anthony Burgess's *A Clockwork Orange*:

There was me, that is Alex, and my three droogs, that is Pete, Georgie, and Dim, Dim being really dim, and we sat in the Korova Milkbar making up our rassoodocks what to do with the evening, a flip dark chill winter bastard though dry. The Korova Milkbar was a milk-plus mesto, and you may, O my brothers, have forgotten what these mestos were like, things changing so skorry these days and everybody very quick to forget, newspapers not being read much neither.   (Burgess 1972: 5)

Note that speaker meaning here, though not conventionally determined, is still *recognizable and intended to be*. Words like 'rassoodocks' and 'skorry' have a meaning discernible to the reader, not through any straightforward relation to conventional associations, but rather through their intentionally-selected syntactical position in the text. This mimics that of other words, with which, it emerges, they are intended to be taken as synonymous. The same is true of Jonathan Safran Foer's *Everything is Illuminated*, in which the Ukrainian narrator Alex relies upon a thesaurus for his vocabulary:

My legal name is Alexander Perchov. But all of my many friends dub me Alex, because that is a more flaccid-to-utter version of my legal name. Mother dubs me Alexi-stop-spleening-me!, because I'm always spleening her. If you want to know why I'm always spleening her, it's because

---

[30] It is true that we are working out what Antoinette means here, but that, I suggest, is wholly dependent on what Rhys intends her to mean.

I'm always elsewhere with friends, and disseminating so much currency, and performing so many things that can spleen a mother. (Safran Foer 2002: 1)

Though extreme intentionalism allows that speaker meaning may deviate from direct appropriation of sentence meaning, a sensible version does not allow that speaker meaning could deviate from conventional meaning to the extent that the reader could not reasonably be believed to recognize what the allegedly determinative intention was. Had it been that in some interview, Douglas Adams claimed that the Vogon poem 'Oh Freddled Gruntbuggly' in *The Hitchhiker's Guide to the Galaxy* ('Oh freddled gruntbuggly, Thy micturations are to me, As plurdled gabbleblotchits on a lurgid bee') was intended to prompt imaginings about glossy chestnut mares cantering on a beach, then, since he could not plausibly have believed that readers would recognize this intention via such an utterance, we would have been entitled to say that he was mistaken or joking about his own intentions. This follows from the condition upon the having of an intention noted earlier: to intend someone to do something, one cannot believe that it is impossible for that person. For an author to reflexively intend that her utterance of x should be a reason for her readers to F-imagine that p, she cannot believe that achieving this is impossible; yet if she believes her choice of words and sentences is thoroughly and arbitrarily at odds with conventional rules, in a way undetectable to the reader, then she will believe achieving this is impossible. Neither Burgess nor Foer fall foul of this constraint—they each had good reason to believe that readers would recognize the syntactical position of words such as 'skorry' and 'spleening' in their texts, and *work out* what the authors intended such words to mean, based on their knowledge of other more familiar words which tended to fit this context.

We can now see that the worry that extreme intentionalism must have it that sentence and word meaning could be arbitrarily changed simply by a speaker's intentions, is an illusion.[31] First, there is no suggestion that conventional sentence meanings themselves get changed by individual speakers' intentions (or, *pace* Grice, by speakers' intentions at all). Secondly, in cases where a speaker intends to use a sentence in a way which deviates from its conventional meaning, she can only genuinely intend this if she does not judge that the hearer stands no chance of understanding her intention. This rules out any arbitrary meaning changes which look in principle unrecognizable.

---

[31] It is sometimes objected to me in conversation: couldn't a severely irrational person genuinely believe that [arbitrary sound x] could communicate meaning M to hearer H, and so reflexively intend that x produce F-imagining in H? My response is that, in cases of such severe breakdowns of rationality, notions of utterer's meaning become very unclear, both for fictive utterance and for ordinary conversation. It is not clear even if such cases should be treated as of a piece with ordinary utterer's meaning. If wished then, my position can be taken to apply to only those fictions not produced by people severely impaired by false beliefs about what the sounds or marks they make may communicate (after all, this accommodates nearly all fictions, and certainly all published ones). See Irwin (2015: 146) for someone who feels more relaxed about attributing intentions to radically irrational agents.

1.12 Extreme Intentionalism and Miswriting

Within the objection I am now considering, there was an additional though related worry expressed: that extreme intentionalism ruled out the possibility of misspeaking or miswriting. This too is misplaced.

On the intentionalist view of conversation, a central sort of case of misspeaking, including malapropisms, happens where a speaker intends to use a conventional word or sentence meaning—that is, she intends to communicate the very meaning of that word or sentence, as conventionally understood, via the use of that word or sentence— but makes a mistake and unintentionally uses the wrong word or sentence instead. In that case, in working out what the speaker meant, we fairly standardly advert to what she was intending to say; which is how we can say that 'mis' speaking occurred at all. Equally, a central case of miswriting by an author with respect to a fiction is where she intends to use a conventional word or sentence meaning, but makes a mistake and unintentionally uses the wrong word or sentence. Here again, intentionalism explains the possibility of miswriting, rather than being incompatible with it.

Some argue that where misspeaking or miswriting occurs, the meaning which should be prioritized is the conventional one originally and mistakenly conveyed. See for instance:

[S]uppose someone says: "You are a very perspicuous fellow." The best hypothesis is that the speaker intends to say that the person addressed is perspicacious (that is, someone with acute judgement), but it does not follow that the speaker did say this. In fact, it seems quite certain that he did not but rather uttered the nonsense that the person in question is expressed very clearly.   (Stecker 2006: 437)[32]

However, this seems at odds with actual practice. Granted, there are *some* contexts in which what a speaker says first, in terms of sentence meaning, is taken to determine what act has been committed, even if it contains an inadvertent slip. One example seems to be in card games:

A player might let slip the word "redouble" without meaning to redouble; but if the circumstances are appropriate and the play strict, then he has redoubled (or he may be held to have redoubled)...Forms can take charge, in the absence of appropriate intention.

(Strawson 1964: 457)

Strawson goes on to describe this case as 'essentially deviant or nonstandard' (*ibid.*). But in any case, neither conversation nor the writing of fiction looks like this sort of case. If they did, in the case of conversation there would be no asking speakers what they really meant, and often deferring to the answer; and in the case of fiction, no patient editing of manuscripts, no proof-reading, and no correcting of typos and other slips in subsequent published editions. Literary practice clearly allows that authors can notice and

---

[32] This is actually presented as an objection to hypothetical intentionalism (see Chapter 3) but apparently would apply to extreme intentionalism as well.

correct mistaken forms of expression to better fit their governing intention. The right conclusion to draw, with respect to fiction as well as conversation, is that speaker meaning is favoured over sentence meaning as a determiner of utterance meaning, even in cases where in practice the text as it is fails to produce the intended response.

1.13 Summary

In the first part of this chapter, I introduced extreme intentionalism, and set up some preliminaries about intention, F-imagining, and other basic matters. I then focused on the relation between extreme intentionalism about fictional content and a Gricean position on speaker meaning in conversational utterance. We saw how, according to each of these views, what is communicated is determined by an author's reflexive intentions to produce certain states of minds in her audience or readership: in the case of fictional content, F-imaginings, and in the case of conversational utterance, beliefs (at least in some central cases). The precise nature of those intentions can be discerned partly by considering conventional sentence meaning, but also by considering what goals, both ultimate and instrumental, the speaker or author has in producing her utterances, and her likely beliefs about how best to achieve those goals. I also discussed the nature of an intended readership, and the apparent problem for extreme intentionalism of works positively intended not to be read by anyone.

In the latter part of this chapter, I described four frequently posed challenges to extreme intentionalism about fictional content, and addressed the first of these: that it implies, implausibly, that words mean whatever the speaker intends them to, and that therefore there is no misspeaking or miswriting. Chapter 2 will move towards addressing the second of these challenges, via a relatively detailed discussion of the kinds of strategies which may be employed in the interpretation of fictional content.[33]

---

[33] The rest of my response to that challenge will be found in Chapter 3.

2

Intentionalist Strategies of Interpretation

2.1 Introduction

This chapter is concerned with strategies of interpretation of fictional content. Broadly speaking, it aims to do two things. In the first half, I will argue that, though there are many legitimate strategies of interpretation available, no strategy of interpretation is applied appropriately without exception to fictional texts. This will provide a further source of support for extreme intentionalism, inasmuch as intentionalism provides a good explanation of why this is so: a strategy of interpretation is appropriate for a text only when its author (effectively) intends the reader to use it, and not all authors may share intentions in this respect. With this material in mind, in the latter part of the chapter I will then turn more squarely to addressing the second objection raised against intentionalism towards the end of Chapter 1: that is, that fictions standardly might have perniciously hidden, even undetectable meanings. Against this worry, I will show that there is in fact a range of evidence normally available, to which an interpreter may legitimately appeal.

2.2 Conventions of Sentence Meaning

My general claim, to be defended, is that no strategy of interpretation of fictional content is inevitably appropriate to a given text, or portion of a fictional text. For every application of a given strategy, we need to assume implicitly, or in some cases explicitly look for, a prior sanction offered by the author's intentions.

My first point can be made relatively briefly, since it has already been covered. In Chapter 1 we saw that it is normally appropriate for a reader to interpret a fictional text according to her understanding of conventional sentence meanings. We saw that, in order to convey their communicative intentions to readers, authors have a vested interest in making those intentions clear. Using conventional sentence meaning is a means of partly achieving this. Hence, normally, unless there is evidence to show otherwise, the reader is entitled to think that the author is using sentence and word meaning in a way determined by conventional rules. However, this is compatible with denying that conventional sentence meanings get applied to (certain parts of) fictional texts *automatically*: the Burgess and Safran Foer examples discussed in Chapter 1 showed that this is false. Authors can subvert conventional sentence meaning intentionally, as long as they do so in a way which, they believe, is in principle recoverable by readers.

It is true that even Burgess and Safran Foer appeal in the relevant works to conventional sentence meanings a lot of the time; and that a fiction which made no standard use of conventional sentence meanings would almost certainly fail in generating any imaginings, and so content, at all. So the scope of this claim is best understood as concerning parts of texts, not texts as a whole. Even so, my point has consequences even for those more typical cases where sentences are being used according to conventional norms. Sometimes, the fact that evidence for a particular interpretation includes evidence of conventional sentence meaning is taken by philosophers to show that evidence of convention is *something separate from and additional to* evidence of authorial intention (e.g. Livingston 2005: 155).[1] But this is not right—even where authorial intentions 'mesh' with sentence meaning, *sentence meaning is being used intentionally in a particular way*. The author intends to use conventional sentence meanings straightforwardly, and their presence is a source of evidence about that intention.

So interpreting according to conventions governing sentence meaning is not independent of appealing to intentions. I turn now to a more complex kind of content, generated not by semantic means but by pragmatic means: what usually are called 'implied fictional truths'.

2.3 Implied Fictional Truths

It is well-known that fictions do not only make certain states of affairs fictional via conventional sentence meanings. They also *imply* that certain other things are to be imagined via other means. For instance, in Haruki Murakami's *South of the Border, West of the Sun*, set in 80s Tokyo, there is no explicit mention that the scenario described is a post-Hiroshima one: yet the following sentences effectively tell us so, via their implied reference to the shadows flash-burnt into the walls of Hiroshima:

The four a.m. streets looked shabby and filthy. The shadow of decay and disintegration lurked everywhere, and I was part of it. Like a shadow burned into a wall. (Murakami 2003: 72)

---

[1] Alternatively, there is the position of Richard Gaskin, who argues that: 'the original meaning of a work of literature is a function of the meanings that its component words have in the language at the time of that work's promulgation, of the contemporary significance of the syntactic constructions into which those words are fitted, and of the work's historical and literary context. We may say that an author has the resulting or constructive intention to mean by his work what it objectively means in this sense' (2013: 219). He apparently thinks of a 'constructive' authorial intention as picking out by ostension whatever the work 'objectively' means, in terms of conventional sentence meaning plus relevant historical and literary content. On my view, authors can communicate via pragmatic means fictional truths which could not have been anticipated by reference to conventional and historical factors alone. Moreover, our practice of looking at 'historical and literary context' to recover fictional truth makes sense only on the assumption that it might give us good information about what the author was intending to do.

This fictional truth is not recovered from conventional sentence meaning alone. Consider these further examples, to which I shall return later. In *Jane Eyre* arguably it is fictional that Jane's lack of any maternal figure in early childhood has had an enormous effect on her—though this is not apparent through Brontë's telling the reader directly, anywhere in the text. The percipient reader of Nancy Mitford's *The Pursuit of Love* knows without being told directly that it is fictional that Lord Merlin is gay. And (spoiler alert!) in Sarah Waters' *The Little Stranger*, it is implied though not stated anywhere that the narrator, Dr Faraday, commits vandalism, violent acts, and murder. A theory of interpretation focusing on implied fictional truth should be able to explain these facts.

For the moment, let's just take implied fictional truths as identical to any fictional truths in a text *not* generated directly via an understanding of conventional sentence meanings, but conveyed pragmatically by other means. The question now is: are there any interpretative strategies of which a reader can appropriately make use automatically, to detect the presence of implied fictional truths?

2.4 Fiction Treated as Ordinary Conversation

In Chapter 1 we saw that in the case of ordinary conversation, interpretation of its pragmatic aspects usually involves an appeal to the assumed central purpose of the speaker in engaging in that discourse: arguably, to convey information to the hearer. In contrast, it seems that, in order to understand all of the non-conventional pragmatic aspects of fictional content, it would be inappropriate for the reader exclusively to treat fiction as if it were an information-oriented conversation. For obviously, a fiction very often is written with intentional purposes other than information-oriented ones—for instance, to provide pleasure, a thrill, titillation, horror, and so on—and it is likely, as in fact I will describe shortly, that certain distinct pragmatic implications will stem from understanding it as such.

It is true that *sometimes, for some parts of fictions*, as I shall argue in Chapter 4, the author of a fiction aims to provide the reader with reliable world-relevant information via her text; and in passages where this happens, the application of pragmatic norms inherited from ordinary conversation can be appropriate. However, where it is appropriate, this too is subject to the background understanding that the author *intends to* pass on information, in those passages, thereby making application of the norms in question appropriate. The norms do not get to apply automatically.

One might argue that, at least, *where a fiction explicitly represents a conversation, this* part of the fiction should be interpreted as we interpret ordinary information-oriented conversation (minus any commitment or inference to the truth of what is expressed, in most cases). Much fiction explicitly represents what can reasonably be counted in a loose sense as conversations: either in the form of dialogue, or in the form of letters to another character, or in the form of a first-personal narration to the reader or another character. In many fictions, characters engage in communication and information-exchange. It is therefore reasonable to think that many of the purposes which animate ordinary conversation will often fictionally animate conversations in stories as well; and that therefore, it is often reasonable to apply to fictional conversations those strategies used in interpreting ordinary conversation, in order to find out what is fictionally pragmatically implied by the characters in question.

Take the following extract from *The Power and the Glory*, a conversation between Tench and the whisky priest:

> 'O God, I'd like a drink. *Ora pro nobis.*'
> 'I have a little brandy,' the stranger said.
> Mr Tench regarded him sharply. 'Where?'
> The hollow man put his hand to his hip—he might have been indicating the source of his odd nervous hilarity. Mr Tench seized his wrist.
> 'Careful,' he said. 'Not here.'...
> 'Come to my place,' Mr Tench said.
> 'I meant,' the little man said reluctantly, 'just to see her go.'
> 'Oh it will be hours yet,' Mr Tench assured him again.
> 'Hours? Are you certain? It's very hot in the sun.'
> 'You'd better come home.'
>
> (Greene 1971: 11)

Presumably Greene intends us to interpret this conversation in many of the ways in which we would interpret a conversation composed of identical sentences, were we to overhear it in actuality. We are to infer, for instance, that (it is fictionally true in this text that) 'I meant just to see her go' means 'I only intended to see her go' (we also learn from earlier conversation that 'her' refers to a ship). We are also to infer that 'Oh it will be hours yet', refers to the time 'she' will go; and that 'It's very hot in the sun' means roughly 'Standing in the sunlight makes one very hot' rather than describing, say, the temperature at the sun's surface. Moreover, we are to infer that this is not intended by the speaker simply to be an accurate description of the effect of strong sunlight on human temperature, but to imply that the whisky priest worries about whether he will be able to withstand the heat, if he stands for hours waiting to see the ship go.

Even so, the application of these strategies is not automatic. We apply them on the implicit understanding that we are intended to do so. When it comes, for instance, to the following piece of dialogue in Virginia Woolf's experimental fiction *The Waves*, we do not take ourselves to be intended to treat the lines it contains as we would an ordinary conversation.

'Old Mrs Constable lifted her sponge and warmth poured over us,' said Bernard. 'We became clothed in this changing, this feeling garment of flesh.'

'The boot-boy made love to the scullery-maid in the kitchen garden,' said Susan, 'among the blown-out washing'.

'The breath of the wind was like a tiger panting,' said Rhoda.

'The man lay livid with his throat cut in the gutter,' said Neville. 'And going upstairs I could not raise my foot against the immitigable apple tree with its silver leaves held stiff'.

(Woolf 1951: 106)

The Waves was written with the aim of capturing experience phenomenologically in layered, non-sequential, shifting, and scattered guises. In *The Waves* there is often ambiguity as to who is speaking, and indeed whether there are six distinct characters or one central consciousness. Here the strategies of interpretation look different, because the intentions behind the passage are different: the aim is not to represent the sort of conversation that might be held in the actual world.

Just now I insisted that we should not see conventional meaning as an additional source of information about fictional content, separate from the author's intentions to use it to convey what is to be imagined. The same point applies to pragmatic principles governing the interpretation of ordinary conversation and information-exchange. Let 'S' stand for whatever the set of pragmatic principles and strategies is for uncovering non-conventional speaker meaning in ordinary conversation. The caveat is: S should not be treated as a source of information about fictional content, *separate from* information about authorial intention. Rather, we should think of the author as intentionally calling upon a shared implicit understanding of S to convey what she intends readers to imagine, via certain cues. Fictions are not conversations; they (sometimes) *intentionally represent* conversations. In such cases, the author intentionally relies upon a reader's comprehension of these strategies to pursue the achievement of her intention.

So in sum: in determining implied truth, fiction is not automatically to be treated and interpreted as a kind of conversation. Some parts of it might be appropriately treated this way, depending on context: but if so, this is in virtue of the author's intending us to do this at those points. In §2.8, I will consider a related view of Gregory Currie, which effectively says that a fiction as a whole should be treated as a (one-sided) fictional conversation by a single narrator. First, however, I need to discuss the influential account of David Lewis.

2.5 Treating Fiction as a Counterfactual

Effectively, Lewis suggests that the correct and automatically applicable strategy for recovering non-conventional pragmatic aspects of fictional content—implied fictional truths—is to treat a fiction as a counterfactual. Seeing where this goes wrong will also help us further positively clarify what strategies are suitable for fictional texts in particular, and how extreme intentionalism can accommodate them.[2]

---

[2] A further pay-off of this discussion will emerge in Chapter 6. For there we will see that the manner in which Lewis's theory fails is significant in undermining the attraction of a popular view of how imaginative content is generated in the course of an imaginative episode, according to which it behaves very like belief.

A. Lewis's account

In his account, well-known to analytic philosophers, Lewis asks us to conceive of a series of story-worlds for a fiction F (1983).[3] Just think of a story-world for a fiction F as a 'world' where certain things are true and other things are false, as in our world, though the truths and falsehoods in each case will differ. Use this notion as a kind of helpfully vivid construct, if you like. The story-worlds for F do not all contain the same set of facts: things are true in some of them that are false in others.

Lewis presents the 'explicit' content of a fiction as follows: the explicit content of a fiction F is equivalent to all and only those propositions which are true 'at every world' where F 'is told as known fact rather than fiction' (Lewis 1983: 268). A proposition is 'told as known fact' if it is reported by a teller, to others, in a way which non-accidentally directly reflects true facts in that world. The propositions true at every world where F is told as known fact by and large correspond to those entailed by the straightforward use of conventional sentence meanings.

Lewis's main target is not explicit content, however, but rather implied content. As is well known, he thinks of the interpretation of implied fictional truth as closely resembling the interpretation of counterfactuals: as working out what would be the case, were certain other things the case. What counts as implied content is, roughly, what would be (widely considered to be) the case, were the explicit content of a fiction—roughly, the content directly and easily recoverable from the sentences of the text—true and 'told as known fact'.

He first gives us 'Analysis 1':

A sentence of the form "In the fiction f, φ" is non-vacuously true…[if and only if]…some world where f is told as known fact and φ is true differs less from our actual world, on balance, than does any world where f is told as known fact and φ isn't true. (1983: 270)

Let's see how this works in practice. Grace Paley's 'The Pale Pink Roast' begins

Pale green greeted him, grubby buds for nut trees. Packed with lunch, Peter strode into the park. (Paley 1998: 27)

Let's treat this, artificially, as a complete fiction F rather than a fragment. In our actual world, nut trees have sap in them; and the name *Peter* is applied to males almost exclusively. Is it true in F that nut trees have sap in them? Yes, because a world in which F is told as known fact, and nut trees have sap in them, differs less from our actual world than any world in which F is told as known fact, and yet nut trees do not have sap in them. In that latter world, the laws of biology would have to be substantially different. Is it true in F that Peter is a girl? No, because a world in which F was told as known fact, and 'Peter' was a girl's name, would differ more from our actual world than any world in which F was told as known fact, and yet Peter was a boy's name. The practices of

---

[3] For relatively recent papers on Lewis, see Hanley (2004); Levinstein (2007); and Sainsbury (2014).

naming would be fairly different. Is it true in F that Peter has blue eyes? No, it is neither true nor false: for a world in which F was told as known fact, and Peter had blue eyes, broadly speaking would be just as similar to or just as different from our actual world, as a world in which F was told as known fact, and Peter had brown or green eyes. This is how indeterminacy in fiction is accounted for: what is indeterminate in a fiction (i.e. neither true nor false) is all and only those facts which, if the fiction was told as known fact, would be neither more similar to, nor more different from the actual world, than a world where the same facts did not obtain. The indeterminacy is metaphysical, not epistemological. It is not that there is some fictional truth about Peter's eye colour that the reader does not know. There is no such fictional truth.

On Analysis 1, the implied content of a fiction is, effectively, the joint product of explicit content, and what is necessarily or contingently true in the actual world. Effectively, the reader is licensed to 'import' into the fictional scenario, as fictional truths, any necessary or contingent truths from the actual world consistent with explicit content. Lewis notes that Analysis 1 has an unattractive implication: what is 'imported' into a fiction includes features of the actual world that neither the author nor the readers of the fiction could have heard about or thought of. For instance, application of Analysis 1 has it that $E = MC^2$ is imported into Chaucer's *Canterbury Tales*.

Most find this counter-intuitive. For this among other reasons, Lewis also offers 'Analysis 2':

A sentence of the form "in the fiction f, φ" is nonvacuously true... [if and only if]..., whenever w is one of the collective belief worlds of the community of origin of f, then some world where f is told as known fact and φ is true differs less from the world w, on balance, than does any world where f is told as known fact and φ isn't true.   (Lewis 1983: 273)

'Collective belief worlds' are the sets of beliefs endorsed by most in the community of origin of F, and believed by most to be believed by most (Lewis 1983: 272). The community of origin of F is the community of the text's actual or potential readers, at the time of writing and/or publication. Implied fictional truth is now the 'joint product of explicit content and a background of generally prevalent beliefs' (*ibid.*). What is 'imported' into a fictional scenario from the actual world is only the set of those truths (and falsehoods, for that matter) represented in communal beliefs held by the relevant community of origin. We still get the same interpretative result with respect to our Paley fragment, since most people at the time of the book's publication believed that nut trees have sap in them, and that *Peter* is a name for human males. But we do not get the implication that in Chaucer's stories, $E = MC^2$, since no one in Chaucer's time believed this.

Lewis does not adjudicate between his analyses: others have argued that readers often alternate between them (Walton 1990: 160). For simplicity, I will sometimes talk of the 'Lewisian view', referring to a kind of amalgam of the two analyses: that implied fictional truth is what would follow from explicit fictional content, against a background of *well-known* facts (i.e. facts collectively believed) in the text's community of origin. Though not strictly true, this is near enough accurate for current purposes: it covers all the implied fictional truths predicted by Analysis 2, and many predicted by Analysis 1.

Could Lewis's view be made compatible with intentionalism? No: it is effectively thoroughly anti-intentionalist. Analysis 1 treats fictional 'facts' like real ones: what else is fictionally true is just what else would be true actually, were those facts the case. This plainly removes any reference to a connection between what is implied as true, in a fiction, and the mind that produced it: a historically situated mind which, inevitably, will have only a limited epistemic outlook on the world, and for which many facts will be hidden; while other facts may be, unusually, revealed.

Analysis 2 goes some little way to addressing this, since it recognizes that what counts as implied truth for a fiction must be constrained by what plausibly could be believed collectively by the text's community of origin (which includes the author) at the time. But this still rules out as irrelevant to implied fictional truth any possible reference to the *particularities* of the author's historical situation, in interpreting a work: her goals; her particular beliefs, skills and insights, or lack of them; her personality and style; the literary context in which she wrote; the influences she was subject to; and so on and so on. Since knowledge of a person's particular epistemic outlook, and particular historical context, etc. normally looks highly relevant to ascertaining a person's intentions, especially with reference to what she wishes to convey to others, it looks as if Analysis 2 is also incompatible with being seriously committed to conceiving of fictional truth generation as the recovery of an intentional process.

B. *Lewis's view and the reader's experience*

I turn now to criticism of this view.[4] It will turn out that there are genuine implied fictional truths not explained by Lewis's analyses; and moreover that treating a fiction as a counterfactual in fact produces supposed 'fictional truths' which clash with features of the competent reader's experience and practice. It is therefore not the case that it is automatically appropriate to work out what is fictionally true by treating fiction as a counterfactual. It is, I will argue, sometimes appropriate to do so: but *only where we have a prior understanding that this is what the author intends us to do*.

Lewis himself draws attention to the fact that there are genuine implied fictional truths not explained by his analyses. For instance, they cannot accommodate fictional truths that follow as a result of understanding genre. If a character has prominent

---

[4] For further criticism see Lamarque (1990a), Byrne (1993), Phillips (1999), Woodward (2011), Sainsbury (2014). For attempts to rescue Lewis from some objections, see Hanley (2004) and Levinstein (2007).

incisors in a vampire book, she is often a vampire; yet a world in which a person is a vampire is much further away from the actual than one in which she merely has prominent incisors and is not a vampire. Lewis's own example is of a genre-based story (he does not say which genre) depicting a dragon, in which it is implied that the dragon breathes fire, even though the dragon is never explicitly represented as such (Lewis 1983: 274). Neither of his analyses seems to accommodate this intuition. Since there are no dragons, there is no implication that dragons fire-breathe, either in actuality or in collective beliefs about actuality.

A different kind of implied fictional truths unaccounted for on the counterfactual model is those fictional truths that follow as a result of understanding symbolism. As is frequently noted (Walton 1990: 165; Lamarque 1990a: 336; Levinstein 2007: 68–9) use of symbols can be a means of generating implied fictional truth in a text. We have already seen one example of this in the passage from *Jane Eyre* quoted earlier, describing the famous red room in which she was locked as a child (Brontë 1966: 45). Critics have argued that it is important to understand, as a fictional truth for this text, the psychological effect upon Jane of losing a mother in early life (Rich 1973). This is indicated by a number of symbolic objects included by Brontë in the text, not least the famous womblike red room. But on Lewis's view, the significance of the red room in generating fictional truths about Jane cannot be accounted for, as in a world in which *Jane Eyre* was 'told as known fact', no (collectively believed) facts about Jane's motherless state and its strong psychological effect on her would follow from the fact of Jane's being locked in such a room as the red room, no matter how womblike it seemed. For a reader to grasp symbolic meaning, here too she must relate to the text other than simply as if told as known fact.

This point is illustrated brilliantly in the Nabokov short story 'Signs and Symbols'. One of the story's main characters has 'referential mania', whereby:

[T]he patient imagines that everything happening around him is a veiled reference to his personality and existence. He excludes real people from the conspiracy—because he considers himself to be so much more intelligent than other men. Phenomenal nature shadows him wherever he goes. Clouds in the staring sky transmit to one another, by means of slow signs, incredibly detailed information regarding him. His inmost thoughts are discussed at nightfall, in manual alphabet, by darkly gesticulating trees. Pebbles or stains or sun flecks form patterns representing in some awful way messages which he must intercept. Everything is a cipher and of everything he is the theme. (Nabokov 2001: 599)

His parents attempt to buy him a birthday present that could not possibly be interpreted as meaningful by him, and come up with 'a dainty and innocent trifle: a basket with ten different fruit jellies in ten little jars' (2010: 598). Yet at the end of the fiction, waiting for a call which may or may not be the hospital reporting the death of his son, the father 'spells out' the names of the jellies, one by one—'apricot, grape, beech plum, quince' (2010: 603). Critics have noted both that these flavours ascend in bitterness, and that the term 'beech plum' is redolent of the English translation of Buchenwald, 'beech forest'; along with other strikingly sinister images scattered throughout the text, a possible, unspecified connection between the parents and Nazi Germany is being introduced. Here Nabokov playfully references the facility of fiction to generate fictional truths from a position 'outside' a fictional scenario, via symbols, a grasp of which depends on seeing the fiction as a deliberate construct. Seen from 'inside' the fiction, via the perspective of the parents, the son's referential mania is a madness, a disorder; yet from 'outside' the fiction, Nabokov indicates to the reader with a knowing smirk that the son is right—qua fictional character, his world is a construct in which 'everything is a cipher and of everything he is the theme'. There is no room on Lewis's model to accommodate such sophistication: the son remains mad on that view, and the world remains without any hidden causality or constructed meaning.

Let's turn now to examples of how treating a fiction as a counterfactual produces alleged 'fictional truths' which clash with features of the competent reader's experience and practice. For instance, Lewis's view seems to predict that what Walton has called 'silly questions' (1990: 174–83) should routinely trouble the reader; much more than they in fact do. For instance, in Caroline Graham's *Chief Inspector Barnaby* series, set in the fictional county of Midsomer, gruesome and mysterious murders frequently occur; and yet it is not imagined consciously by most viewers that murder rates are unusually high for this area, something that would seem to follow fairly obviously on the Lewisian model. Equally, the reader who knows about the effects of alcohol does not imagine that in P.G. Wodehouse's *Jeeves and Wooster* books, Bertie Wooster's digestive system is slowly being poisoned owing to the effects of drinking, no matter how many stiffeners he is served by Jeeves, even where the reader would draw this conclusion fairly quickly in 'real life'. Nor does she question what unusual things must be happening to the cells in the body of Hergé's boy reporter Tintin, such that he never ages facially in any of the stories in which he appears, even though this surely would be queried in any analogous actual-world case. In short, the apparent irrelevancy to fictional content of even some well-known facts apparently 'close' in subject-matter to the explicit content of a given text, is problematic for Lewis (see Sainsbury 2014: §1 for related discussion).

One might respond, as Walton does, that where importation of a given set of facts/beliefs from the actual world would generate a silly question in this way, the facts/beliefs in question get 'blocked' before the question can get generated (1990: 181). But if this response was to be adopted by a defender of the Lewisian picture, then it would look rather ad hoc, simply suggesting that in some circumstances, neither of the analyses offered by Lewis is used for detecting fictional truth, but some other strategy is used instead, without saying what. It would be better to aim for a theory that gave us a principled explanation of why silly questions do not in fact arise very often for the competent reader (see also Lorand 2001: 434).

A further issue under this heading is that Lewis's theory populates fictional scenarios unnecessarily in a way irrelevant to fictional interpretation. Whether it is a gothic short story by Angela Carter, a Jeeves and Wooster comedy, a piece of erotica by E.L. James, a 19th-century realist novel by George Eliot, a postmodern work by Paul Auster, a Harry Potter fantasy, or an equestrian sex romp by Jilly Cooper, it is a consequence of the application of Lewis's view that in these stories, no matter what their differences in form or content, it is fictionally true that *the USA has fifty states*, that *Queen Victoria was married to Prince Albert*, that *mercury is a shiny slippery metal*, that *Abraham Lincoln was assassinated*, that *Neolithic man used stone tools*, that *eating oranges is a good way of taking in vitamin C*, that *a primer is usually required first when painting furniture*, that *Yorkshire Pudding is made with flour, milk, and eggs*; that *Aneurin Bevan founded the National Health Service*; that *the Sahara is the biggest desert in the world*, and that *going out into the cold with wet hair can make flu worse*. Assuming these things are true *simpliciter* in the actual world, these things are true on Analysis 1; since they reflect well-known facts figuring in the collective belief worlds of each text's community of origin, most look true on Analysis 2 too.

Yet many—even most—well-known facts about the world simply look irrelevant to plausible interpretations of a given work.[5] It seems to be a reasonable assumption that whatever the implied content of a fiction is, or seems to be prima facie, it should be useful to the reader to reflect upon it, if wished, and to conjoin it in thought with explicit fictional content. Doing this should be a way of fruitfully extending a reader's experience of the work, at least potentially. Yet to the reader of a Carter gothic fairy tale, there seems no conceivable point in conjoining in thought imaginings about the Erl-King or Bluebeard with facts about Yorkshire pudding or the National Health Service. Nothing interesting would emerge about the book: no hidden aspect of character or clever plot development could be revealed. Another way to put the point is that Lewis cannot explain why someone who read a reliably narrated fiction *F*, and spent her time obsessively pursuing *F*'s first four sentences against a background either of reality or of collective belief worlds about reality, would be doing anything inappropriate. And yet, we want to say, surely normally she would be missing the point of the work.[6]

A distinct problem for Lewis is that his view predicts the wrong phenomenology for the experience of the competent reader. Obviously, on any account, the reader's understanding of what is explicitly and implicitly fictional in a given text should develop as the text progresses. Now, on the Lewisian view, the reader must start reading a fiction

---

[5] See Byrne (1993: 25); Phillips (1999: 279). Byrne describes facts such as the presumable chemical composition of the blood test used by Sherlock Holmes in 'A Study in Scarlet', which Analysis 1 would have us treat as part of the story even though unmentioned, as 'implausible detail'.

[6] Walton (1990: 148–50) notes this profligacy and attempts to accommodate it by saying that some fictional truths are more important than others. I shall examine this response shortly.

with a huge number of fictional truths automatically 'imported' from the actual world into the scenario of the text *already*. Recall that on the Lewisian account, the fictional content of a text will include, roughly, whatever well-known facts are true in the actual world which are consistent with what is explicitly true. At the beginning of a text, a reader knows very little about what the text explicitly will make fictional—she has just begun reading. So nearly all well-known facts true in the actual world are consistent with what is explicitly true, for all she knows. At the beginning of reading a story, the scenario of the story must look to the reader very like a portion of the actual world, if Lewis is right. But if this were right, one would expect the reader to feel more surprise when she encounters fictions which, *at their very beginning*, explicitly introduce elements inconsistent with aspects of the actual world. Presumably, the feeling should be somewhat similar to the feeling one has when one encounters some fact in the world inconsistent with some belief one has and feels surprise, as the world contradicts expectations. And yet the reader feels no similar surprise at the beginning of a fictional text. Take for instance the following opening lines:

All children, except one, grow up.   (Barrie 2008: 1)

In a hole in the ground, there lived a Hobbit.   (Tolkien 2013: 7)

Katagiri found a giant frog waiting for him in his apartment. It was powerfully built, standing over six feet tall on its hind legs. A skinny little man no more than five foot three, Katagiri was overwhelmed by the frog's imposing bulk. "Call me 'Frog,'" said the frog in a clear, strong voice.   (Murakami 2002: 1)

Though as openings, these are all undoubtedly attention-grabbing, none evokes any particular sensation of surprise in the reader, I suggest, and nothing akin to the shock of a plot twist. Surprise, I suggest, is hardly ever felt right at the beginning of a fiction, and yet Lewis's view would predict surprise for the beginning of many works, including those quoted above, given their initial explicit content. In fact, rarely does a reader form any concrete beliefs about the implied fictional content of a text, right at the beginning of a text she knows little else about.

Finally, just as Lewis's view does not get the reader's experience of beginnings of fictions right, it also gets her experience of the *ends* of fictions wrong. For Lewis's view effectively entails that, for every fiction, there are many implied determinate facts about what happens in the fictional scenario in question 'after' the fiction has, in terms of explicit content, ended. Again, recall that on the Lewisian account, the fictional content of a text will include, roughly, whatever well-known facts are true in the actual world which are consistent with what is explicitly true. Well-known facts about the actual world include many facts about typical causal conjunctions: what tends to follow what (and what does not). So it apparently would follow from Lewis's view that the reader may reasonably predict what will happen in a fictional text, or fail to happen, 'after' the text's ending, based on her understanding of (what widely are believed to be) causal conjunctions in the actual world. And yet for many fictions, this would not look appropriate.

For instance, *Great Expectations* ends with Pip reporting that

> I took her hand in mine, and we went out of the ruined place: and, as the morning mists had risen long ago when I first left the forge, so, the evening mists were rising now, and in all the broad expanse of tranquil light they showed to me, I saw no shadow of another parting from her. (Dickens 1994: 443)

On one plausible reading, Dickens intends this authoritatively to be predictive of what is the case later in the fiction: that Pip and Estelle do live happily ever after (Dickens in fact replaced the original sad ending with a happier one to please his public; see Eigner 1970). It would be insufficiently satisfying to imagine that Pip merely precariously *believes* he has a happy future with his love. This is so, even though it presumably is part of most communal belief worlds, even at the time of the text's reception, that predictions about one's own future can easily be wrong. On the Lewisian view, we should interpret the future as possibly containing a parting for Pip and Estelle; however, on a more plausible reading, it does not.[7]

In another case, Charlotte Brontë's *Villette* ends with Paul Emanuel, the lover of Lucy Snowe, being caught in a terrible storm, the 'perfect work' of 'the destroying angel of tempest': the sort of storm which, according to most people, would sink a ship were it to happen in reality. So in the Lewisian picture, this is what the reader should predict for the couple. Yet Brontë, deliberately, refuses to resolve the ending explicitly:

> Here pause: pause at once. There is enough said. Trouble no quiet, kind heart; leave sunny imaginations hope... Let them picture union and a happy succeeding life. (Brontë 1985: 596)

On the Lewisian picture, presumably it is fictionally true that Emanuel has drowned, and that Lucy is withholding this fact in order to leave hope in the reader. Yet, perversely, if this were right then the competent reader would have little hope left, contrary to the apparent intention of Brontë. The interest of the passage is diminished if we fail to recognise the ambiguity here: that we genuinely are supposed to be unsure whether Lucy is merely hiding the death of her lover from us, or whether it is indeterminate whether he dies or not.

Many of the objections just canvassed rest on the assumption that a plausible theory of fictional truth should fit with the reader's psychological experience of interpretation. Now, a defender of Lewis might counter that Lewis in fact is not interested in giving an account of what the interpreter does psychologically as she interprets fiction; he is interested only in the metaphysical facts about fictional truths, which are generated as he says they are. But this could not be right. Lewis must in fact be offering a theory with a psychological dimension, for if he were not, it would be hard to see what justification his metaphysical view could have. Unless he was at least prima facie

---

[7] Other examples of 'closed fictional futures', and their relation to the Lewisian view, are discussed in Le Poidevin (2001).

describing the psychological process involved in interpretation, why else should we be tempted to accept that the implied fictional truths of a text are any that counterfactually would follow from explicit fictional content plus actual world-truths, or beliefs about them? Yet now that we have looked more deeply at some of the psychological facts about actual readers as they interpret, we have seen that his theory falls short as a general claim.

C. Extreme intentionalism again

It is notable how, without explicitly engaging in any discussion of the relation between the Lewisian view and intentionalism, certain critics of Lewis with a background in philosophy of language have tended to produce alternatives to his view in a recognizably 'intentionalish' vein. For instance, Alex Byrne has proposed as an alternative to Lewis's view that:

It is true in fiction F that p... [if and only if]... the Reader could infer that the Author is inviting the Reader to make-believe that p.   (Byrne 1993: 33)

Here the 'Reader' and 'Author' are somewhat idealized figures, so that the position looks more like hypothetical intentionalism than actual intentionalism, but still, the move is strikingly in the right direction.[8] Meanwhile, John Phillips also offers a noticeably intentionalist formulation:

A sentence of the form 'In the fiction F, Φ' is true if and only if, it is reasonable for an informed reader to infer from the text that, under ideal conditions, the author of F would agree that Φ is a part of F.   (Phillips 1999: 287)

In fact, an extreme intentionalist picture is easily able to explain the features of fiction that the Lewisian view could not. It can explain why the reader does not tend to get bogged down considering 'silly questions' such as why mortality rates in Midsomer are so high, or what damage is being done to Bertie Wooster's liver by his copious drinking. Quite simply, the reader grasps, correctly, that in those cases she is not intended by the author to consider such questions. That this is so can be indicated, wholly negatively, by the fact that we can find no authorial goal which would be served by intending that such questions be considered. In the case of the *Chief Inspector Barnaby* series, no plotting ever relates to high mortality rates in the county, nor could this 'fact' conceivably relate to any theme. But equally it might be indicated by the fact that we *can* find relevant authorial goals which would be *thwarted* by intending that such questions be answered: arguably, in the *Jeeves and Wooster* series, the comic tone intended by Wodehouse would be darkened and so spoilt, were the question of a potentially serious illness afflicting loveable Bertie to be raised in sombre medical terms.

---

[8] Hypothetical intentionalism will be discussed in Chapter 3.

Equally, extreme intentionalism does not populate fictions unnecessarily in a way irrelevant to fictional interpretation. What makes actual world facts about Yorkshire pudding irrelevant to an Angela Carter gothic short story is that Carter did not instruct her readers to imagine anything about Yorkshire pudding, as indicated by the fact that there is no evidence in the story nor in any separate source that she intended such facts to be relevant.

Relatedly, extreme intentionalism predicts that a reader should not import actual-world facts into a story automatically in a wholesale way, right at the beginning, because she should wait to see more precisely what, she judges, the author instructs her to import. Her policy should be to *wait and see what else is made fictional, and by what means*, before forming any concrete beliefs about implied fictional content for a text. This is why she is not surprised at opening situations which would be surprising, were they true in the actual world: because of a recognition that the author is free to make fictional whatever she intends to make fictional, in a way in which people are not free to manipulate reality.

Extreme intentionalism also explains why the reader is not, at the end of a fiction, always prone to predict what will happen next, based on beliefs about typical causal conjunctions in the actual world, or beliefs about them: because in some cases (as with *Great Expectations* and *Villette*), she judges that the author does not intend her to do so. The author is not tied slavishly to reproducing in implied fictional content, whatever would be (widely believed to be, or believed by a fictional narrator to be) the case in reality, given what is explicitly true. She has the power simply to *stipulate* certain things.[9]

In short: extreme intentionalism can accommodate many features of the reader's experience, which Lewis's view cannot.

D. Partial application of the Lewisian analyses?

An important point for the present purpose is as follows: fictions should not be treated as counterfactuals *automatically*, for treating them this way often results in an inappropriate account of what fictional truths are implied by that text. This is not to deny that sometimes, fictions or parts of fictions are appropriately treated as counterfactuals. But where they are, as before, this is subject to the author's intention that this be the case.

Lewis is not alone in thinking that interpretation of any given fiction should 'import', as implied fictional truths, most actual world facts (or what is believed communally about them). Others have argued for a 'principle of minimal departure' (Ryan 1980: 406) according to which 'we reconstrue the world of a fiction and of a counterfactual as being the closest possible to the world we know'. Lamarque and Olsen, even after being highly critical of Lewis's approach, agree at least that:

---

[9] See Phillips (1999: 280).

> Fictional states of affairs (objects, events, personages) can be assumed to be like ordinary states of affairs (object, events, personages) failing indication to the contrary. (1994: 95)

However, I maintain, this is false as a general point about fiction.

It is actually highly unusual for a fiction *as a whole* to be intended to work as a counterfactual. Granted, some works have as *one* of their aims the exploring a of some particular counterfactual—consider for instance Pat Barker's *Regeneration*, which draws extensively on first-person testimony of World War 1, and can be partly understood as an attempt to explore what it would be like to be in the trenches. But even in this work, there are implied fictional truths which cannot be recovered counterfactually via the Lewisian method. For instance, a motif of an eyeball (painted on a prison cell door; found enucleated on the ground after battle) coveys several fictional truths about the protagonist symbolically (Bond 2016).

Meanwhile, of course, many fictions are not aimed at exploring counterfactuals at all: they have alternative aims. This is a point noted by Nathaniel Hawthorne, who compares the genre of 'Novels' (in the 19th-century sense of the term) and 'Romances':

> When a writer calls his work a Romance, it need hardly be observed that he wishes to claim a certain latitude, both as to its fashion and material, which he would not have felt himself entitled to assume had he professed to be writing a Novel. The latter form of composition is presumed to aim at a very minute fidelity, not merely to the possible, but to the probable and ordinary course of man's experience. The former—while, as a work of art, it must rigidly subject itself to laws, and while it sins unpardonably so far as it may swerve aside from the truth of the human heart—has fairly a right to present that truth under circumstances, to a great extent, of the writer's own choosing or creation...He will be wise, no doubt, to make a very moderate use of the privileges here stated, and, especially, to mingle the Marvelous rather as a slight, delicate, and evanescent flavor, than as any portion of the actual substance of the dish offered to the public. He can hardly be said, however, to commit a literary crime even if he disregard this caution. (Hawthorne 1999: x–xi)

As Northrop Frye also observes: 'The romance is the nearest of all literary forms to the wish-fulfilment dream' (Frye 1957: 187). Equally, fantasies, erotica, horror stories, and fictions aimed at moral education may not be aimed at exploring counterfactuals at all, but have some other aim, in the pursuit of which the counterfactual aim would be irrelevant or actively harmful. In an escapist love story, where a couple wander off happily into the sunset, it would not be consonant with the intended warm glow to infer that they stand a 42 per cent chance of later getting divorced. Equally, where a character in a detective novel walks into a deserted building alone and unarmed in pursuit of a psychopath, it would probably not be conducive to preserving tension to dwell on the fact that she is committing a disciplinary offence by not informing her unit or calling for back-up. When reading erotica, it would be fairly pointless and indeed antithetical to most people's purposes to think about the resulting stains on the sheets. And so on.

Despite all this, it will often be appropriate to apply something like Lewis's analyses *defeasibly*, in working out what else one was intended to imagine at a particular point. One might, say, be trying to recover an implied fictional truth about a particular causal relation. For instance, in *Memento Mori* by Muriel Spark, elderly characters are plagued by phone calls reminding them they will die. The reader naturally wonders what is fictionally the case about the source of these phone calls. In that case, a reader may well consider what else would (be commonly believed to) be the case in the actual world, were such phone calls to occur, *in order to come up with a defeasible hypothesis about Spark's intention*. This is because *one way* for an author to signal to a reader that she is to imagine that *p*, given scenario *S*, is by indicating intentionally that at least with respect to this part of the story, things function as they (commonly are believed to) do in the actual world, where the author also expects the reader to believe that if *S* was to occur in the actual world, then *p* would be the case.

However, it must also be remembered, equally there may be evidence that the author in fact does not intend the reader to use this strategy in a particular place. As it happens, it seems likely from surrounding evidence (of which more below) that Spark wants us to imagine that Death himself is making the phone calls in *Memento Mori*, and not a prank caller. This again emphasizes the defeasibility of the Lewisian strategy. Depending on what she wants to do with a text, an author can make it fictional that events are linked by God, or by the Devil, or magic, or astrology (D. Davies 2007: 55). A counterfactually generated causal relationship will look appropriately imputed to a fiction, because it apparently complements the author's wider aims at that point. Yet again, the appropriate application of Lewis's analyses is inevitably subject to the understanding that the author in question has intentionally sanctioned their use at the relevant point.

2.6 A Sparsely Populated Fictional Scenario?

In this section I shall digress from the main narrative to discuss a consequence of my own intentionalist position, and emphasize a difference from Lewis's. That is, it follows from my view that for most fictions, many—even the majority of—actual-world contingent facts are metaphysically indeterminate for a fiction.

Hence I disagree with such commentators as D. Davies (2007: 50) when he writes that in Holmes stories, it is true automatically that Watson has ten toes, or that in *Pride and Prejudice*, it is true that characters 'exercise normal biological functions'.

This initially may sound strange. However, the impression of strangeness should be mitigated partly by noting that the claim is *not* that such things are fictionally false either, nor that it is fictionally true that they are not the case. The claim is rather that such things are metaphysically indeterminate for the fiction in question. Moreover, to say a certain state of affairs *S* is 'metaphysically indeterminate for a fiction' is emphatically *not* to say that, *within the scenario of the fiction*, alongside truth about characters and events, it is also true that *S is metaphysically indeterminate*, so that (*ex hypothesi*) the reader is somehow to *imagine that S* is indeterminate. The claim that *S* is metaphysically indeterminate for a fiction is a claim made from 'outside' a fictional scenario, relating to the fiction as a fiction—an intentionally constructed product. It should also be remembered that on Lewis's view too, there is much that is metaphysically indeterminate for a given fictional scenario: remember the case of the Paley fragment and Peter's eye colour. There is no fact about the matter about Peter's eye-colour and nothing to imagine about it, either way, though of course if the reader wanted, she could harmlessly take an imaginative stance on the matter.

A defender of the Lewisian picture may respond that all or most actual facts get imported as fictional truths, but that some fictional truths are more important than others (Walton 1990:148–50). However, there is now a problem: namely, to discern in a principled way which ones are important (Walton 1990: 15). Importance is usually relevant to some set of purposes. One attractive way to decide which fictional truths are important or not would be to advert to what the author was trying to do: important fictional truths would be ones which contributed to the achievement of the author's aims. Interpreting the important fictional truths in a text would be a matter of working out which fictional truths the author intended the reader to prioritize in her thinking about the text, where this depended on evidence provided by the text as well as, where one had it, knowledge of the author's aims for the text and other relevant context. Unimportant fictional truths would be those which did not conceivably pertain to anything the author positively intended the reader to imagine, where again this would be ascertained in relation to knowledge of the author's aims and other relevant context, as well as the text. But if this was the route chosen, then it would be unclear what we lose by bypassing talk of unimportant fictional truths altogether and saying that unimportant fictional truths are not fictional truths at all (see Lorand 2001: 434 for a related point). The story I propose about fictional truths misses out no fictional truths that the rival story says are important.

Sometimes empirical evidence is offered which purports to show that in a large number of cases, readers take fictional scenarios, not to be sparsely populated as I claim they are, but rather as richly filled with entities and facts from the actual world. For instance, Neil Van Leeuwen reports that

[P]sychologists Deena Skolnick Weisberg and Joshua Goodstein (2009) provide direct evidence that individuals following a story import elements of what they take to be reality (in other words, their beliefs) into their understanding of what happens in the story. They had subjects read stories and then simply asked them questions about what else would be true "in the story." They found subjects held that mathematical, scientific, conventional (about social norms), and contingent facts were true in the stories, even though these were not given by the text. (Van Leeuwen 2013: 227)

Yet on further scrutiny, such evidence turns out to be relatively untroubling for my claims here. Weisberg and Goodstein (2009) describe how subjects are offered three stories: 'Close' 'Middle' and 'Far'. In 'Far' there are explicitly many violations of actual-world causal and physical laws. In 'Middle' there are only a few; and in 'Close' there are none. After reading each story, participants were then presented with a list of 21 actual-world facts, including mathematical, scientific, 'conventional' (to do with e.g. mores and etiquette), and 'contingent' ones (e.g. geographical ones), and asked to rate them as definitely or probably true or not true in the story. The study found that participants judged the relevant facts as 'significantly more likely' in the Close world than in the Middle world, and as 'significantly more likely' in the Middle world than in the Far world. With respect to all worlds, there was variation in the degree to which particular kinds of facts were judged as imported: in all cases, mathematical facts were more likely to be judged as imported than scientific facts, scientific facts more likely than conventional ones, and conventional ones more likely than contingent ones. (It should also be noted that by no means did participants judge as automatically imported actual-world facts, even in the Close world: even mathematical facts were not judged as automatically imported by all.)

Given these data, and the variations of importation of actual-world facts between types of fictional scenario, an alternative interpretation to that of Van Leeuwen looks easily available. That is, it seems reasonable to think that the implicit aim of participants was to anticipate what the author *intended them to imagine*, rather than automatically to import actual-world facts willy-nilly. With respect to Far and Middle worlds, participants presumably took the explicit presence of alien causal laws (etc.) to signal the intention that the importation of unmentioned actual-world facts positively would be inappropriate; and even in the case of the Close world, they were not confident enough to import all such facts automatically, assuming it more likely that mathematical facts were intended to be imported than contingent ones. Hence these empirical facts about readers' practices look consistent with my position.

2.7 'Explicit' and 'Implied' Fictional Content and Unreliable Narration

One more digression is called for at this point, to make a further critical point about Lewis but also to note an amendment to my own view. As we have seen, Lewis effectively posits fictional interpretation as involving two distinct stages: *first*, we treat the explicit content of a fictional text as if it were told as known fact, and *then* we see what further implied content is generated. But actually, as many have noted, cleanly identifying a kind of first-order 'explicit' content of fictional sentences, whose meaning is not partly dependent on content which occurs elsewhere in a text, is difficult to do (Walton 1990: 174; Woodward 2011: §4; Sainsbury 2014). Most obviously, this is true of certain kinds of unreliable narration. Sometimes the fictional content of a set of utterances in a text—including whether they state some fictional truth(s) directly, or merely describe another's narration of some particular, possibly false claim—will partly depend on further content, even implied (unstated). This sort of case makes the idea that there might be a basic kind of content in this text which, if 'told as known fact' would generate other more 'hidden' content, look rather murky.

Take the aforementioned example of unreliable narration in Sarah Waters' *The Little Stranger* (again, I apologize for the spoiler). It is never stated in this text but only implied that, unbeknownst even to himself, the narrator Faraday is the murderer.[10] This is implied by, among other things, the use of a striking image at the end of the work, where Faraday gazes into a window of the house in which he has committed his crimes and thinks he sees a ghostly malevolent presence for a moment; but then he realizes that he sees 'only a cracked window-pane, and that the face gazing distortedly from it, baffled and longing, is my own' (Waters 2009: 449). As a result, the implication retrospectively entails that the reader is not ultimately entitled to take at face value all the earlier parts of Faraday's own narrative.

Rather than maintain a clean distinction in principle between explicit and implied fictional content, better, then, to make one's general aim, as a reader, to attempt to recover what the author in question intended her readership to imagine. In doing this, we can make a rough distinction between content which is relatively quickly recovered, and content which takes longer to recover. We can call this a distinction between 'explicit' and 'implied' content if we like, and indeed, I will continue to use this terminology. But it must be remembered throughout that the ease or speed with which authorial instructions are reliably recovered from a piece of text, in a particular case, is compatible with readers' applying complex understanding of authorial techniques (and as we have seen, this may include an understanding of techniques which have nothing obviously to do with any inference from actual-world facts). That such understanding comes easily, or that her strategies of interpretation get applied automatically, does not mean that no relatively deep interpretation can be occurring.

Meanwhile, the possibility of unreliable narration forces an amendment of the basic articulation of extreme intentionalism I gave earlier, as follows. Let's focus upon the example already introduced. Consider the following sentences from *The Little Stranger*, fictionally uttered by Faraday, at a point before most readers suspect he is unreliable. It concerns events that fictionally take place on one Wednesday 7th April in the 1940s.

My first sight of Mrs Ayres's swollen, darkened face made me shudder, but worse was to come, for when I opened up her nightgown in order to examine her body, I found a score of little cuts and bruises, apparently all over her torso and limbs. Some were new, some almost faded. Most were simple scratches and nips. But one or two, I saw with horror, had the appearance almost of bites. (Waters 2009: 396)

---

[10] Online discussion of the book takes this claim to be controversial; nonetheless I think it clearly consonant with various aspects of the book.

This passage and those surrounding it imply that Faraday has not seen these injuries before; and that therefore he is not the perpetrator of them. As noted, it turns out later in the text to be the case, arguably anyway, that in fact Faraday inflicted these injuries on Mrs Ayres, though to the end he persists in refusing to recognize this.

Let's call the stage of reading at which this passage occurs 'stage N' in the text, and the later stage of reading at which it is implied that Faraday is the perpetrator 'stage N + 1'. And let's call the fictional proposition that *on Wednesday 7th April Faraday was having his first sight of Mrs Ayres's injuries* '*F1*'.

So: on the basis of 'My first sight of Mrs Ayres's swollen, darkened face made me shudder' plus several other utterances in the text, the reader at stage *N* is intended by Waters to imagine that *F1* is true. Yet at stage *N+1*, given further plot revelations, she is intended by Waters to 'retract' that imagining, as it were, and imagine instead that *F1* is false. Thus, even though Waters reflexively intends readers to imagine that *F1* is true, it seems that strictly speaking it is not part of the fictional content of the text overall. This looks like a counterexample to my initial formulation, which made a reflexive authorial intention that readers imagine that *p* sufficient for fictional content that *p*.

In order to accommodate this sort of case, let us distinguish between two sorts of authorial intention. The first is the authorial intention that an utterance *x* in a text, *once it is encountered for the first time, persistently* (be disposed to) cause a given propositional imagining that *p* in a readership *R*, throughout *R*'s experience of the text. (The reference to 'be disposed to' is in order to accommodate the fact that no utterance reasonably could be intended to result in a reader's consciously imagining its content throughout the whole of her experience of the work; this would be incompatible with limits on conscious attention.) That is, the author intends readership *R* to imagine that *p* as a result of utterance *x*, and moreover, would be happy for *R*, once *R* has read *x* for the first time at the appropriate part of the text, consciously to imagine that *p* at any subsequent point in her experience of the work.[11]

A contrasting sort of authorial intention is the intention that an utterance *x* in a text, *once it is read, temporarily* cause a given propositional imagining that *p* in a readership *R*, for some portion of *R*'s experience of the text amounting to less than all of it. Waters utters 'My first sight of Mrs Ayres's swollen, darkened face made me shudder' intending that at that stage in the reader's experience, it only temporarily cause the imagining that *on Wednesday 7th April Faraday was having his first sight of Mrs Ayres's injuries*. Waters does not intend the reader to be disposed consciously to imagine this by the time she reads the last page of the novel (in fact she intends the reader to imagine its negation, I assume).

---

[11] Of course, utterances do not tend to work in isolation to convey fictional truths, and especially not implied ones taking longer to recover, so the talk here of single utterances causing discrete propositional imaginings is somewhat misleading; but is left for the purposes of simplification.

With this distinction in mind, we can then adjust the original formulation of extreme intentionalism thus:

> An author *Au*'s utterance *x* (or set of utterances *S*) in fiction *F* has fictional content that *p*, if and only if *Au* utters *x* (or *S*) intending that, once *x* (or *S*) is read for the first time: i) *x* (or *S*) *persistently* should (be disposed to) cause propositional imagining that *p* in her intended readership *R*, for as long as she is thinking of *F* at all; ii) *R* should recognize this intention; and iii) *R*'s recognition of this intention should function as part of *R*'s reason to propositionally imagine that *p*.

More on this case and unreliable narration generally will be found in Chapter 5, where I discuss its implications in relation to my account of fiction. Now, however, I return to one of the main themes of the chapter: establishing that there are no general strategies of interpretation automatically applicable to a fiction. I shall now consider a rival view to Lewis's: that of Gregory Currie.

2.8 Treating Fiction as a Fictional Conversation

Currie argues that *p* is implied fictional content for a fiction *S*

> [i]f it is reasonable for the informed reader to infer that the fictional author of *S* believes that *p*. (Currie 1990: 80)

The 'fictional author' is a construct, posited imaginatively as author of the text in front of one simply in order to help interpretation of implied fictional content. The reader is supposed to imagine this fictional author as the sincere and truthful author of a non-fictional text, identical to the fictional one she is reading. It will be reasonable for an informed reader to infer that a fictional author of a given text believes that *p*, either when *p* is explicitly in the text, or when a belief in *p* is 'implied' (were the text a genuine report) by what is explicitly in the text, plus certain relevant facts available to an informed reader.

These facts are often pretty minimal. An informed reader is 'a reader who knows the relevant facts about the community in which the work was written' including 'knowledge of what people in that community tended to believe' (Currie 1990: 79). She is permitted to use this knowledge in constraining her interpretations of what the fictional author of this text might have believed. Sometimes, the fictional author can be taken as equivalent to the fictional narrator (1990: 124). In that case, at least, the reader presumably may know quite a lot about the fictional author (as, for instance, the reader knows quite a lot about Jane Eyre, who narrates her own story in Brontë's work). But in other cases, there is no obvious fictional narrator; or else the fictional narrator is unreliable. In the latter case:

> we move to the level of an unobtrusive narrator who, by putting words in the mouth of the explicit narrator in a certain way, signals his skepticisim about what the explicit narrator says. (Currie 1990: 124)

Here, as with the case where there is no obvious narrator in a text at all with which to identify the fictional author, on Currie's view the reader is not permitted to imagine anything very concrete about the author's epistemic outlook, aside from that for which there is evidence in the text, in conjunction with general knowledge about what sort of beliefs someone writing in the relevant period conceivably might have had (1990: 78).

Earlier I suggested that Lewis's Analysis 2 could be read as marking a limited and still insufficient move in the direction of some version of intentionalism. Currie's view can be read as a move further towards intentionalism, since, effectively, it characterizes implied fictional content as, not what would be taken as implied from the explicit content of a text in conjunction with the collective beliefs of the text's community of origin, but rather as what might be taken to be *conversationally implied from* that explicit content by a *particular reporter*, were she reporting it as true. Since we usually do not know whether a given reporter would share in any widely-held beliefs of her time, we cannot include as implied fictional content, on this model, any propositions which, the community collectively would judge, would follow from explicit content, but for which there is no direct evidence in the text that the 'fictional author' believes them. Application of Currie's model therefore can result in interpretations of content more tailored to an individual epistemic outlook than could be the case for Analysis 2, which appeals only to the epistemic outlook of a group.

For instance, Currie is not committed to treating as implied fictional truths the content of any belief prevalent in the collective belief worlds of the intended audience which is consistent with what is described in the text, as Analysis 2 would have it; let alone any actual-world consequence of those descriptions, as Analysis 1 would have it. His theory is more selective than this: where it is reasonable to think, based on textual evidence, that the fictional author knows about a topic, we can include that knowledge as fictional truth; where it is not, we cannot (1990: 84).[12] Presumably, then, we can say that if we have no textual evidence that the fictional author of F has beliefs about Yorkshire pudding, furniture, and Neolithic man, for instance, then these are not included as fictional truths for that text.

To this extent Currie's view is closer to intentionalism than Lewis's Analysis 2. However, it is still not close enough.[13] As just noted, effectively Currie characterizes implied fictional content as what might be taken to be conversationally implied as believed by the narrator of that explicit content, were she reporting it as true. This means that, like Lewis's view, it cannot accommodate any fictional truths generated via techniques not transferable from the interpretation of ordinary conversation; something that we have already seen is problematic.

For instance, to return to the example of *Jane Eyre* and the red room, it is near impossible to make sense of a sincere and truthful reporter, Jane Eyre, conversationally

---

[12] So I disagree with Phillips that 'Currie, like Lewis, thinks a belief that is prevalent in the community of origin of a fiction, in the absence of any manifest denial of this belief in the text, must be true in the fiction. So Currie, following in the footsteps of Lewis, imports irrelevant propositions into fiction' (284).

[13] See also D. Davies 2007: 66–9 for further criticism.

implying her belief that she herself was much affected by the loss of her mother, by truthfully describing her belief that she had once been locked in a red room. There is no practice in ordinary conversation of mentioning objects symbolically to this sort of effect. An analogous point can be made about an implicit appeal to genre conventions. Equally, Currie is unable to explain how in *Great Expectations*, it might be fictionally true that Dickens has (possibly) fixed the future to guarantee Pip and Estelle's happiness. Were the text imagined to be the sincere and truthful report of the narrator Pip's beliefs, it would look unreasonable to attribute to Pip the belief that he possessed the power to guarantee the future, or to hold it metaphysically suspended (see Le Poidevin 2001).

In brief: Currie's view cannot accommodate those plausible cases where grasping what is implied as fictionally true involves treating the text otherwise than as if it were a conversational report of belief or fact. The strategy he offers should not be applied automatically. It might be applied in *certain cases*, perhaps: for instance, in some first-personally narrated fiction for young children, where the only implied fictional truths are those that, there is reason to think, the fictional narrator might believe. But again, in such cases, the appropriate application of a strategy such as Currie's is subject to the background understanding that this is what the reader is intended to do.[14]

2.9 Treating Fiction as Subject to Genre Conventions

I turn now to the influence of genre classification on fictional truth. As a prompt for discussion, I will use a passage by Neil Van Leeuwen, who writes of certain fictions that:

contextual cues, like mention of magic or spaceships, trigger the use of genre truth attitudes for purposes of inferential elaboration on initial imaginings...Just as looking and smiling trigger a toddler's understanding of pretense, mention of magic and hyperdrives trigger the use of genre truth attitudes in understanding a story and drawing inferences. (Van Leeuwen 2013: 228)

Now, one claim that Van Leeuwen is apparently making here is A) that classification of a text in a given genre (as fantasy, or as sci-fi, for instance) 'triggers' certain implied

---

[14] An adaption of Currie's view is offered by Peter Alward, who argues that '"In fiction F, S" is true... [if and only if]...the theory which best fits the narrator of F's reports, the evidence for her reliability, and relevant background information includes the proposition that S' (2010: 358). Effectively he thinks we should treat a fiction as the product of a fictional narrator who is a 'fact-teller', but attend to not just what that narrator says or implies, but also what she 'reveals', against a context of relevant background information which includes 'genre conventions, inter-fictional carryover, and authorial and critical discussions of story, as well as facts about the actual world and beliefs prevalent among members of the author's community' (2010: 362). On my view, once it has been conceded that information about genre conventions, authorial and critical discussions of stories, symbols, and so forth, are relevant to fictional interpretation, we might just as well dispense with the complicated work of trying to establish how a fictional narrator who is a fact-teller might 'reveal' fictional truths in the light of such aspects, and concentrate instead more simply on how an author, who is often not a fact-teller, might imply them by the use of those same means.

fictional truths—or as he would put it 'genre truth attitudes for purposes of inferential elaboration'—automatically. This point might also look present in the worry of Lewis, which we saw earlier, about a story which, simply by virtue of belonging to a particular genre, implied that the dragon who was a character in it breathed fire, though this was never stated. I shall come to this claim shortly. But Van Leeuwen might also here be saying something else (and even if he is not, it is worth investigating): B) that certain markers, irrespective of whether or not they are intended, can, on their own, be the basis for accurate fictional genre classification. In that case, genre categorization would not depend on an author's intending to write in that genre. And in conjunction with claim A), this might seem to pose a problem for intentionalism. For from A)—the claim that genre classification 'triggers' certain implied fictional truths automatically— it follows that there are some fictional truths generated in a fiction which have nothing *directly* to do with authorial intention. Now, one apparent way for the intentionalist to deal with this challenge would be to say that *genres are always invoked intentionally*: it may be that once a text belongs to a certain genre, this 'triggers' certain fictional truths automatically, but these can still be characterized as intentionally generated fictional truths insofar as genre membership is always intentional. However, if, as claim B) has it, genre membership is sometimes accidental and non-intentional on the part of the author, this route looks blocked.

Actually, I will suggest, B) is true: it is true that genre membership is sometimes accidental. However, I will argue, this does not threaten intentionalism, because A) is false: it is not true that genre classification triggers certain implied fictional truths automatically and non-intentionally. I will deal with these points in turn.

First, some background on genres, worthwhile as a corrective against occasional tendencies of philosophers to over-simplify when writing about them. We first should note that the category of *literary* genres, generally, includes many instances that apparently have no bearing on fictional truth at all: for instance, poetic genres such as sonnets, epithalaliums, and villanelles. The present topic is *fictional* genres: for instance, the romance, the detective novel, the *Bildungsroman*, and so on. We should also note that even fictional genres are discussed by theorists in terms other than fictional truth. Equally, theorists may focus upon other important aspects: e.g. what symbols, imagery, or linguistic forms tend to be used in that genre; what comment is made on art, or literature; what intertextual references or allusions are apparent; and so on (Dubrow 1982).

In most cases, it seems that a given fictional genre is 'governed' by a relatively large number of conventions, some of which are sufficient for genre membership but few or none of which are necessary. As just noted, these conventions may refer, not just to characteristic fictional content, but also to characteristic imagery, symbolism, linguistic form, and intertextual reference, etc. It will be rare that any single convention is necessary for or essential to genre membership, and even rarer that one be sufficient. For instance, Frye characterizes the romance genre as involving, not only certain plot elements (adventure or quest; conflict and overcoming) but also structural ones;

a characteristic point of view (the hero's), characteristic imagery; certain psychoanalytic associations; characteristic symbolism; a lack of complexity of characterization; a black and white morality; and so on (1957: 186–205). There is no suggestion that a romance has to exhibit absolutely all of these features to count as such, and only one seems to be 'essential' according to Frye (i.e. 'adventure').

Rather than necessary, better to think of each of these conventions as, in some degree, well-established or 'standard' for the genre, in the sense delineated by Walton (1970); and of their explicit subversion as 'contra-standard' for that genre. The contra-standard subversion of *several* genre conventions can result in a text which thereby is disqualified from membership of the genre in question. But the contra-standard indifference to or even subversion of a single (or even a few) well-established genre conventions can normally still be present in the production of a text in the genre in question. For instance, Sarah Waters' *Affinity* is still a neo-Victorian melodrama despite featuring lesbians rather than heterosexuals, as is standard.

Against this background, the apparent thought of Van Leeuwen's in the passage above, that a single element—for instance the 'mention of magic'—might carry with it firm implications for genre membership, is rather an over-simplification. It is perhaps true that sometimes, for *some* genres, a single piece of fictional content is necessary for genre membership, and not just standard, so that its absence would result in disqualification from the genre category. For instance, as we have seen, Frye argues that 'the essential plot of romance is adventure' (1957: 188). And the modern genre of 'chick-lit' is a genre specifically written for and marketed to heterosexual female readers, in order (broadly) to provide them with comically romantic 'escapist' works concerning heterosexual protagonists. Here it does seem to be a defining presupposition of the genre that the protagonists be thoroughly and enthusiastically heterosexual. However, obviously, neither of these elements is *sufficient* for genre classification, on its own. Spy thrillers are adventures and often have heterosexual heroes but that does not make them romances. Magical realist works often include magic but are not fantasies. Generally, several elements at once will drive genre classification, and not only one or a few.

We can now return to the question: can a text fall into a given fictional genre, even though the author did not intend it to? The answer, I think, is yes. That is, an author can intentionally produce certain features in her text, the presence of which is, unbeknownst to her or otherwise unintentionally, sufficient to make the text an instance of the genre in question. I do not say that this is typical but it does look possible. For instance, Frye convincingly classifies certain poems of Wordsworth and Walt Whitman as falling into the genre of pastoral elegies, even though these authors convincingly disassociated themselves from readings based on genre convention at all (Frye 1963: 125–6). Frye so classifies them on the basis that certain intentionally-produced elements in the poems fit, as a matter of fact, with many characteristics archetypical of pastoral elegy. Equally works could fall into a genre, where the genre-relevant features were products of unconscious influences upon the authors, rather than deliberate incursions into the genre as such. For instance, arguably many plot features in 'women's romantic fiction' are less products of a deliberate intention to work in that genre, than products of centuries of exposure to patriarchal stereotypes.[15]

Another instructive example is as follows. Kazuo Ishiguro's work *The Buried Giant* has been classified by many as falling into the fantasy genre, on the basis that it includes ogres. Ishiguro has been clear that if so, it counts as 'inadvertent' fantasy, cogently explaining the presence of ogres as due to a different sort of purpose:

> My guiding principle when writing *The Buried Giant* was that I'd stay within the parameters of what somebody in a primitive, pre-scientific society could rationally believe. So if you don't have a scientific explanation for why somebody dear to you has got ill, it seems to me perfectly sensible to go for an explanation that went something like, "A pixie came in the night and gave my dear wife this illness, and I only wish I'd done something about it, because I heard something moving around that night and I was just a bit tired and I thought, well, it's a rat or something"...If it was within the imaginative world of the people of that time, I'd allow it literally, in my fictional world, but I wouldn't allow a flying saucer or a Tardis, because that was outside their realm. (Gaiman and Ishiguro 2015)

So: it generally seems possible that an author may intentionally produce [a text with aspects *x*, *y*, and *z*], where unbeknownst to her or otherwise unintentionally [a text with aspects *x*, *y*, and *z*] thereby counts as an instance of genre *G* (not least, at the very start of a genre tradition!). And as an instance of this phenomenon, it may be that an author intentionally produces [a text with fictional content *p*, *q*, and *r*] where unbeknownst to her [a text with fictional content *p*, *q*, and *r*] thereby counts as an instance of fictional genre *G*.

However, as described briefly above, this raises an apparent worry for intentionalism, in conjunction with a further claim (also apparently endorsed by Van Leeuwen in the quote above): that membership of a given genre can render certain implied fictional truths in a story automatically present, irrespective of what the author intends about those fictional truths. For we now seem to have a state of affairs where a fiction can count as a member of genre *G* despite the author's not intending this, whilst at the same time being a member of *G* can generate certain fictional implications for a text automatically, irrespective of what the author intends. This makes it look as if fictional truth can be generated unintentionally. However, as I shall now argue, this is not in fact a worry. It is not true that being a member of a given genre generates certain fictional implications for a text automatically, irrespective of what the author intends.

When we look at actual cases of competent fictional interpretation we do not find genre-based automatic content-generation of the kind posited by philosophers. What we find instead are other things, with which it might tend to be confused. The first is the banal fact that when a reader *starts* reading a fictional text, expectations of genre make it reasonable to *predict* what fictional truths the text will make *explicit* (not implied),

---

[15] I am very grateful to Laura Gibbon for this point.

before the reader has read them. If, for instance, it seems to be a vampire novel—as signalled by the cover, the publisher's blurb, or the fact that it is written by Stephenie Meyer or Anne Rice—it is reasonable to suppose that there will be vampires in it. But this is not a case of genre membership itself generating implied fictional content; it is a case of defeasible assumptions about genre membership generating defeasible expectations about fictional content. Since, as we have seen, genres have few necessary conditions, it would be unwise to make one's expectations about fictional content too concrete: a vampire book may at a minimum need vampires but it need not be gothic (*Nice Girls Don't Have Fangs* by Molly Harper) and the vampires need not be evil (*Twilight* by Stephenie Meyer), for instance.

A second thing which might be mistaken for genre-based automatic content-generation is the use of stereotypes or stock characters. Recall that Lewis worried that a story written about a dragon might make it fictional that a dragon breathes fire, even though no fire-breathing is represented explicitly, and nothing would follow about dragons either way against a background of well-known facts. Where the story is a 'perfectly typical instance of its stylized genre' (1983: 274), he worries that it is true that the dragon breathes fire, even though this is not ever said explicitly. Yet actually, when we look more closely, we see that whether or not it is fictionally true that the dragon in Lewis's example breathes fire is not to do with whether the text in which it appears counts as an instance of a particular genre, but rather with its generally being a stereotype that *dragons breathe fire* (this is surely a, if not the, best-known 'fact' about dragons). For instance, there is no more reason to think that this question arises for a fantasy containing a dragon more pressingly than for any other genre where a dragon is present (e.g. Chinese mythology).

Now, on the intentionalist view I espouse, the inclusion of a dragon in a fiction, even given knowledge of the relevant stereotype, does not in fact automatically license any particular inference of fictional fire-breathing, on its own. We also need additional evidence that this is what is intended by the author (e.g. because it furthers some narrative aim or is suggested by other evidence). If elsewhere in the story, there is a description of a scorched patch of earth next to the dragon; or repeated playful reference to metaphors of fire and heat; or some other relevant indicators are present, then this, plus our knowledge of the stereotype, would count as a reason to think that the author intended us to think that the dragon breathes fire. But either way, where an implied fictional truth about fire-breathing is licensed, it is not simply because the genre of fantasy is being exemplified.

Compare the related use of stock characters. In the intentional construction of a stock character, an author tends to imply deeper fictional characteristics by the explicit mention of superficial ones conventionally associated with the former (e.g. *flamboyance* with *being a homosexual*; *being a schoolma'am* with *being morally upright*; *being a 'painted lady' in a Wild West brothel* with *having a heart of gold*). Earlier I said it was implied but not stated explicitly as true in Mitford's *The Pursuit of Love* that Lord Merlin is gay. What *is* explicitly stated is that Lord Merlin's whippets wear diamond necklaces, and that he dyes pigeons every year in bright colours, drying them in the linen cupboard (Mitford 1949: 37). Relying on the reader's understanding of the stock character of the gay man, Mitford intended her readers to draw the inference. However it is still conceivable that, had other evidence suggested that Mitford was interested in writing a different kind of book, it would not be appropriate for the reader to take these facts as fictionally causally connected to homosexuality.[16] Not every inclusion of a 'flamboyant' man (relative to actual Western culture) in a fiction automatically licenses a fictional association with homosexuality. To judge whether there is one, genuinely, we have to look at other features of authorial context, including checking the extent of her acquaintance with social and literary stereotypes, what she was trying to achieve in the text, what genre she took herself to be working in, and other particularities of her context (for more on stock characters see Walton 1990: 162–3).

A third phenomenon with which genre-based automatic content-generation might be confused are cases of the following structure: i) as previously described, an author of a text T intentionally and explicitly makes some propositions p and q fictionally true in T; ii) by the explicit inclusion of p and q in T, plus additional relevant indicators elsewhere where applicable (e.g. formal means, symbols), the author implies certain unstated fictional truths r and s in T; iii) the presence of p, q, r, and s in T are at least part of the reason to classify T as in genre G. (As noted, other reasons for genre classification might be generated by non-fictional elements of the text.)

Now, as my description here makes clear, this is not a case where genre membership 'automatically' produces certain implied fictional truths. Rather it is a case where explicit and implied fictional truths plus other markers imply genre membership. However, the latter might be confused with the former because of a further feature of many such cases: namely, in cases where T counting as an instance of G is apparently known and intended on the part of the author, and not inadvertent, then the classification of T as G hermeneutically supports the reader's thought that r and s are implied as fictionally true in T.

For instance, in my earlier example of a text in which characters explicitly have prominent incisors, this (plus other relevant cues: e.g. they do not like sunlight, or avoid garlic; a dark tone; gothic imagery) is intended to imply the fictional truth that the characters are vampires. Such fictional truths, both explicit and implied, give reason to think that the text is in the vampire genre. So far, there is no suggestion that the genre 'triggers' any implied fictional truths, but only that fictional truths are (partial or total) indicators of genre.

The impression that a text is in the vampire genre is likely to be reinforced for the reader not just by fictional content, but also by markers such as illustrations, a certain

---

[16] Moreover, contra Lewis, by describing Merlin's flamboyancy Mitford is not merely making it fictional that *it is likely* that Merlin is gay, but *determining* that he is (see also Phillips 1999: 280). So here, as in the earlier case of Dickens apparently guaranteeing Pip and Estelle's future (or at least, possibly guaranteeing it), it looks as if we have a case where the author determines what is implied as fictionally true stipulatively, in a manner wholly unrelated to any inferences from prior sets of facts, or collective beliefs about them.

style of dust jacket, publisher's blurb, etc. But this is because publishing editors read the books they publish; normally the way books are branded is driven by the fictional content within (though not always: see Shipley 2008). Readers looking at branding, blurb, and so on, may usually reasonably assume the author is or would be happy with them as fitting with her own conception of her text, and so take these features, along with the text's explicit fictional content, as a further endorsement that the book is indeed in a given genre. (Of course, as already noted, this assumption might be false in a case where the text is only inadvertently in a certain genre, and being marketed in a way that does not reflect the author's positive intentions in that respect; but for the most part, such cases are unusual.) The point for present purposes *is that evidence that a text is intended by its author to fall within a given genre may hermeneutically reinforce the reader's confidence about what fictional truths are implied but unstated in the text.* Yet, as described, this is not a case where genre classification alone automatically produces fictional content, so much as one where the realization of it—at least partly driven by appreciation of fictional content—hermeneutically reinforces the thought of certain fictional truths as implied.

So: in practice, we have not found one convincing example of a text in a given genre's 'automatically' producing certain fictional truths, whether or not the author intended them. What we have found is either: assumptions about genre producing expectations or predictions about explicit fictional content; or the intentional use of stereotypes and stock characters producing implied fictional truths; or genre classification reinforcing the reader's understanding of what implied fictional truths are intended, but only where these are implied by other means within the text too.

2.10 Fictional Content and Hidden Meaning

So far in this chapter I have mostly been arguing (with some important digressions along the way) that there are no automatic strategies of interpretation of fictional content, applicable generally to all works, independently of facts about authorial intention. I take it that this is a further source of support for extreme intentionalism, since it furnishes a good explanation of this fact. For extreme intentionalism predicts that a given strategy of content interpretation is appropriate for a given text only when its author effectively intends the reader to use it. Meanwhile authors may not always share intentions in this respect. Not every author intends to use sentence meanings straightforwardly; or to explore some counterfactual; or to produce a text to be interpreted as a fictional conversation. Even within a given fictional genre, authors can be selective in observing associated conventions concerning fictional content. Hence appeal to these strategies should not be automatic but instead should be based on reasonable assumptions about authorial intention.

I turn now to addressing the second of the challenges laid down to extreme intentionalism in Chapter 1: namely, that it entails that fictions may have hidden, even undetectable meanings. Among other things, I will shortly argue, some of the material of previous sections will help us establish that this is not the case in any deeply worrying sense.

The challenge comes in several versions. On one version, the objection is harnessed to the point, debunked in Chapter 1, that from extreme intentionalism it must follow that words and sentences can be made to mean whatever their author intends, by arbitrary fiat. If this were so, then since it would follow that readers could not possibly tell in some cases what an author intended to communicate—for words might be used by her in ways radically at odds with their conventionally-bestowed meanings, in unpredictable ways—it would then be the case that fictions might have hidden meanings (Irvin 2006: 117–18). Yet we have already seen that this is not a serious worry. This is due to the general constraint upon the having of intention also emphasized in Chapter 1: for an agent to intend to A, or to get someone else to A, she must not believe that A or getting someone else to A is impossible. Hence, words and sentences cannot meaningfully be used by authors in ways which, those authors must acknowledge, would be impossible for readers to decipher. 'Intentions' that words and sentences communicate wholly private, stipulative, and arbitrary meanings are not a worry.

A different version of this sort of worry focuses on cases of miswriting (or misspeaking). The worry here is that if extreme intentionalism was true, then in cases of miswriting, since we only ordinarily have access to the text and can't ask the author, the 'true' intended meaning must be hidden. I will address this worry in Chapter 3, in the context of a wider discussion of certain hidden and failed intentions and how they relate to content.

A third version of the objection has it that generally, a person's intentions in writing something can be difficult to detect, and only really identifiable by asking them directly (an extreme version of this suggests that we could only ever get access to them by mind-reading). Since readers typically are not in contact with authors, there might be no evidence available to the reader about what an author's intentions actually were, in writing the fiction. The author might not have expressed any views about her intentions, or might have given out misleading information about them. In the case of fictions written long in the past, the chances of evidence being available are even slimmer (Beardsley 1992: 34). If intentionalism, whether extreme or moderate, entails that the meanings of fictions could be such that even competent readers could not access them, then so much the worse for them, it is suggested.

Now, this chapter has already given us reason to think that this worry is rather overstated. For effectively we have seen that much valuable information about authorial intention comes from relatively 'local' features of the text itself: sentence meanings; apparent appeal to ordinary conversational implicature at particular points; the apparent exploration of counterfactuals at particular points; the apparently intentional use of genre; and so on. Even though there is no automatic means of interpreting such aspects, they each nonetheless at least offer good evidence to a reader of what the author may well have intended, subject to confirmation in other ways. But this is not the only source of evidence available; far from it. Another equally important source of information about authorial intention is evidence about wider authorial purpose, as I shall now explain.

2.11 Fictional Content and Authorial Purposes

A. Wider purposes and more local intentions

In Chapter 1, I stressed the close connection between an author's goals and purposes in writing a text, and their intentions, and suggested that evidence of the former can be good evidence of the latter. I also noted how goals, and so intentions, may 'nest': an agent may intend to C in order to B in order to A (and so on). Consideration of those ultimate goals may well cast light on what is being intended 'lower down' the chain. For instance, in a very simple case, say that I see a friend running along the street. The additional knowledge that she has an appointment in London that day that she wants to keep will give me some reason to think she is running for a train, rather than for some other reason.

Possible goals in writing fiction are numerous. One may intend to write a fiction in a particular genre, or to create a new one; to write a fiction that will sell lots of copies; that will improve one's gifts as a writer; that will explore a given theme; that will express one's feelings, that will entertain one's kids, or send them to sleep; that will explore one's past; that will make some moral point; that will illustrate some philosophical position; that will cement one's reputation (and so on). Goals can be various with respect to the same fiction, and may interact: e.g. in order to sell many copies, one may aim to write in a particular popular genre.

As we also saw earlier, this is not to say that an author must consciously appraise her goals before writing begins, or even during the writing process. An author's true purposes in writing a piece of text may not be immediately apparent to her.[17] The right sentence may—in the words of A.E. Housman—just 'flow' into her mind, or on to the page, apparently unplanned (Housman 1933: 49), so that only *afterwards* might she realise how it fits some purpose of hers, newly formed or already existent, and decide to include or retain it. Moreover, as acknowledged, in certain cases an author may not be aware of her intentions consciously, even after writing. This may be because the agent positively represses knowledge of such intentions; or more banally, because she does not attend to them. To say intentions may be unconscious is, I take it, still compatible with saying that they are potentially recoverable in principle, given the right sort of attention and/or analysis. That writers sometimes do not engage

---

[17] 'I never consciously place symbolism in my writing...Better to let the subconscious do the work for you, and get it out of the way...During a lifetime, one saves up information which collects itself around centers in the mind: these automatically become symbols on a subliminal level, and need only to be summoned forth in the heat of writing. Thus locomotives can be dragons, or dragons locomotives, at will, if one desires. I trust my subconscious implicitly. It's my good pet. I try to keep it well fed with information through all my senses, but never look directly at it.' (Ray Bradbury, cited in Funke Butler 2011)

in the right sort of analysis to become aware of their own true intentions does not mean that they are not in principle available; both the reader and the author may make more or less reasonable hypotheses about them, based on available evidence (Grice 1957: 388).

A fortiori, there is no suggestion that the means of execution of a given goal must be well worked out at the beginning of writing:

Certainly not all the steps [need be present in the original conception]. But there must be something, some major object towards which one is to approach.
(E.M. Forster, quoted in Furbank and Haskell 1953)

There is a point of departure, and there are some characters. It often happens that the first characters don't go any further and, on the other hand, vaguer, more inconsistent characters show new possibilities as the story goes on, and assume a place we hadn't foreseen.
(Francois Mauriac, quoted in Le Marchand 1953)

Equally, new purposes and intentions may emerge in the course of revisions: in redrafting, restructuring, deleting, and adding.

The important point for our purposes is that an author will often (come to) intend that her readers imagine certain *particular* things, in order to achieve some ultimate goal of hers. For instance, where an author's aim is to explore the theme of 'loss'— e.g. 'loss of love, loss of self, loss of God' (Edna O'Brien, quoted in Guppy 1984)—she will intend, and so instruct, her readers to imagine certain concrete events which, she judges, illustrate that theme. Where an author's aim is more prosaically simply to sell lots of books, she will instruct her readers to imagine certain things which, she judges, will increase the appeal of the book and so its sales. Where her aim is to produce a fiction in a certain genre, she will instruct her readers to imagine certain concrete things which fit with 'markers' of the genre in question. And so on. In fact, most cases are bound to be more complicated: an author might intend to include some particular fictional content in order to achieve a particular effect in a paragraph, where achieving this effect is a means to some further end, which is itself a means to some further end, and so on. Usually, a given piece of content will be at most contributory to a given goal, along with other features of the text (e.g. other content; stylistic features; structural features), though in rare cases it may be entirely responsible for achievement of the aim in question: for instance, an author aiming to shock his audience may achieve this via the inclusion of one shocking fictional event alone.

Because of all this, a reader is entitled to, and indeed would be foolish not to, use evidence of authorial purposes as evidence for her interpretations of fictional content. Some hypotheses of content will fit well with presumed purposes; other hypotheses will not. We have already seen that in interpreting fictional content, at relevant points, among other things, the reader can appeal to facts about: the sentences used and the associated linguistic conventions; conventions governing the interpretation of conversations; counterfactuals based on actual-world information or collective beliefs in conjunction with certain explicit content; stereotypes and stock characters and their conventionally associated characteristics; genres, and the sorts of fictional truths they tend to be associated with. (This list is not supposed to be exhaustive.) However, none of those facts, considered on its own, will 'automatically' generate given kinds of fictional content: in every case, what is being made fictionally true by the use of that strategy, at a fine-grained level, will be ascertained only by also considering the author's goals in writing the text.

To make clearer the influence of assumptions of wider authorial purpose, I will focus on an area relatively under-explored by me so far: the interpretation of symbols and their relation to fictional content. Let's look at two examples. One of Flaubert's documented aims, in writing *Salammbô*, a novel set in pre-Christian Carthage, was to 'examine, in an unfamiliar context, some of his own feelings and anxieties about contemporary France' (Green 1982: 59). Flaubert's anxieties concerned the moral corruption he believed to be widespread in 19th-century France. Partly for this reason he described in *Salammbô* not just the corruption of Carthage, but repeated images of decay, disease, dead bodies, and flies buzzing (Green 1982: 62–3). Equally, to emphasize Carthage (and by association, France) as a disordered, chaotic society always on the verge of breaking apart, at times he described the opposing armies of Carthaginians and mercenaries as chaotic, and at other times as highly ordered (Green 1982: 65). These fictional details included by Flaubert at the level of content look instrumentally related to his ultimate intentions/goals for the text, by being directed towards the achievement of further instrumental intentions first.

Meanwhile, in *Villette*, there is copious use by Brontë of symbols of enclosure, interpreted by many critics as representing, among other things, the confinement of Victorian middle-class women, and the repression of female desire. The garden at the *pensionnat* in Brussels where Lucy Snowe teaches is a central, Edenic image. It contains a further enclosure, an alley where Lucy is permitted to roam but pupils are forbidden; its plants are described in various suggestively erotic terms. Lucy sits in the garden; nature arouses her from feelings of passivity and depression. She recalls:

At that time, I well remember whatever could excite—certain accidents of the weather, for instance, were almost dreaded by me, because they woke the being I was always lulling, and stirred up a craving cry I couldn't satisfy. (Brontë 1985: 176)

On one reading of this passage, the sensuous imagery used to describe the garden and Lucy's relation to it make it the case that Lucy's 'craving cry' is expressive of sexual and romantic longing (Newton 1985: 119). The interpretation of what this moment implies, in conjunction with the use of symbols of enclosure, is complemented by external evidence, from Brontë's letters, of repressed sexual desire towards Constantin Heger, a married teacher at the actual *pensionnat* in Brussels which Brontë attended from 1842 to 1844, and with whom she was in love:

Day or night I find neither rest nor peace. If I sleep I have tortured dreams in which I see you always severe, always gloomy and annoyed with me. I do not seek to justify myself, I submit to every kind of reproach—all that I know—is that I cannot—that I will not resign myself to losing the friendship of my master completely—I would rather undergo the greatest physical sufferings. (Brontë 1844)

It seems reasonable, partly on the basis of this biographical evidence about her own experience long prior to writing, to assign to Brontë the purpose in that text of representing repressed sexual desire (among many other simultaneous purposes).

It should be noted that the aim, in uncovering authorial purposes and so intentions, on this view, is *not* to psychologize the author for the sake of it, as is sometimes implied (Levinson 2006: 306). The author may well have many reasons to write a given fiction, only some of which will be relevant to what we should say about its content. In the cases where a given reason turns out to be irrelevant, it is not of particular interest to the interpreter.

It should also be noted that there is no suggestion that one must *first* identify an author's probable purposes in writing a fiction, and *then* use this knowledge to interpret the content. In practice, understanding a fiction's probable purposes and recognizing the fictional content which serves those purposes will be hermeneutically linked: in coming to understand the content, one comes to understand some of the purpose; in coming to understand the purpose, one understands some of the content (Sainsbury 2014).

B. Evidence of authorial purpose

Noting the important role of ascertaining wider authorial purpose in attributing fictional content opens up the possibility that a range of extra-textual evidence plays an important role in interpretation: for instance, letters of the author, diaries, interviews, reported conversations with third parties, holograph drafts or the 'avant-texte' of the manuscript, and so on. This material is useful in at least two potential respects: a) because it might be a place where the author clarifies her intention with respect to a given piece of fictional content in a particular place; but more likely b) because it can give us information, directly or indirectly, about what the author's goals were, in writing the text, and this can also be a source of evidence of authorial intention with respect to fictional content, indirectly.

Such material is often used by literary critics in interpretation. For instance, a critic relates of the avant-texte of Flaubert's *Salammbô* that:

It's in the partial plans and notes...that the central themes are worked out. In them, Flaubert expands scenes or character sketches or merely jots down a few words to indicate a possible line of development; and since these rough preliminary notes express his ideas in their barest form without heed for style...they frequently reveal his preoccupations more readily than do their carefully transformed counterparts in the finished novel. (Green 1982: 50)

Equally, knowledge of an author's *other fictions* can help a reader determine what is fictionally the case in a particular text, by providing evidence of possible authorial goals, shared across works. For instance, according to at least one critic, appropriately interpreting the notoriously opaque *Pale Fire* depends on knowing facts about Nabokov's other works: the fact that it is common in his work for ghosts to intervene from beyond the grave can be used as evidence for an interpretation according to which the character Shade does so, in this work (Boyd 1997: 203–4).[18] Equally, as mentioned earlier, in Muriel Spark's *Memento Mori*, it is implied, though never stated definitively (the possibility is raised, tentatively, by one character) that Death is responsible for making a series of nuisance phone calls, reminding people that they must die. This conclusion is partly motivated by consideration of Spark's wider oeuvre, in which there are frequently supernatural interventions and the exploration of religious themes.

One might also appeal to evidence furnished in biography, as with the Brontë example just now. For another example, consider C.S. Lewis's *The Lion, The Witch and the Wardrobe*. Aslan the lion dies and is resurrected: we are told that this occurs by virtue of magic 'deeper' than the Deep Magic of the White Witch, going back to 'the darkness before Time dawned' (Lewis 1959: 148). But given what we know of Lewis's Christian beliefs, and so on, it is wholly reasonable to suppose it is also implied as fictional that the causal explanation of Aslan's resurrection has a Christian God as its source, though this is never stated in that text.

Authorial interviews are another good source of evidence about authorial purpose. It is sometimes assumed that there would be something wrong with an intentionalist position which took, as evidence for the author's intentions in a given fiction, what she herself said about them (e.g. Stecker 2006: 431). But this looks arbitrary. Just as in conversation, we may permissibly seek clarification from the speaker about what she 'really meant' where there is ambiguity, so too may we permissibly seek clarification from an author, where we can get it. As already noted, we take it as unexceptionable that where there is no reason for repression, and given relevant concept mastery and appropriate careful attention, an agent introspectively scrutinizing her own current or recent mental states, including intentions, has some degree of enhanced first-personal authority with respect to them. But this is not to say we accept pronouncements uncritically, or that there is not a time limit on their authority, given limits on memory. In given circumstances, where pronouncements apparently clash with available evidence, authors may reasonably be judged to be confused about their intentions, or deliberately obfuscatory, or forgetful. Just as we may undercut, in certain circumstances, a conversational partner's description of her own intentions in a given action, by adverting to other evidence (what she has said in the past, what she may have told others, and so on) so too might we ignore an author's own pronouncements about her intention in a given case in favour of an interpretation which draws on other evidence instead (see Chapter 1).

---

[18] Needless to say, the Lewisian model cannot accommodate this: were (somehow?) *Pale Fire* 'told as known fact', no facts about Nabokov's other fictions could be relevant to its interpretation.

Sometimes, a caricatural picture is offered as a possibility, of an author radically disrupting an established understanding of her text simply by saying, in an interview or diary, that the text means something completely different, for which there is absolutely no corresponding evidence in the actual text. Yet discussion in Chapter 1 has made it clear that this is hardly a serious possibility: for to have a genuine reflexive intention in the first place that readers imagine certain things in response to a text, the author has to believe that readers could detect this intention via the text that she is producing. If, therefore, there is no detectable evidence whatsoever in the text that a text has fictional content that p (and even conflicting evidence that it does not have fictional content that p), then the author's claim that she nonetheless seriously intended readers to imagine that p in response to it looks suspect and normally should be rejected.[19]

In sum: working backwards, evidence of authorial goal, arrived at via extra-textual evidence such as holograph drafts, interviews, letters, and diaries, can help the reader come up with plausible interpretations of what the author might have intended her to imagine in particular cases, as a means of arriving at that goal.

2.12 Summary

One of the main tasks in this chapter has been to argue that there are no automatically-applied strategies for interpreting fictional content: that at every stage, the appropriateness of a given strategy is subject to assumptions about authorial intention. Along the way, I have discussed and rejected the theories of fictional truth of David Lewis and Gregory Currie, as well as a picture of fictional scenarios as profligately strewn with objects from the actual world. I have also clarified the relation between unreliable narration and my intentionalist position.

At the same time, however, I have stressed that a reader defeasibly can bring to bear her knowledge of factors such as conventional sentence meaning, conversational implicatures, fictional genres, stereotypes, stock characters, and culturally popular symbolic associations (among other things) upon the evidence provided by a text, in order to work out reasonable hypotheses about what the author intended her to imagine, via the use of such techniques and devices in that text. Equally, in interpretation a reader may legitimately make reference to extra-textual evidence about authorial purposes concerning the text, since such purposes are bound to be pursued via the fictional content of the text itself. Hence the popular complaint that somehow extreme intentionalism forces reference to private, or hidden, intentions, for which the reader has little or no evidence, has been shown to be a straw man for most typical cases.

In Chapter 3, among other things I shall discuss particular cases where there seems genuine reason to think that the author's intention is more hidden, and what we should say about them.

---

[19] It is true, of course, that there will be cases where the fictional content of a text is ambiguous, or even temporarily hidden, but eventually brought to light with reference to extra-textual evidence of the author's intentions. This is perfectly admissible and indeed reflects standard critical practice. I will discuss these sorts of cases in Chapter 3.

3

Extreme Intentionalism and its Rivals

In this, my final chapter on extreme intentionalism, I turn my attention to three of its main rivals: 'modest' intentionalism, hypothetical intentionalism, and value-maximizing theory (a variety of anti-intentionalism).[1] I will first address an apparent source of support for all three, and in particular, a central motive for modest intentionalism: the thought that extreme intentionalism takes an implausible stance towards unsuccessful authorial intentions that a text have a certain content. I will argue that, rather than being on the back foot with respect to unsuccessful intentions, extreme intentionalism is in a better position to accommodate these than its rivals. With this point established, and having removed the main obstacle to moderate intentionalists' becoming more 'extreme', I shall move on to general criticisms of hypothetical intentionalism and value-maximizing theory, thereby further generating support for my own view.

3.1 The Problem of 'Unsuccessful' Intentions

In Chapter 1 I identified four common objections to extreme intentionalism. The third of these was the complaint that extreme intentionalism implausibly entails that there are no genuinely unsuccessful intentions that a text should mean something. Critics complain that if an intention that a text means such-and-such fails for some reason, then such-and-such should not be counted as part of the meaning of the text. But extreme intentionalism seems to make success simply a matter of having the right intentions, irrespective of whether they are successful or not.

The apparent power of this worry depends partly upon a historical tendency of intentionalists to fail to articulate properly the nature of the intention that determines meaning (that is, fictional content). If we take that intention to be the rather vague 'intention that a fiction mean that p' then, confronted with the scenario where this intention is unsuccessful, it looks simply obvious that in that case, the fiction will not mean that p; for how could it, when the intention that this be the case has failed? It is

---

[1] Considerations of space preclude my covering all available rivals to extreme intentionalism. For a survey of alternative varieties of hypothetical intentionalism, see Irvin (2006). For a criticism of anti-intentionalism based on deconstruction and/or post-structuralism, see Lamarque (1990b).

implicitly assumed that the only situation in which a meaning-determining intention can be unsuccessful, is if the relevant meaning is not present.

This worry is partly mitigated, however, if, as in my account, the relevant intention is specified in a way that removes reference to 'meaning' in its specification. Instead, as we have seen, the relevant intention is to reflexively intend *that readers imagine certain things as a result of one's utterances*. On this construction, I will argue, the fact that one has this intention, but it fails, need not automatically result in one's utterances failing to have the content in question.

In fact, once the authorial intention is properly specified, immediately we can see a situation which can cause an authorial intention to 'fail' but with no obvious bearing on fictional content. One obvious way in which it can fail is where it is recognized as such by intended readers, but the readership apparently *has difficulty imagining what they are intended to*. This covers cases of imaginative resistance. (The topic will be dealt with at length in Chapter 4.) The apparent fact that readers cannot easily imagine a proposition apparently contained in a text would not count, for most, as a reason to deny that it is part of the text's content (an exception is Weatherson 2004, though he apparently argues this from intuition).

However, there is an apparently more threatening version of the worry about unsuccessful intentions still available. This is the worry that an author might reflexively intend that readers imagine that *p* as a result of reading her text, and yet that intention be one for which there is no evidence in the text itself. In that case, the objection goes, surely we should allow that the author's communicative intention has failed; in which case we should deny that the text has fictional content that *p*. In other words, on closer inspection, this sort of objection turns out to be a further instance of the objection generally discussed in Chapter 2: that extreme intentionalism countenances hidden intentions, and so hidden meanings, in an unacceptable way.

This sort of objection is a central source of motivation for 'modest' (or 'moderate' or 'partial') versions of actual author intentionalism. On this view, an author's intentions are determinative of fictional content only in certain circumstances, but not always (Carroll 1992, 2000; Stecker 2006; Livingston 2005). A central circumstance in which moderate intentionalists have it that authors' intentions cease to be determinative of fictional content is where they are unsuccessful, in the sense of being radically hidden. They therefore make it a condition of a text having a given fictional content that this content 'mesh with' or 'be supported by' features of the text itself.

The intentions of authors that the modest actual intentionalist takes seriously are only those intentions of the author that the linguistic/ literary unit can support (given the conventions of language and literature).   (Carroll 2000: 76)

Intentionalists of a moderate or partial variety—such as myself—agree that intentions are fallible and therefore do not necessarily determine the content of a story. It follows that any plausible intentionalist or authorial account of fictional truth must include a success condition. Thus we can say that inferences as to implicit story content must 'mesh' with the explicit features of the text or other expressive items, and some authorial intentions and plans may simply be incompatible with the latter. (Livingston 2005: 199; see also 147)

Perhaps oddly, at least one modest intentionalist makes it a condition upon a successful content-generating intention that it must straightforwardly observe the conventions of sentence meaning:

> The meaning of an utterance is the meaning successfully intended by an utterer, or, if the utterer's intention is not successful, the meaning is determined by convention and context at the time of utterance. Furthermore, an utterer successfully intends a meaning X just in case the utterer intends X, the utterer intends that the audience will grasp this in virtue of the conventional meaning of the utterer's words or an extension of the meaning permitted by those conventions, and the first intention is graspable in virtue of those conventions or permitted extensions of them. (Stecker 2006: 429)

The apparent fear here is that, if we allow that authors of fictional texts can use sentences in ways that deviate from their ordinary conventional meanings, readers will not be able to detect those meanings. Yet in Chapter 1 we saw examples where passages within texts deviate from established conventions governing sentence meanings and yet remain intelligible in terms of authorial intention. Burgess's *A Clockwork Orange* and Safran Foer's *Everything is Illuminated* both systematically deviate from conventional sentence meanings to some extent, and yet there is no sense that the meanings are 'hidden' for long, in any worrying sense. Of course, they do not do so arbitrarily. Still, it would be implausible to insist that somehow the content in such passages was 'governed' by ordinary conventions, or even a 'permitted extension of them' rather than an intentional playful and wholly new adaption of them. (It would also be disingenuous to put this intelligibility down vaguely to 'context' rather than admitting that the reader is intended by the author to use her understanding of context—most obviously, the syntactic resemblances between unfamiliar terms and known ones, and in the Safran Foer case, some indirect semantic associations too—to work out the author's intentions.)

Moreover I have stressed throughout that—just as in ordinary conversation, on most accounts—*whether or not* an author produces an utterance or set of utterances consistent with conventional sentence meanings, the content of those utterances is determined by authorial intention (either to use those conventions straightforwardly, or not). So on both counts it is implausible to insist that being 'consistent' with linguistic 'conventions' is somehow a separate and additional constraint upon fictional content. A text can intentionally deviate from linguistic conventions without those intentions being hidden, and there is no reason thereby generated to deny that the text has the content the author intends it to have.

Still, an apparent more general worry remains: a text might be written with certain intentions, for which there is no evidence in the text. For instance, Carroll offers us the case where an author writes 'green', but intends 'black', arguing that in this case, the text means 'green' not 'black' (Carroll 2000: 85). Presumably here he is partly worried by the thought that no reader would ever be able to tell that 'black' was originally intended. Meanwhile, hypothetical intentionalists are motivated by this sort of worry to reject actual author intentionalism completely (see Currie 2004: 125; see also Currie 1993: 418; Levinson 2010: 145).

Thus this issue connects with one discussed in Chapter 2. In that chapter I argued that, despite worries to the contrary, there were ordinarily several sources of evidence about fictional content readily available to interpreters, both 'internal' and 'external'. Hence there was no reason to think that, *in general*, authorial intentions were hidden. However, a worry remains that in some *particular* cases authorial intentions are wholly hidden from their intended audience, and in these cases they cannot be the determinant of fictional content.

It also connects with a further complaint, also first aired in Chapter 1 as the fourth of four popular challenges to extreme intentionalism: that it unacceptably 'decentralizes' the text, potentially, as a source of meaning. In extreme form, the objector is concerned that if extreme intentionalism were true, we might do away with the text altogether, and just consult the author about what she meant. This is clearly a straw man: the text contains or implies all the propositions which the author intends the reader to imagine; short of reproducing the text orally, it is unclear how an author could successfully convey those intentions in some other form. But a more moderate version of the objection connects with the worry that extreme intentionalism entails that parts of the text are radically hidden: hence, the worry goes, in those cases at least we must move away from the text towards 'external' forms of evidence, and this is unacceptable given existing practices of valuing fictional texts as a central source of their own meaning.

3.2 The Structure of Unsuccessful Intentions

Many cases of unsuccessful intentions have a similar structure. I have already noted that intentions can 'nest': I can intend to do A in order to do B in order to do C (e.g. I intend to raise my arm in order to throw the dart in order to hit the target). Let's call A and B 'instrumental' intentions and C (in this case) an 'ultimate' intention.

Now, intentions very often fail because the means by which an agent seeks to achieve her ultimate intention (or at least, an instrumental intention further down the chain) inadvertently fails. For instance, I intentionally raise my arm and throw my dart but inadvertently wobble and miss my target. In this sort of case my action(s) count(s) as intentional under some descriptions and not others. Under the description 'raising my arm' or 'throwing something' my action(s) count as intentional, but under the description 'missing my target' they do not (I did not intend to miss my target; I intended to hit it).

In the case of fictional content, lots of cases of unsuccessful intentions are like this: an ultimate (or less instrumental) intention that readers imagine certain things fails, because of some inadvertent interference from the world. Communicating is not a 'basic' action: that is, it always takes place via some instrumental means. The case just mentioned by Carroll is like this: the author has the ultimate, or at least less instrumental, intention of saying 'black' and getting readers to imagine something black, but instead inadvertently automatically writes 'green'. Meanwhile, in a malapropism an utterer might intend to say 'You are a very perspicacious fellow' but inadvertently mix up 'perspicacious' with 'perspicuous' and say 'You are a very perspicuous fellow' (Stecker 2006: 437).

These cases just mentioned involve an author intending to communicate that a certain thing be imagined by readers, via an explicit description of it. Other cases involve an author intending a certain thing to be imagined, but rather than stating it explicitly, attempting to imply it. In a detective novel, an author might write intending all her 'clues' to point to a particular character as murderer; but inadvertently create a text that can be read as being intended to point to a different explanation.[2] Or consider that one might attempt to make it fictional that an event in a story is 'sad' (or falls under some other evaluative description) not just by stipulating this, but by describing enough detail that the reader herself feels sadness, and then makes the inference. This intention too can fail, as arguably in *The Old Curiosity Shop*, where Dickens intended readers to imagine that *the death of little Nell was sad*, at least partly by making them sad as they read about it. However, at least according to Oscar Wilde's famous pronouncement, Dickens' means of execution failed to produce this effect.[3] Equally, in *Uncle Tom's Cabin* Beecher Stowe intended it to be imagined that her main character was a strong and courageous person, by way of describing a character who was supposed to evoke this reaction in readers spontaneously; yet many have found him to be a servile racial stereotype, no doubt owing to Beecher Stowe's unconscious adoption of white cultural influences.[4] And in her novel *Possession*, A.S. Byatt intended to make it fictional that her character Randolph Ashe writes fine poetry, by the means of including in the text actual poems, of which she intended it to be imagined that Ashe has written them; yet in fact those poems have been roundly judged by her actual readers as poor.

Shortly, I will discuss cases with this sort of structure in more detail, and assess whether they entail or make likely that the author's original unsuccessful intention is not still evident in the text. In the meantime, though, we need to distinguish these cases of unsuccessful intentions from other cases.

---

[2] I owe this example to Manuel Garcia-Carpintero. Arguably Waters' *The Little Stranger*, discussed in the previous chapter, is in fact a real-life case of this, judging from the amount of online comment which fails to acknowledge Faraday as the murderer.

[3] Famously, Wilde is reported to have said that 'one must have a heart of stone to read the death of Little Nell without laughing'.

[4] I owe this example to Amber Leigh Griffioen.

3.3 Intentionally Controlled Ambiguity or Selective Communication

There are famous cases of fictions where an author deliberately makes it ambiguous which of two scenarios is the case in her text. One is Henry James's *The Turn of the Screw*. On one reading of the text, the ghosts are real and the governess sane; on another, the ghosts are a figment of the governess's disordered mind. James deliberately makes it ambiguous which of these scenarios is the reliable one. I shall discuss the implications of this sort of case for what James intends us to imagine in Chapter 5; the point to retain for now is that this is not a case of ambiguity of relevance to the issue of unsuccessful intentions.

A further distinction to be made is between inadvertently unsuccessful communication and deliberately selective communication, to a small group but not the whole of a text's readership (some instances were introduced in Chapter 1). When Lewis Carroll tells us in *Alice in Wonderland* that Alice says:

> four times five is twelve, and four times six is thirteen, and four times seven is—oh dear! I shall never get to twenty at that rate! (Carroll 1928: 21)

one explanation offered is as follows. Alice executes the first calculation (4x5) with a number base of eighteen (which gives 12), and then adds 3 to the last number base each time to get her next base and do her next calculation. Yet at the point in the series of calculations at which the number base becomes 42, and one might expect the sum arrived at to be 20, it is not (Gardner 2000: 23). If this is the right interpretation of Carroll's intention, and assuming Carroll realized that only a few *cognoscenti* could possibly recognize this as the explanation of why Alice will 'never get to twenty', then it isn't a mark of any failure of Carroll's intention that most readers do not recognize it.[5]

Finally we need to distinguish unsuccessful intentions from cases where an author deliberately has masked her original intentions for a text in later amendments to it. It is suggested that evidence of the character Rhoda's lesbianism exists in holograph drafts of Woolf's *The Waves*, and that subtle traces remain in the finished novel (Oxindine 1997). Their subtlety is ascribed to Woolf's anxiety following the obscenity trial of Radclyffe Hall's lesbian fiction *The Well of Loneliness* in 1928, at which Woolf testified on behalf of Hall. It took the emergence of evidence of Woolf's own lesbian relationships, and of her anxiety about prosecution for obscenity, plus scrutiny of the holograph texts, in order to bring this aspect of the text to the reader's attention. Without wanting to pronounce on the issue of whether it is fictionally true in the final text that Rhoda is a lesbian (i.e. whether Woolf ultimately intended readers to imagine this as they read the text), the fact that few readers till recently have picked up on the

---

[5] For discussion of cases where an author intends to convey some particular 'secret' meaning to a small group of readers, but not to others, see Carroll (2000: 91).

point is not due to a *failure* of Woolf's to communicate it properly, since clearly she was at least ambivalent about doing so.[6]

3.4 Inadvertently Unsuccessful Intentions

I move to cases more pertinent to the present issue. But just before I do, we should once again note a point already emphasized. That is: for an agent to intend to achieve *A*, she has to believe that she can or could achieve *A*. Accordingly, for an agent to intend someone else *S* to achieve *A*, she has to believe that *S* can or could achieve A. When applied here, this means that for an author to have the relevant reflexive intention I have cited, she must believe that readers can or could recognize her utterance as conveying that intention (quite possibly with the help of additional information about the author's context, as insisted upon above). Where an author does not satisfy this condition—say, where she arbitrarily insists that readers find content in her fiction which, she would acknowledge if pressed, they could not possibly be expected to recognize, even given additional information—her 'intention' has failed, in the sense that it was never a genuine intention in the first place. If 'intentions' fail in this sense, then, obviously, the fiction does not have the 'intended' meaning.

For instance, J.K. Rowling has stated after the publication of her Harry Potter series that her character Dumbledore is gay. As Irwin (2015) notes, whether this is a fictional truth in her books depends on whether there is reasonable evidence that in fact she did intend to communicate this point at the time of publication. Since the evidence within the text seems to be scant to the point of non-existence, it is an open question whether Rowling seriously could have believed she had provided readers with enough material to notice Dumbledore's sexuality, and so genuinely intended readers to imagine it.

Earlier I listed cases where there was a genuine ultimate/less instrumental authorial intention to communicate to readers that they were to imagine something, but nonetheless that intention failed. The cases described had a similar structure: the author intentionally did *A* in order to achieve *B*, but doing *A* did not in fact achieve *B* because of some inadvertent interference from elsewhere. Through inadvertent misspeaking or malapropism, or failing to anticipate how readers would interpret one's text in a certain respect, or unconscious promulgation of racial stereotypes, or a failure to anticipate readers' emotional responses to certain descriptions, what the author does to produce effect *B* in fact does not produce it. Now, the worry about extreme intentionalism seems to be that in such cases the original authorial intention that *B* should be achieved gets radically hidden (for after all, *B* was not achieved). But in fact this is not true for most or perhaps even any cases: *for there will usually be evidence potentially available of the person's trying to do B by A-ing, even if they have not succeeded in doing B.* I may try to make a beautiful wedding cake, which turns out via my incompetence to be an ugly

---

[6] For a comparable case, see the Henry James stories 'The Author of Beltraffio' and 'The Pupil', discussed in detail by Toibin as cases where a 'gay subtext is hinted at and then withdrawn' (2002: 31).

mess, but nonetheless the choice and placing of certain decorations, the texture of the icing, and so on, will allow a viewer to reconstruct my original intentions, even though they were unsuccessful. Attempted assassinations may fail but they usually leave ample evidence of their perpetrator's intentions. So too when an author tries to communicate some fictional content, but fails, the nature of her actions usually still provides evidence of what her goal was originally.

Of course, there may well be evidence of failed authorial intention 'external' to the text too, but even without this there is highly likely to be partial evidence of trying in features of the text itself. The speaker meaning behind inadvertent malapropisms—e.g. (to change the example) 'we're all cremated equal'—is, despite the deviation from sentence meaning incurred by malapropisms, easily recognized in practice by hearers, and in fact still taken to be what determines meaning in that context, rather than sentence meaning (Davidson 2006). Equally, misspelling a word is nearly always consistent with identifying in context the intended word, especially since misspellings tend to somewhat resemble, phonologically or lexically, their well-formed versions (Predelli 2010: 339). The same is true of automatic slips of the tongue or pen, which are usually phonologically or semantically similar to the intended word or phrase choices (Sorenson 2011: 401). Mistakes tend not to occur arbitrarily but can usually be related by interpreters, semantically, lexically, or phonologically, to words which would have expressed the governing intention better; and even where they cannot, other context usually often supplies the clue to speaker meaning.

I take it that similar points, suitably modified, can be applied to the Dickens example, for instance. In *The Old Curiosity Shop*, the sentimental overstatement, the heavy-handed symbols of Nell's innocence and virtuous nature, and so on, clearly attest to an intention to make the reader feel sad about Nell's death. A similar point might even be made of the detective novel we considered earlier, in which the intended murderer (call him 'Jack') is consistently overlooked by readers in favour of another explanation, owing to the author's failure to communicate her intention well. Perhaps if still alive and asked, the author would correct the reader's impression; or perhaps there is other evidence in the author's life or accompanying works which might help establish what she meant. But more importantly, for this example to be plausible at all, it is not, presumably, that there is absolutely no 'internal' evidence in the text that Jack is intended to be the murderer, even once one has access to additional external evidence to that effect. It is much more likely that the relevant 'internal' evidence will become salient only to a reader who has the testimony in mind, than that it does not exist at all.

To see this last point more clearly, we should consider an actual-world case, of an authorial intention being 'hidden' to contemporary commentators and only emerging as a possibility late in the text's history. A passage in Jane Austen's *Emma* describes the party's walk after a picnic 'in the middle of June'. Emma sees Harriet and Knightley talking as they walk, and Emma reflects that

[t]here had been a time...when Emma would have been sorry to see Harriet in a spot so favourable for the Abbey-Mill Farm; but now she feared it not. It might be safely viewed with all its appendages of prosperity and beauty, its rich pastures, spreading flock, orchard in blossom, and light column of smoke ascending.   (Austen 1990: 325–6)

Many readers have presumed that Austen's governing intention in so writing was to fictionally represent the vista in June, as Emma, Harriet, and Knightley looked at it. For the observant among them, then, the inclusion of blossom in June, out of season, has seemed strange (Sutherland 1996: 17). However, Sutherland interprets the last sentence of this paragraph—partly based on Austen's care in authenticating details elsewhere in her oeuvre—as representing a 'montage' cycling through several seasons in a compressed way, including Spring (Sutherland 1996: 18–19). In this case, if Sutherland is right, the 'evidence' of Austen's intention has been there all along, only unnoticed. So too, it is likely that in the detective case, the 'evidence' interpreted one way will support the thought that Jack is the murderer, and read another it will not.

So, to extrapolate: there nearly always seems to be evidence available both within a text and without it, about what the fictional content of the text is, even if as a matter of fact that evidence is contingently obscured to a given group of readers, or perhaps even all, at a given time.

An objector might worry: what about Carroll's case, where an author 'wrote 'green', but intended 'black' (2000: 85)? Let's assume that no other evidence in the text might suggest to the reader that 'black' was intended instead of 'green' (the thing described is not *the night sky* or *a cat* or *a thundercloud*; the thing described is not described as 'black' elsewhere in a way that would reveal the error). The trouble here is that quite properly, I have allowed that 'external' evidence can also count as potential defeasible evidence of those intentions. The assumption is that the slip is inadvertent; presumably then, the author, if still living, would recognize it as such and admit to it, if asked. This means that had the reader had access to this evidence, she would recognize 'green' as a slip, and that the true intention was 'black'. After all, 'green' and 'black' are both colours—the mistake is comprehensible on grounds of semantic similarity.

Of course, readers may not *as a matter of fact* have access to this information about what the author would have said, if asked; perhaps as a matter of fact she was never asked and did not notice, and perhaps she is now dead or otherwise unavailable for comment. But that an author's intention might in certain circumstances fail to be recognized by readers owing to a contingent lack of evidence is not itself an argument against intentionalism. In certain cases, we can properly say that some aspect of the content is hidden. As we will see later in this chapter, this is not a feature any plausible theory of fictional content can avoid.

In some cases, through limits on our knowledge, a text may remain ambiguous. Assuming Sutherland is right, Austen presumably did not mean for her intention to be masked or interpreted as a mistake. In these sorts of case, the author intends her readers to imagine that p in response to her fiction, and does not intend that they should imagine that q, but this intention is inexpertly conveyed, so that the text presents ambiguous evidence, applicable perhaps to p and q, as the right imaginative response. This too looks like a kind of failure of intention, but it is not one that gives us reason to doubt extreme intentionalism. The relevant failure seems to be that the author has failed in her presumable intention that utterance x be recognized by her readers as intended to produce the imagining that p in them, *unambiguously*. An author can be legitimately criticized for failing to get her content-generating intentions across unambiguously, when presumably she had intended them to be unambiguous. But that a certain aspect of a text's fictional content is contingently partly obscured from current readers does not yet look like a reason to deny that the fiction has the relevant content at all.[7]

I suppose someone might persist: what about the (presumably very rare) case of a fiction where an author so radically misunderstands some communicative norm that the text is unrecognizable as an attempt to appeal to it? For instance, say an author so totally misunderstands what is required to write a fiction that conveys content p in a particular way, that no one at all could recognize the text that she produces as a manifestation of this intention. Does the text still have content p? The issue here is that the original complaint, that 'no-one at all could recognize the text that I produce as a manifestation of this intention', still looks overstated. For, assuming we are talking about rational agents, even tortuously bad and initially thoroughly confusing prose can be disentangled so that certain intentions behind it become apparent, once we allow external evidence of authorial intention to bear upon our readings of it, and so to reveal certain patterns and other aspects within it as significant.[8] Of course, normally there is very little value in painstakingly reconstructing the intentions behind very bad fiction. But I still see no reason to deny that in such a case fictional content would still be identical to what the author intended readers to imagine.

We now have an answer to the challenge, described earlier, that extreme intentionalism 'decentralizes' the text as a source of meaning. As I have acknowledged, it is perfectly true that an authorial intention with respect to what is to be imagined can be hidden, and detectable only once the reader has access to extratextual evidence from the author's life (interviews, evidence from diaries, and so on). But this is not a case of

---

[7] Assuming the reader has access to two interpretations of a piece of text, each of which look epistemically possible to her as reflective of the author's true intention but between which she cannot decide, she can at least imaginatively engage *with each of them in turn*. Hence, assuming one of these interpretations is the right one, she can imagine what she is intended to, even though she also imagines what she is not intended to. A reader of *Emma* can, for instance, *first* imagine that the fruit trees Emma is looking at are blossoming in June, and then imagine that they blossom only in Spring. One of these, we are assuming, will be what Austen intended her to imagine. So the reader still may comply with the relevant authorial intention. There is a disanalogy here with ordinary information-bearing conversation. Namely, where an utterance x is made in ordinary conversation with the reflexive intention to convey belief that p to an auditor, and yet the auditor finds x ambiguous in respect of two readings p and q, the hearer cannot believe both; belief, unlike imagining, is not acquired at will to this extent.

[8] See also footnote 31, Chapter 1.

external evidence 'decentralizing' the text, so much as making existing aspects of it salient that were previously hidden. Even the case of miswriting which is indiscernible in principle given surrounding context, the offending word can count as an undoubtedly poor but still existent piece of 'evidence' for the relevant true governing intention, once discovered externally. The worry that the text could be 'jettisonable in principle if we could get more directly at what the author had in mind to tell us' (Levinson 1992: 223) is unfounded.

3.5 Unsuccessful Intentions, Hypothetical Intentionalism, and Aesthetic Criticism

The framework I just offered with respect to contingently unsuccessful, hidden intentions furnishes the critic with an important tool in aesthetic assessment of fictional texts. Extreme intentionalism allows that there can be a mismatch between a) fictional content—understood as what the author intends readers to imagine—and b) the extent to which the text effectively communicates that content, or produces some desired effect from it. Hence we can criticize an author who includes misspellings or slips of the pen in her text as being sloppy in her means of communicating content. We can criticize an author whose audience fails to understand some piece of content intended to be unambiguous, as being insufficiently clear and/or failing to anticipate the responses of readers properly. And so on.

Oddly, one prominent critic of actual author intentionalism, Gregory Currie, accuses it of just the opposite. He writes:

> An interpreter for whom letters, diaries, and other sources have suggested an interpretation of which the text is a defective embodiment has ceased to be an interpreter of the text in question and has become the interpreter of another, hypothetical work: the text that would have been written if the author's intentions had gone well.
>
> (Currie 2004: 125; see also Currie 1993: 418; Levinson 2010: 145)

His complaint here seems to be that actual author intentionalism ignores problematic communication of content in a text, instead reconstructing the text in an idealized way. This is simply not true, however. And even more puzzlingly, this *is* true of Currie's own favoured position, hypothetical intentionalism (1993, 2004).

According to this theory, fictional content is determined not by speaker meaning, nor by sentence meaning, but by a third, 'utterance meaning'. Utterance meaning is determined by *what would be* interpreted as the speaker's meaning, by certain epistemically well-positioned and aesthetically sensitive readers, given certain restrictions on the evidence they can call upon in the process. That is, interpretation is a matter of working out, in conjunction with appropriate evidence, what 'an appropriately informed, sympathetic, and discriminating reader' would take the text to be intended to mean, given the restrictions in question (Levinson 2006: 302). Opinions amongst hypothetical intentionalists diverge about what should be admitted as appropriate evidence. According to Levinson, for instance, a lot of information about the actual author and her historical and cultural context should be admitted into the epistemic background against which interpretation is supposed to occur; according to Currie (1993, 2004), less so (I will discuss this shortly). However, hypothetical intentionalists of all stripes seem to agree that the evidence which appropriately may be called upon in anticipating these idealized response *excludes* 'essentially private—which is not to say epistemically inaccessible' information about the actual author not available in the public domain (2006: 306); e.g. a 'secret diary' (1992: 230) or other source.

Though it is rarely commented upon (though see Carroll 2000: 92–3 for related points), this exclusion of 'private' evidence from interpretation means that, potentially, a text's content can change over time according to hypothetical intentionalism, as previously 'private' evidence comes into public view. To return to an example given above, let's just assume, probably contrary to fact, that Woolf intended readers of *The Waves* to notice unambiguously that Rhoda was a lesbian. Extreme intentionalism would have it that on that basis, Rhoda's lesbianism is part of the fictional content of the text. On this view, what the private information about Woolf's love life, holograph drafts (etc.) have done is to make epistemically accessible to readers previously-overlooked evidence of this intention within the text. Hypothetical intentionalism, meanwhile, would have it that prior to public dissemination of private information about Woolf's lesbian affairs, the holograph drafts and so on, Rhoda's lesbianism definitely was not part of the fictional content of *The Waves* (since it could not be detected in the text without the help of these sources). Only after the emergence of this information did this aspect of fictional content come into being. This would be a metaphysical, not an epistemic claim.

Some hypothetical intentionalists reject as irrelevant to interpretation, not just private information unknown to the public, but also any detailed information about the author's context at all. For instance, as we saw in Chapter 2, Currie thinks that fictional content should be interpreted by reference to the construct of a fictional author who reports the text as fact. Fictional content is equivalent to what this fictional author could reasonably be taken to believe, given the details of the text. In the process of interpretation, readers are permitted to attribute to the fictional author general knowledge about what sort of beliefs someone writing in the relevant period might conceivably have had (1990: 78), but in many cases not a lot else. Now, obviously, the more the hypothetical intentionalist sheers off private information in principle from the domain of interpreting fictional content, the more she moves away from the aim of reconstructing authorial intention. This is problematic, not least because in some cases authors can intend to imply certain fictional truths whose grasp will depend upon a full understanding of their own individual context—background, influences, personal beliefs, and so on.

To take just one example: Marilynne Robinson's *Gilead* is explicitly narrated by a character, Rev. John Ames, who luminously describes a complex Christian faith.

However, Ames is not thoroughly reliable: there are facts in the fiction he does not know.[9] Towards the end of the work, Ames writes:

> It has seemed to me sometimes as though the Lord breathes on this poor grey ember of Creation and it turns to radiance—for a moment or a year or the span of a life. And then it sinks back into itself again, and to look at it no one would know it had anything to do with fire, or light. That is what I said in the Pentecost sermon. I have reflected on that sermon, and there is some truth in it. But the Lord is more constant and far more extravagant than it seems to imply. Wherever you turn your eyes the world can shine like transfiguration. You don't have to bring a thing to it except a little willingness to see. Only, who could have the courage to see it?
> (Robinson 2005: 280)

It is very tempting to read this, not just as the articulation of an epistemically limited and possibly false perspective of John Ames, but also as authoritatively reflecting something true in the fiction. In *Gilead*, it is *true* that the Lord is constant and extravagant, and that wherever you turn your eyes the world can shine like transfiguration. It is tempting to say this because *we know that Robinson is a Christian writer, and that this view is one she holds*. Indeed, in an interview Robinson has said:

> Ordinary things have always seemed numinous to me. One Calvinist notion deeply implanted in me is that there are two sides to your encounter with the world. You don't simply perceive something that is statically present, but in fact there is a visionary quality to all experience. It means something because it's addressed to you. This is the individualism that you find in Walt Whitman and Emily Dickinson. You can draw from perception the same way a mystic would draw from a vision. (Fay 2008)

Yet there is no obvious room for this interpretation on Currie's view. For Currie, Ames can only be describing his own defeasible perspective, not an authoritative one. A similar point can be made for any plausible interpretation of the content of a book which depends on facts about the particular author's context; e.g. character, personal creed, or individual influences. In brief, to get a rich enough account of what is fictionally true according to standard critical literary practice, we often need to attend to particularities of the author's actual context, which some versions of hypothetical intentionalism would ignore.

Let's now return to Currie's earlier accusation made against extreme intentionalism: that it involves reconstructing the text in an idealized way which precludes criticism of the author's mistakes in communicating content. In fact, this objection seems much more aptly directed towards hypothetical intentionalism itself. On Currie's view:

> '[i]nterpretation of the text aims to postulate communicative intentions for which the text can be seen as an adequate vehicle, and these will not always be the intentions the author actually had'
> (2004: 125)

---

[9] This is arguably indicated by, among other things, Ames's fictionally unwitting but metafictionally significant use of words from *King Lear* at the end of the book (Churchwell 2014).

But now it looks as if there is precisely no room for identifying and so criticizing any mismatch between what the content is and how it is expressed in the text! If acknowledging that a given text can be a 'defective embodiment' of its author's intentions is an important desideratum of a theory of fictional content, as Currie suggests it is, then actual author intentionalism achieves this more easily and straightforwardly than hypothetical intentionalism does.

A similar point applies to value-maximizing theory, which has it that the fictional content of F is determined in relation, first to conventional meanings of words and sentences in F, and after that, to whatever interpretation of F's fictional content would maximize the value of the text (S. Davies 2006). I will discuss this view in depth shortly, but for the moment, we should note that this thoroughgoing move away from authorial intentions makes it unclear how we could criticize, say, *Possession* for including actually-bad poetry which is fictionally good—for presumably, for most, it would make the text more valuable to think it included deliberately bad poetry, than that it did not.

3.6 Hypothetical Intentionalism and Fiction as 'Public'

I turn now to another aspect of hypothetical intentionalism: the thought that a fiction, qua artwork, is an essentially 'public' object.

The point can be put something like this. Let us grant that in ordinary conversation, interpretation of speaker meaning may potentially advert, unproblematically, to the speaker's own pronouncements about what she means, diary entries, or even secret thoughts. But still, the case is essentially different with fiction. Fictions, qua artworks, are essentially 'public' entities, in a way that utterances in conversation are not (for approving discussion, see S. Davies 2006; for relevant criticism, see Carroll 2000: 86–93).

One wonders why the allegedly 'public' nature of fiction should negate the idea that its content is determined in relation to speaker meaning. Say that I speak with a loudhailer to a large crowd, none of whom I know personally. My speech is public, one-sided, and directed towards unknown auditors. Yet it does not follow from any of this that my meaning should not be determined by relation to my communicative intentions. Moreover, if I misspeak during the speech, there is no suggestion that what my utterance meant must have been what it seemed to idealized hearers to mean, rather than what I intended.

Perhaps the insistence that the text is a 'public' one, and that 'private' evidence is inadmissible with respect to its nature, is at least partly grounded in the thought that the meaning of a text is governed by publicly understood *conventions* (this seems to be the case with Levinson; see 2006: 306). Yet, as has been repeatedly emphasized in Chapter 1 and elsewhere, conventions in fact play only part of the role of contributors to meaning, and where they do so directly, they might not have. We cannot just assume convention or rules will settle every interpretative question, in conversation or in fictive utterance. So: that fictions are public in this sense is not incompatible with private evidence being appropriate to their proper interpretation.

The thought of a fiction as essentially 'public' is perhaps motivated instead by the worry that to say otherwise, and so to make meaning determined by actual authorial intentions, leaves the interpreter in a particularly insecure position: what will gauge the correctness of her view, or otherwise—the intentions and purposes of the author—is something that contingently may never be revealed. This, of course, is true. Extreme intentionalism predicts that often a reader will know that she does not know for sure what the content of the text is. However, the salient point for present purposes is that hypothetical intentionalism is not immune to the possibility of meanings about which we cannot be sure either; quite the contrary, in fact.

To see this, note that obviously, most actual readers do not approximate to the idealized 'appropriately informed, sensitive, and discriminating' readers whose hypothesized responses are supposed to be determinative of meaning according to hypothetical intentionalism, and they know that they do not. Hence most readers are not entitled to straightforwardly take their own hypotheses about the likely intentions of an author who produced *this* text as equivalent to its content. Instead, according to hypothetical intentionalism, they should be making hypotheses about *the hypotheses of idealized readers about the likely intentions of an author who produced this text*.

Perhaps even *expert critics* should not take their own responses about content as inevitably mirroring or determining that content, according to the implicit commitments of hypothetical intentionalism. For even where critics tend to have access to all relevant 'public' information, they still disagree with each other about certain works' content (consider the controversy about the content of *Pale Fire*, described in Boyd 1997). Moreover, they may not be sure that they are experts.

It seems there is no easy way, according to hypothetical intentionalism, for a reader to 'check' whether her interpretation matches an optimal one—for where should she find such information about what the optimal interpretations *really are*? At least actual author intentionalism allows the possibility in some cases of an author's easily confirming or denying a reader's interpretation. Hypothetical intentionalism does not allow anything like this. If anything, there seems to be greater lack of certainty with respect to interpretation, given hypothetical intentionalism, and not less.

3.7 Extreme Intentionalism versus Value-maximizing Approaches

I turn now to the 'value-maximizing' view. A reminder: this says that interpretation of fictional content, and indeed of art more generally, does or at least should take place in virtue of considerations about what would make the text most artistically valuable. As one prominent advocate of the view, Stephen Davies, writes:

> the maximizing theory assumes that interpretations seek what is artistically valuable in the works they target and that, when it comes to adjudicating among work-compatible interpretations, those that make the text out to be artistically more meritorious as literature are to be preferred.   (S. Davies 2006: 242)

If we add the assumption, reasonable within this context, that for every text, there will be more than one interpretation associated with maximum value for that text (or at least—more realistically, I assume—more than one interpretation of significantly high value, where assessments of the value of such interpretations are incommensurable with one another) then value-maximizing theory entails endorsement of 'critical pluralism' (S. Davies 2006: 245). Critical pluralism says that, for some or all fictions, there might be more than one equally good interpretation of its content (Kieran 1996). In contrast, extreme intentionalism is a monistic position: if it is true, then critical pluralism about fictional content must be false.

At least one of the motivations for value-maximizing theory seems to be well accommodated by extreme intentionalism. That is: that the experience of fiction is valuable partly because the reader does not merely robotically recover what the author intended her to think, but plays an active role in 'contributing' to the meaning of the text (something obviously emphasized in what are known as 'reader-response' theories in literary studies).[10] Now, it is certainly true, according to extreme intentionalism, that the reader does not *robotically* recover authorial intentions, because, as already emphasized, these intentions can be relatively well-hidden, ambiguous, or multiple; so that the matter of recovering them need not be robotic or automatic. So here too there is an active role for the reader to play. Admittedly, the intentionalist will balk at describing this role as one of 'contributing' to textual meaning, rather than 'discovering' it. But generally, discovery (e.g. of new mountain routes, theories in physics, or animal species) can be active and difficult, and experienced as valuable because of those facts.

A critical question for the value-maximizer is whether, on this view, readers are said to seek out what *they themselves* would consider valuable in an interpretation, or rather, what, they believe, some privileged group of experts would consider valuable. I take it that the latter claim would have some unfortunate consequences: not least, that potentially a large gap would open up between the typical competent-but-not-expert reader's interpretation of a text, and the 'correct' one (i.e. the one that experts would agree upon). This is because—in a problem analogous to one facing hypothetical intentionalism—competent-but-not-expert readers are unlikely to have an easy grasp of what experts would find most valuable as a text's interpretation. An additional problem here is one raised by Levinson (2002) with respect to Hume's 'Of the Standard of Taste'—what reason does the ordinary reader, whose preferences are likely to deviate from those of experts with respect to a given text, have for accepting that the latter is the source of the 'correct' interpretation, since presumably it will not be perceived as a source of value *to them*, given those preferences? In any case, it is clear from Davies's formulation that his claim, at least, is that readers are to interpret in ways which enhance the value of *their own* experience (S. Davies 2006: 241), rather than in ways which attempt to anticipate the enhancement of others' experiences.

---

[10] This point was pressed by a referee.

This is not, of course, to say that content of a given text must vary from reader to reader; a value-maximizing theorist might conceivably be a relativist about fictional content in this way, but more likely she will think that there are facts about what would maximize the value of the text, that are separate from particular readers' preferences and/or assessments of value. Even so, it remains true on this view that readers, in their everyday acts of interpretation, are acting in the light of their perception of value, and this is what I want to critically focus upon.

In the characterization initially given of the theory, I wrote that 'the value-maximizing view says that interpretation of fictional content, and indeed of art more generally, *does or at least should* take place in virtue of considerations about what would make the text most artistically valuable' (my italics). I will now argue that both are implausible because as a matter of fact, value-maximizing *could not* be the complete story about how the reader discerned fictional content, or tried to.

According to value-maximizing theory, in interpreting content, a reader will respect the conventional meanings of words and sentences; beyond that, she will interpret in a way that maximizes the value of her reading experience, and so of the text (for her, at least). Now, as we saw in earlier chapters, in ordinary conversational contexts, conventional sentence meaning vastly underdetermines what is meant by a speaker; it excludes all sorts of non-conventional conversational implicatures. These, I argued, get determined by reference to what the speaker intended. Is there any coherent way of construing the interpretation of conversational utterance, beyond the conventional, as involving 'maximizing the value' of the utterance? Only in the innocuous and limited sense that the hearer adopts some sort of principle of charity, according to which she attributes to speakers something like a desire to convey maximally true information in a non-misleading way, along the lines of the Gricean 'maxims' discussed in the previous chapter. But this is very different to interpreting utterances in the light of perceptions of what would count as making the utterance most valuable to me. An interpreter who did this would presumably, potentially 'hear what she wanted to hear', quite literally. She could, for instance, ignore irony if it detracted from the value of a statement to her; or treat a literal statement as ironic. She could interpret ambiguous sentences in ways which best suited her ends. This would not be an effective means of communication, by any stretch.

Now this on its own is not a mark against value-maximizing theory, which after all is a theory of fictional content, not conversational utterance. But at the very least this serves to highlight how radically different, according to the value-maximizing theorist, ordinary conversation and fictional utterance must be. It also shows that the value-maximizing theory is committed to denying that fiction-making is in any way *communicative*. Of course, on my own view, the interpretation of fictional content is *somewhat* different from that of ordinary conversation; in the latter, one is working out what one is intended to imagine, whereas in the former, one is working out (roughly, probably with several exceptions) what one is intended to believe. But both are in a sense still communicative; and the practice of interpreting fiction is not radically distinct from that of interpreting conversation, with similar skills involved in each case.

Turning now more squarely to value-maximizing theory as it applies to fictional content: according to this view, as I have said, fictional content is interpreted in the light of considerations about what would give the text most value. One immediate problem with this is that it is implausible to think that, with every new paragraph, readers make some sort of decision about how to interpret it based on considerations of value-maximizing. A reader who generally prefers science fiction to 19th-century realism nonetheless would not read the opening paragraphs of *Middlemarch* as concerning an alien who has come to inhabit the body of 'Miss Brook', no matter how much reading it this way would enhance her enjoyment and, in her opinion, increase the text's aesthetic value.[11] A reader who felt depressed and did not wish to feel worse would not read the initial stages of Toni Morrison's *Beloved* as a farce, or as a bad dream. Indeed, to say that the reader interprets according to her perception of what would be most valuable is to imply that she has some notion of available choices; but for many paragraphs and even chapters, the reader will simply have no idea about any relevant possible alternatives.

In fact, the questions cited by value-maximizing theorists as ones of genuine interest to fictional interpretation—for instance 'is the marriage between Othello and Desdemona consummated, and if not, does this make Othello's jealousy more understandable and his bad judgement more plausible?' (S. Davies 2006: 245)—tend to emerge at a relatively late stage of reading, after a lot of basic interpretation has already been done.[12] In order to ask ourselves whether Othello's marriage is consummated, for instance, we already have to have understood many, many of the utterances which compose it. Perhaps, like others before her, the value-maximizing theorist assumes that all this work can get done by the reader's understanding of 'conventions' (see S. Davies 2006: 242). But as we have seen, this simply is not true. So there is a huge explanatory gap in the theory of value-maximizing: according to what principle does the reader interpret each paragraph, as she reads, where she is not yet in any reasonable position to apply considerations of value?

The objection just raised says that for much of a text's content, it would be impossible for value-maximizing theory to provide a good account of how readers reach conclusions about it. The next objection says that for other aspects of fictional content, though it might be *possible* that value-maximizing theory was a good account of how it was generated, as a matter of fact readers *do not* apply considerations of value in reaching conclusions about such content. For even late on in a reading, where many of the 'basics' have been established, a reader will not conceivably suddenly introduce explicit considerations of value into her interpretation of fictional content without the *obvious*

---

[11] See also Carroll (1992: 119–20).
[12] The other questions cited by Davies are not about fictional content at all, but about what the fiction tells us about the real world.

presence of ambiguity. It may be tempting to free-associate the sort of plot one would like, on reading a novel, as Gregory Woods does when he reads Orwell:

> whenever I read *Nineteen Eighty-Four* I cannot help imagining, between its lines, the spectral presence of another novel, a gay novel called 'Nineteen Forty-Eight', in which two young Londoners called Winston and Julian fall in love with each other and struggle to sustain their relationship under the continuous threat of blackmail, exposure and arrest...
>
> (Woods 1998: 266)

But no one would seriously propose that this is the text's *content*, because there is no ambiguity signalled in the text as to the character Julia's gender identity.

So the most plausible version of value-maximizing theory must say that *where a text is ambiguous*, we choose the possible reading we perceive to have most value. But even this is not yet wholly accurate. As we saw earlier, ambiguity of fictional content comes in two varieties, deliberate and non-deliberate. In the case of deliberate ambiguity—as with *The Turn of the Screw*—clearly the competent reader does not tend to interpret according to her preference, even if as a matter of fact she hates ambiguity and would prefer a more settled ending. This leaves us with the case of non-deliberate ambiguity, such as in the example from Austen's *Emma* that we looked at in the previous chapter. Is it the case in that text that apple blossoms appear in June, or not? This sort of case, I suggest, is the only remotely plausible case for value-maximizing theory, since it does seem that at least sometimes, at such a point, the reader is likely to apply value-maximizing considerations (hence the plausibility of Davies's *Othello* example above).

Yet there is now a two-pronged problem for the value-maximizing theorist. On the one hand, she lacks a convincing and non ad hoc explanation of why the reader value-maximizes here but not earlier or elsewhere. On the other, her rival the extreme intentionalist *has* a convincing explanation of this fact: namely, in such a case, *value-maximizing is a somewhat reliable (though not infallible) means of ascertaining what the author really intended the reader to imagine*. For: a lot of the time, an author's purposes include producing a text of value, and equally, many authors have a grip upon what would count for readers as a valuable text. In the case of Austen, given our prior knowledge of her as a masterful practitioner, on balance it makes more sense to think she deliberately constructed a montage of seasonal images than that she intended to describe an anomalous natural event. The ambiguous passage is of greater value if read that way, and it fits with what we know of her to read this as meant.

I have said that in cases of non-deliberate ambiguity, value-maximizing considerations are likely to apply 'sometimes'. As this suggests, even here they are not inevitably likely to apply. We can see this in the case of morally repellent literature. Once we have removed the author's intentions in such cases as irrelevant, there are usually other interpretations open to the reader, which would remove the objectionable attitude from the text, as it were, and thereby enhance the value of the reader's experience.

Take the following passage from a Sherlock Holmes story[13] (also to be discussed in Chapter 4):

> I don't think that any of my adventures with Mr. Sherlock Holmes opened quite so abruptly, or so dramatically, as that which I associate with The Three Gables.... The door had flown open and a huge negro had burst into the room.... His broad face and flattened nose were thrust forward, as his sullen dark eyes, with a smouldering gleam of malice in them, turned from one of us to the other. "Which of you gen'l'men is Masser Holmes?" he asked.... He swung a huge knotted lump of a fist under my friend's nose. Holmes examined it closely with an air of great interest..."I've wanted to meet you for some time," said Holmes. "I won't ask you to sit down, for I don't like the smell of you, but aren't you Steve Dixie, the bruiser?" "That's my name, Masser Holmes, and you'll get put through it for sure if you give me any lip."
> "It is certainly the last thing you need," said Holmes, staring at our visitor's hideous mouth.
> (Conan Doyle 1960: 1023)

It would presumably enhance many non-racist readers' experience of this text to treat this passage as describing a man of colour, Steve Dixie, who simply coincidentally *happened to have* such properties as 'sullen dark eyes with a smouldering gleam of malice in them' and a 'hideous mouth', rather than to read it in the way it was clearly intended by Doyle: as suggesting that these properties were possessed by Steve Dixie *because* he was a person of colour. Value-maximizing theory would suggest that this is what we will or at least should do. But of course (I assume) readers do not, nor should they, seek to neutralize the morally objectionable in fictional contexts by finding alternative readings which enhance the value of our experience of the associated texts.

So I conclude that value-maximizing theory fails. It cannot account for large amounts of fictional content. Meanwhile, of the fictional content it could arguably account for (i.e. some cases of non-deliberately ambiguous content) extreme intentionalism can account for that too, and arguably with a stronger rationale.

3.8 Extreme Intentionalism and Post Hoc Meanings

The main motive for value-maximizing theory, as compared to actual authorial intentionalism, is supposedly that the former but not the latter can accommodate the full range of meanings competent interpreters tend to find in/attribute to texts.[14]

When we have exhausted the meanings that authors successfully intended as regards their works' meanings, still many plausible, interesting, and apparently legitimate interpretations are not accounted for. By excluding unintended meanings, the actual intentionalist unduly restricts the literary interpreter.   (S. Davies 2006: 233)

---

[13] Notwithstanding that it is not particularly ambiguous.
[14] See the Introduction for a list of kinds of meaning that extreme intentionalism is not supposed to account for.

One kind of meaning which might seem to favour value-maximizing over extreme intentionalism is 'post hoc' ones. These often involve analysis of a fictional text in terms of historical or theoretical entities about which the original author could not possibly have known.

For instance, one might cite Terry Eagleton's Marxist reading of *Wuthering Heights*; Eagleton states that Heathcliff 'represents a turbulent form of capitalist aggression which must historically be civilised' (1988: 115). However, on closer inspection, this is not best understood as a claim about fictional content, but rather about structural similarities between the character Heathcliff and a capitalist archetype. It seems compatible with this reading to suppose that Brontë intentionally represented her character Heathcliff as having characteristics x, y, and z. This in turn has allowed Eagleton later to recognize that Heathcliff, qua possessor of characteristics x, y, and z, embodies several features of capitalist aggression as he conceives of it, and to that extent 'represents' such aggression. In the same way, one might say that actual people in the world 'represent' certain forces or ideas, even where they are unaware of them.

Or take Jonathan Culler's Barthes-inspired deconstructive reading of Flaubert's *Madame Bovary* in terms of ideas from post-structuralism (Culler 1974). Culler argues that certain passages in the novel undermine the notion, inherited from Balzac amongst others, of an omniscient authorial narrator; and more radically, even the notion of a single coherent self. In passages such as the opening one of the novel, describing schoolboy Charles's ludicrous and extravagant hat, Culler argues that details are accumulated to the extent that their symbolic import teeters under its own weight and becomes meaningless, reinforcing the post-structuralist conception of meaning as fragmented and deferred. Again, though, this is not about the nature of fictional content in *Madame Bovary*, but about its consequences. Actually, it is perfectly possible that Flaubert had, as one of his goals in writing *Madame Bovary*, the undermining of notions of Balzacian realism, including the notion of a stable point of view and the possibility of omniscient description, without conceiving of that goal, anachronistically, as 'post-structuralist' or 'deconstructive'. In other words, Flaubert and post-structuralists such as Barthes might have shared aims—or as another critic puts it, a shared 'project'— without problem (Schor 1980: 29). But even if Flaubert had no such aims, and just *accidentally* produced a text which could be read in this valuable and interesting way, this would not threaten my view, which is about the nature of fictional content directly, and not about the extent to which fictional content happens to illuminate contemporary philosophical theories of language.

Both the cases just discussed involved pointing out illuminating resemblances between some aspects of fictional content and some theoretical postulate (a form of capitalist aggression as conceived of by Marxism; language as conceived of by post-structuralism). Roughly this sort of explanation can also be applied to a famous stick with which intentionalism is often beaten: namely, that it is supposedly fictionally true in Shakespeare's *Hamlet* that Hamlet has an Oedipus complex (Jones 1910). After all, it is said, he exhibits all the symptoms. Yet this is not something Shakespeare could have intended to be imagined, given his historical context. Arguably, an Oedipus complex is an entity essentially characterizable in relation to a web of Freudian theoretical concepts coined for the first time in the late 19th and early 20th centuries. Hence Shakespeare could not have direct cognitive access to the concept of an Oedipus complex, as such, and so could not have had intentions which explicitly name one. So extreme intentionalism cannot accommodate this or other similarly derived 'meanings'.

Granting all this for the sake of argument, the intentionalist cannot admit a reference to an Oedipus complex as part of *Hamlet*'s fictional content, I agree. However, she can accommodate the intuitions that lead people to think that *Hamlet* contains this as a fictional truth. That is, she can say that he intended the audience to imagine that Hamlet suffers from certain problems: namely, excessive grief at the loss of his father; jealousy of his mother's new lover; anger at his mother's fast remarriage, and so forth. Meanwhile, those same characteristics are also picked out by later Freudian theory as symptomatic of an Oedipus complex.

A supporter of extreme intentionalism might wonder: could Shakespeare somehow *indirectly* intentionally pick out an Oedipus complex, even though he could not directly refer to one in thought, given his historical context? Unfortunately, I think not. This is because intentions look referentially opaque: co-referring terms cannot be freely substituted into their content without a change in the nature of the intention. Say that I intend to kick this thing, but unbeknownst to me, this thing is a Stradivarius; it does not follow that I intend to kick a Stradivarius (for discussion, see Aune 1977: 97–8). However, though it is not therefore a fictional truth in *Hamlet* that Hamlet had an Oedipus complex, it is also not fictionally false in *Hamlet* that this is so. Rather, it is simply fictionally *indeterminate* whether Hamlet had an Oedipus complex or not; no intentions specify the matter either way. Where some matter is fictionally indeterminate in a fiction, audiences may often harmlessly imagine something specific about the matter, going beyond the fictional content of the text. For instance, where a fiction F instructs a reader to imagine a tall woman, readers might tend to imagine a tall woman *with brown hair*, though the fiction has not specified either way. In that case, I assume, no one would be tempted to say that it is part of the fictional content of F that the woman in question has brown hair.

Where a person K intends someone else J to do A, J can comply and do A by means of B without its following that K intended J to do B. For instance, if K intends J to give her £100, and J achieves this partly by robbing a bank, it does not follow that K intended J to rob a bank. One way for a post-Freudian reader to actually achieve the intention described above would be to imagine that Hamlet had an Oedipus complex. This is a means of doing what she is intended to do, even though it is not the case that Shakespeare intended her to imagine this, in particular. This then, I think, is how we should explain the intuitions which have led some to think it must be part of *Hamlet*'s fictional content that Hamlet has an Oedipus complex. Some readers harmlessly imagine this, as a way of imagining what they are intended by Shakespeare to imagine. They 'harmlessly' imagine this, because even though the text does not instruct them to, it does not instruct them not to either. (For more on 'acceptable' interpretations of fictions which are neither true nor false, see Stecker 1994.)

So to sum up: many cases of 'unintentional' literary meaning which on the face of it might seem to be counterexamples to extreme intentionalism can in fact be ignored, since they do not concern fictional content (directly anyway). On the other hand, I will now argue, other cases which do concern fictional content directly can be accommodated fairly easily by extreme intentionalism. For instance, one thought apparently troubling to the extreme intentionalist is that there can be alternative and incompatible interpretations of fictional content with respect to a given text, relative to different theoretical perspectives. And yet on closer scrutiny, I will argue, extreme intentionalism can accommodate many such cases.

3.9 Extreme Intentionalism and 'Layers' of Meaning

To exemplify, I shall focus on a short story by Angela Carter. Carter was a teacher and scholar on Sade, Freud, the fairy tale genre, Romanticism, the Gothic, science fiction, the history of literature generally, and gender representation in literature. She used her works to explore themes related to these areas of interest. As one critic notes: 'Typically, Carter...presents us with an amalgam of discourses' (Farnell 2014: 272).

Carter's story 'The Bloody Chamber' is a reworking of Perrault's Bluebeard fairy tale, itself an articulation of an earlier myth. The original tale concerns a woman seduced into marrying an older man. He bans her from entering a certain room in his house. Curiosity gets the better of her and she enters, only to find the remains of murdered past wives hidden there. Her husband catches her in the act and prepares to kill her too, but she is rescued by her brothers. Carter adds several variations: the murderous husband is now 'The Marquis', a collector of exquisite aesthetic objects and pornography, who turns the heroine into an object to be both admired and violated; the rescuer is now the heroine's avenging mother; and a blind piano-tuner, Jean-Yves, is introduced as a second husband for the heroine, once the rescue is achieved.

Critics have noticed a panoply of possible influences upon the story, including: the fairy tale of 'Bluebeard', pornographic fiction, Freud (Sheets 1991: 642), the biblical story of Eve, the myth of Pandora's box, the marital Gothic (Pyrhönen 2007: 97), magic realism (Farnell 2014: 283), 'and transgressive vampirism' (Sceats 2001: 110). Furthermore, in the light of evidence from Carter's wider writings and interviews, her documented background as a scholar, and clues within the text, critics have made various, sometimes conflicting claims about the fictional content of the story. To take one example, it is reported that many readers interpret the heroine's reunion with her mother in classical Freudian terms, as a regression rather than a development towards separation. In contrast, Robin Sheets has argued through a neo-Freudian lens that the reunion 'challenges the Oedipus modes of development which privilege separation over dependence' (Sheets 1991: 654) and so counts as a positive, liberating event.

Faced with these inconsistent readings, an onlooker might be forgiven for thinking that we must have moved away from any connection with what Carter intended the reader to imagine. Yet we should recall that single actions generally can be subject to several explanations simultaneously (see S. Davies 2006: 231). An agent might do *A* in order to fulfil several purposes at once. Equally an author might use a single set of utterances to fulfil several purposes at once (Currie 2004: 129), either conveying that certain content is to be believed as well as imagined, or—more pertinently here— effectively constructing 'layers' of content by instructing the reader to conjure different and perhaps even competing imaginative scenarios via the same set of words. It is not such a stretch to think that, in this case, Carter deliberately intended both inconsistent readings simultaneously: the first relative to a classical Freudian background, the second relative to a more feminist neo-Freudian one. Some aspects of the text favour the first reading; other aspects favour the second. After all, Carter was a particularly self-aware author immersed in the history and teaching of literature and psychoanalysis, who self-consciously constructed her texts to be saturated with intended meanings. As Margaret Atwood has put it: 'Carter always knows what she's doing with words' (1994: 134).

Whether or not this is plausible of Carter in this example, generally, extreme intentionalism can allow that texts or parts of texts can have 'layers' of content. That is, they can give rise to several partially overlapping sets of intended imaginings simultaneously— each discernible with reference to some distinct purpose of the author's for the text. It is not incomprehensible that an author might deliberately set out to generate even incompatible pieces of content simultaneously. In fact, we have already seen this in a much simpler case, in the earlier discussion of *The Turn of the Screw*, where effectively James instructs readers to imagine both that the governess is sane, and that she is mad, but not at the same time.[15]

Roughly along lines proposed by Levinson (2006: 304) we can still treat all such aspects of content as integrated into one single global interpretation. In that sense, a single global interpretation may include—either deliberately or inadvertently—two or more 'subsets' of instructions to imagine certain scenarios—where the reader does not in fact conjoin in imagination those scenarios or treat them as two aspects of some larger, more inclusive, scenario. She does not respond to both subsets at the same time, though she responds to each in turn.

Critical pluralism is the view that there is more than one equally acceptable interpretation of a text. Critical monism says that there is only one. Extreme intentionalism is in a sense a monistic position, though as already emphasized it is restricted to fictional content and not applied to other kinds of meaning. It says that the single right interpretation of fictional content is identical to what the author reflexively intended readers to imagine. But as we have just seen, this is compatible with a single text's giving

---

[15] I will return to this sort of case of a 'multiple fiction' in Chapter 5.

rise to several conflicting interpretations, in the sense of sets of imaginings each intended by the author to be communicated to readers for a distinct purpose.

Sometimes it is assumed that critical pluralism must be true, on the grounds that fictional texts are too rich to accommodate any single interpretation:

> there need not be any one coherent pattern, any single or correct theory or explanation, which alone captures and makes sense of the evidence available…we would not expect any one interpretation to accommodate uniquely the evidence that the text provides for our reasoning.
> (Lamarque 1990a: 341–2)

If Lamarque meant by 'interpretation', 'reading of a text's fictional content relative to one particular authorial purpose and related intentions', then this could happily be conceded for many texts. Even so, in a broader sense, a fictional text can still have only one single interpretation or explanation. Once we allow that a single global interpretation or explanation of a text might simultaneously accommodate, for one text, several 'layers' of content each relating instrumentally to distinct further purposes of the author, then it is not so obvious that monism is false.

So to sum up the last two sections: many of the cases which have attracted philosophers to value-maximizing theory are, on closer inspection, harmless to the extreme intentionalist. Either they do not concern the nature of fictional content directly at all; or they do, but can be accommodated by the idea of a single author's having multiple intentions with respect to the same passages within a text.

3.10 Hypothetical Intentionalism, Value-maximizing, and Justified Belief

I have tried to show that neither hypothetical intentionalism nor value-maximizing theory is a plausible alternative to extreme intentionalism; and furthermore, that the latter can account for at least many of the cases that tempt some towards value-maximizing theory as a contender. In this final section of the chapter, I shall introduce a further objection to both.[16] The same objection applies to any view which denies that actual authorial intentions are determinative of fictional content.[17]

According to hypothetical intentionalism, as we have seen, it is not the case that the actual author's intentions are the source of fictional content in a text. Instead, fictional content is determined by the facts (whatever they are) about what would count as an optimal interpretation of the text according to an idealized readership (etc.). But this raises a problem. As I will argue more thoroughly in the next chapter, often fictions can be an intentional source of belief, as well as imagining. Some utterances in fiction are

---

[16] With kind permission of the editors, this section reproduces some material from Stock (2016b).

[17] For instance, it applies to David Davies's view of meaning as identical to 'hermeneutically enriched contextualized conventional meaning'. This says that the meaning of an utterance is the meaning that 'would be ascribed to our utterance by appropriately skilled interpreters able to draw on knowledge of linguistic conventions, context and interpretative intelligence' (D. Davies 2007: 82).

not only reflexively intended to produce imagining in readers, but they are also simultaneously intended to communicate true belief. I shall now argue that this fact cannot plausibly be accounted for by hypothetical intentionalism.

A central way for fictions to make belief appropriate is via authorial testimony.[18] The production of testimony, generally, is an intentional speech act, I will assume. In the paradigm case, for some proposition *p*, the utterer of 'p' intends to transfer the belief that *p* to the hearer (or reader) of her utterances. For instance, when I tell my students that they will have an exam on Thursday, I intend to produce in them the belief that they will have an exam on Thursday. Moreover, a piece of testimony purports to be a source of independent warrant for the hearer's belief in its truth: the hearer is supposed to believe what is said at least partly on the say-so of the utterer. When a teacher tells her pupil that Mount Everest is the highest mountain on earth, the student need not have access to an independent check of the truth of this belief. Following Pritchard, I shall characterize a *testimony-based belief* as 'any belief which one reasonably and directly forms in response to what one reasonably takes to be testimony and which is essentially caused and sustained by testimony' (2004: 326).

Fictions sometimes contain pieces of testimony (Green 2010). Here's a clear example, from Karen Joy Fowler's *We Are All Completely Beside Ourselves*, informing the reader about some concrete historical events:

Nonhuman animals have gone to court before. Arguably, the first ALF action in the United States was the release of two dolphins in 1977 from the University of Hawaii. The men responsible were charged with grand theft. Their original defense, that dolphins are persons (humans in dolphin suits, one defendant said), was quickly thrown out by the judge.

(Fowler 2013: 305)

But testimony-in-fiction need not be confined to the concrete. It can also take the form of general statements, as in the following examples, from *Daniel Deronda* and *Anna Karenina* respectively:

There is a great deal of unmapped country within us which would have to be taken into account in an explanation of our gusts and storms. (Eliot 1986: 321)

Happy families are all alike; every unhappy family is unhappy in its own way. (Tolstoy 1995: 1)

In cases such as these, the utterance made is stipulated as true of fictional events in the story in question, and extends at least that far (that is—on the view I favour—the reader is intended to imagine that such general claims are true of all the characters in the text). However, it also seems clear from context that each author intends her utterance to extend beyond the fictional scenario she describes, to the actual world. The utterances in question make some state of affairs true in the fiction *and* alert the reader to some

---

[18] Anyone sceptical that fictions can contain testimony will have to wait until Chapter 4, where I argue for this point more directly.

state of affairs in the actual world, according to the author. In other words, I take it, we can take such utterances as effectively offering a conjoined instruction 'imagine that *p* and believe that *p*'.[19]

One might worry here that, despite appearances, there are no genuine cases of testimony-in-fiction because authors of fictions, as such, do not and indeed cannot intend to convey belief in the requisite manner. I will examine such arguments extensively in the next chapter. So for the moment the reader will just have to take it on trust (!) that fictions can contain testimony, or at least accept it for the sake of argument. Alternatively, the cautious reader can skip ahead to the relevant parts of Chapter 4.

Now, an important point to note for present purposes is that generally, where testimony is involved, the justification of any beliefs arising on the part of hearers/readers significantly depends upon facts about the utterer. Here, in a sketch, are three rival models of how testimony is thought to operate, in terms of the justification of any resultant beliefs on the hearer's part.[20] The first, the 'a posteriori model', says that a piece of testimony is justified where there is accompanying empirical evidence for its truth. The accompanying evidence might be about the speaker in particular: her sincerity, or trustworthiness, or reliability, or expertise (this sort of evidence is emphasized by Fricker 1995). Or, perhaps, the evidence might be more general: e.g. inductive evidence of a general correlation between testimony (that is, intentional speech acts aimed at transmitting belief) and truth. Either way, on this sort of view one has no 'presumptive right to believe in what one is told just as such' (Fricker 1995: 399).[21] One must have access to positive reasons to believe in a piece of testimony, albeit perhaps not consciously (Fricker 1995: 406).

The second model, the 'a priori model', says that testimony is justified because there are a priori reasons (that is, based on reasoning rather than empirical evidence) to think that testimony is good evidence of truth. For instance, one might argue that the function of reason itself depends upon reliance upon apparently rational sources (Burge 1993: 469). There are other variations too (see for instance Coady 1994). The important point is that on this general sort of view, one does not need empirical evidence to justify belief in the truth of testimony. However, it is also important to note that, nonetheless, one might encounter empirical evidence which forces *doubt* about the truth of testimony in a particular case; in which general a priori grounds for justification will be greatly weakened. So one should monitor for doubt accordingly (see Faulkner 2007: 877).

On a third view, which we can call the 'Assurance model', testimony does not derive its justification from any connection to empirical evidence, nor from a priori reasons

---

[19] For an account of how it is possible to simultaneously imagine and believe that *p*, see Chapter 5.
[20] This is not supposed to be exhaustive. The taxonomy is largely modelled on that of Moran (2005).
[21] The view counts as 'reductionist' in the terminology of many surveys, since it says that the justification for believing in testimony that *p* depends on further justification derived from inference, memory, and/or perception (Fricker 1995: 394).

in the sense just outlined (Moran 2005). Moran argues that the previous two models each effectively treat testimony as a kind of evidence of a person's (true) beliefs, and moreover not specially different from other kinds of non-verbal or verbal behaviour which might count as evidence for a person's (true) beliefs. Yet in fact testimony, when treated as a form of evidence of true belief, looks more susceptible to manipulation than, for instance, non-verbal behaviour typically is, since testimony is deliberate: the utterer has chosen to reveal something, which she otherwise might have withheld. This seems to make that behaviour less reliable as a form of evidence than it would have been, had it been non-deliberate (2005: 6). Instead, Moran proposes, we should make a virtue out of the freely-given, deliberate nature of testimony by treating it as partly deriving its justification from its intentional nature. In testimony, the speaker presents the claim as one she is responsible for: she 'offers a kind of guarantee for this truth' (2005: 11). It is a special kind of assertoric speech act which derives its justification from 'the speaker's attitude toward his utterance and presentation of it in a certain spirit' (2005: 23). That is (adapting Grice), Moran suggests that in a piece of testimony 'p', the utterer of 'p' intends both that hearers believe that *p*, and that they think of her as assuming responsibility for the utterance as a reason to believe that *p*. An analogy is made with promise making: a promise is not offered as or taken as evidence for what will happen, except in odd cases, but rather as an assurance that it will (2005: 24).

How does extreme intentionalism, as a theory of fictional content, accommodate the presence of testimony in fiction? Relatively easily. Take the utterance from *Daniel Deronda* cited earlier. Effectively, on this view, Eliot reflexively intends the reader to imagine that it is true of the characters in that novel, that *there is a great deal of unmapped country within them which would have to be taken into account in an explanation of their gusts and storms*. She also intends the reader to imagine whatever implicitly follows from this in conjunction with other parts of the text and/ or background knowledge. But simultaneously she intends the reader to *believe*, of humankind generally, of which she and the reader are part, that *there is a great deal of unmapped country within us which would have to be taken into account in an explanation of our gusts and storms*.

Where a single utterance *u* functions like this simultaneously both as a vehicle of fictional content *p* (i.e. is an instruction to imagine that *p*, roughly) *and* as a piece of testimony, what is the relation between the fictional content of *u*, and the content of *u* considered as a piece of testimony? My view as just sketched out makes a pleasingly simple story available. Recall that, as detailed in Chapter 1, on one popular Gricean view, adapted just now by Moran, the content of a conversational utterance, including a piece of testimony, is determined in relation to what the speaker intends the hearer to believe. If this is right, then it looks as if there is at least one close affinity between how conversational testimony gets its content, and how fictive utterance gets its content, according to extreme intentionalism. Namely, both are determined by the intentions of a speaker. There is therefore a relatively seamless story available about how a single utterance might function both as a piece of testimony and a fictive utterance. In both cases the reader is working out what the author intended her to do. Moreover, as we have already seen in Chapter 2, it seems plausible that there will be a significant overlap in the strategies by which an author simultaneously conveys her intention that the reader believe something, and that she imagine something. Or to put it another way, there will be a significant overlap in the methods by which the reader detects the relevant intention. In both cases normally she will appeal to conventional sentence meaning; but in both cases she also may move beyond sentence meaning, using her understanding of pragmatics and non-conventional implicature as well.[22]

At this point, a problem for both hypothetical intentionalism and value-maximizing starts to emerge. We can put the point in terms of a dilemma.

I shall start with hypothetical intentionalism. On one horn of the dilemma, the advocate of hypothetical intentionalism attempts to interpret the content of testimony-in-fiction (but not, presumably, testimony generally) in a way that resembles the way that, she alleges, fictional content gets interpreted: that is, in terms of the putative intentions of some hypothetical utterer of those sentences, given a restricted body of knowledge about her and her context. The problem with this is that it would seem to sever any link between testimony-in-fiction and the production of *justified* beliefs in readers.

To see this, let's look again at the three models of justified testimony introduced earlier. Most obviously, there is a clash with the Assurance Model, according to which testimony gets its justification from being an intentional act of assurance on the part of the actual utterer, who takes responsibility for the truth of what is said. If we were to treat testimony-in-fiction as, effectively, the product of some hypothetical person who *might have* made utterances of this form, in a way which potentially deviated from what the actual author intended by the utterance, then there would be no coherent way of taking this hypothetical utterer as responsible for her utterances in the way demanded by this model of justification. (Analogously, were we to interpret the content of a promise according to what a hypothetical utterer might have meant by it, in a way which potentially deviated from what the actual utterer actually meant by it, there would be no obvious sense in which trust in the actual utterer's promise would remain a live option.) Value-maximizing is just as problematic here, if not more so, for fairly obvious reasons: if the hearer is simply to construct the meaning of the testimony-in-fiction according to what would be most valuable to her, the crucial relationship with the actual author again appears to have dropped out altogether.[23]

---

[22] Note that I am not claiming that the strategies will be the same in each case. Many content-discerning strategies seem relevant only to fiction, as I have argued in Chapter 2. For instance, working out what a fictional passage means symbolically does not seem to have any analogous procedure in the interpretation of conversational utterance.

[23] An additional point is that, in fact, it seems that readers can build up (one-sided) relationships of what looks like trust with particular authors, who they come to recognize as wise and authoritative on certain areas or matters, emphasizing that neither hypothetical intentionalism nor value-maximizing theory could be right here.

Meanwhile, on the a posteriori model, there are also problems connecting the content of testimony-in-fiction, construed in terms of hypothetical intentionalism or value-maximizing, with justification. Recall that on this model, a piece of testimony is justified where there is accompanying empirical evidence for its truth. If the claim is that for justification to obtain, the evidence in question must pertain to empirical facts about the actual utterer of the sentence (e.g. her sincerity, trustworthiness, reliability, or expertise) then straight away we see how the hypothetical intentionalist or value-maximizer attempting to analyse the content of testimony-in-fiction in terms of her preferred theory cannot easily appeal to any such factors. For she is (on this horn of the dilemma) not interested in the actual author at all. If on the other hand the supposedly justificatory facts in question concern inductive evidence of a *general* correlation between testimony and truth, then this isn't of much help either. For surely any such observed correlation must be thought of as holding between testimony *as ordinarily conceived*—i.e. as an utterance whose content is essentially connected to the actual utterer and her intentions—and truth. Were someone to claim that there was a reliable connection between testimony-in-fiction, conceived of as getting its content via hypothetical intentionalism, or even value-maximizing theory, and truth, then this would look empirically rather under-researched, at the very least.

Perhaps this last point won't convince everyone; but no matter, since a further point can be made which applies to all theories of testimonial justification, including the a priori one, about which I've said nothing yet. That is: on all of these models, empirical evidence of an actual author's dishonesty/insincerity/unreliability etc. will reduce or remove justification altogether. The point plausibly extends to testimony-in-fiction too: where we already know that an author of a fiction is unreliable epistemically, generally, it would normally be a bad idea to believe any testimony she produces in the context of her text.

Neither hypothetical intentionalism nor value-maximizing theory could account for this. The way in which one's knowledge of a given utterer's personal unreliability—knowledge of her insincerity, obtuseness or dishonesty, for instance—tends to undermine credence in that utterer's testimony would be inexplicable, were the testimony in question's content determined in a way which had nothing to do with the actual utterer's intentions. For, were the content of testimony-in-fiction determined in terms of the would-be responses of some idealized readership about what someone who wrote this text might have intended, as hypothetical intentionalism has it, or in terms of what would be most valuable to the reader, as value-maximizing theory has it, then of what relevance could it be to the justification of any resulting beliefs, that the *actual* utterer of the testimony was insincere or dishonest in some way? None, it seems to me.

Thus far I have been exploring the first horn of a dilemma, according to which the content of testimony-in-fiction is determined according to either hypothetical intentionalism or value-maximizing theory; in which case, as I have argued, problems emerge for any secure connection to justified belief. On the other horn of the dilemma, the content of testimony-in-fiction is interpreted according to the standard story for testimony generally i.e. in terms of the intentions of the actual utterer, as briefly sketched above. The problem here is that there looks to be a fairly radical disconnect, according to hypothetical intentionalism and value-maximizing theory, in terms of the respective ways in which testimony-in-fiction gets its content and the way in which fictive utterances get their content. The former gets its content by reference to actual author intentions; the latter does not. And yet, I have argued, the very same sentence can function both to convey a fictive utterance and to convey a piece of testimony. If there was such a radical disconnect between strategies of interpretation, it seems that it would likely manifest in the reader's experience of such a sentence to a greater degree, since such different criteria for meaning are supposedly involved in each case. A piece of testimony-in-fiction would presumably be experienced more like a single utterance which functions for an interpreter both as an intentional utterance, on the one hand, and on the other, as evidence of some non-intentional phenomenon, such as dementia, or the unconscious use of a dialect one was studying; requiring a shift from seeing the utterance as essentially intentional in the latter sort of case. And yet, I suggest, reading testimony-in-fiction is not like this. One seamlessly and relatively automatically understands both what one is supposed to imagine and what one is supposed to believe.

So, I suggest that, on this horn of the dilemma, hypothetical intentionalism and value-maximizing theory anticipate a split in the reader's interpretative practice and associated experience of testimony-in-fiction which we do not standardly find.

Earlier I pointed out that extreme intentionalism has a story readily available about the crossover in strategies used by the reader to interpret both fictive utterances and testimony-in-fiction. There is no predicted threat of a split in the reader's experience here, even though the strategies used to interpret fictional content and testimony-in-fiction will often differ somewhat. Roughly, fictional content is produced via reference to the actual author's intentions that readers imagine certain things; while the content of testimony-in-fiction is produced via reference to the actual author's intentions that readers believe certain things. But in both cases we are still dealing with actual authorial intentions, and moreover, it is likely that many of the methods by which one is deciphered will also apply to the other.

In conclusion: both hypothetical intentionalism and value-maximizing theory have a hard time properly accounting for the role and experience of testimony-in-fiction. Either they cannot accommodate its potential function in the production of justified beliefs in readers, or they cannot accommodate the reader's experience of interpreting testimony-in-fiction in a way which seems continuous with the experience of interpreting fictive utterance. This, then, I take it, is yet another reason to prefer actual author intentionalism over its two main rivals.

3.11 Summary

This chapter has focused on defending extreme intentionalism against its main rivals in the analytic tradition: 'modest' intentionalism, hypothetical intentionalism, and value-maximizing theory. I first addressed the thought, instrumental in motivating those rivals, that extreme intentionalism takes an implausible stance towards unsuccessful authorial intentions that a text should have a certain content. I argued that in fact, extreme intentionalism is in a better position to accommodate unsuccessful intentions than are its opponents. I then made some general criticisms of hypothetical intentionalism and value-maximizing theory. In particular I focused on the limited extent to which each can accommodate the plausible thought that fictions often contain reliable testimony, and can act as a source of justified belief. Also in this chapter, I addressed the significance of 'post hoc' meanings; and argued that extreme intentionalism, though a monistic position, is compatible with many of the critical judgements which tend to tempt people towards critical pluralism.

4

Fiction, Belief, and 'Imaginative Resistance'

4.1 Introduction

I have now concluded my direct defence of extreme intentionalism. In the second half of this book, I will indirectly support the position further by showing how it can fruitfully be invoked in the context of a range of other questions in the philosophy of fiction and imagination.

But first, there is some business left over from an earlier argument to attend to. In the last chapter, I offered, as an objection to hypothetical intentionalism and value-maximizing theory, the charge that they cannot account for the way authors include testimony about the world in their fictional works, and the fact that readers can sometimes get justified beliefs from such testimony. I promised to defend the claim that authors can convey justified beliefs via testimony in fictions, and now I will make good on this promise. This focus on belief will take us away temporarily from the connections between fiction and imagining; but the shift will pay dividends indirectly, insofar as in the second half of the chapter it will help us to arrive at an explanation of the phenomenon of what has come to be known as 'imaginative resistance'. Effectively I will argue that imaginative resistance can be explained in terms of a rejection, not of a given instruction to imagine something, as many have thought, but instead, of a rejection of an implied invitation to believe something.

Both as a preliminary to that discussion and as an adjunct to the last, I will now discuss fictions that contain and promulgate beliefs in a reader, via testimony. I will argue that, perhaps despite appearances, testimony in the context of fiction can be an epistemically 'safe' source of justified belief about the world; or at least, in this respect it is on an equal footing with testimony generally.

4.2 Testimony-in-fiction

As I suggested in the last chapter, authors can intentionally communicate beliefs via their fictions; not only, banally, beliefs about the fiction in question itself or the person who wrote it, but also, more interestingly, beliefs about the world. One way this can be done is via testimony.[1] (For examples and a basic description of testimony, see the last chapter.)

This is not to say that all non-accidentally true sentences in fictions are included in order to give rise to empirical belief. To take just one example: the events of Muriel Spark's story 'The Ormolu Clock' are inspired by something that happened to her in a guesthouse in a village in the Austrian Alps, where a man stared into her room from an adjoining hotel (Stannard 2009: 215–17). The story contains detail which (arguably, anyway) truthfully describes Spark's own experience at the hotel; for instance:

> Ordinarily I got up at seven, but one morning I woke up at half past five and came down from my room on the second floor to the yard, to find someone to make me some coffee.   (Spark 2001: 342)

Yet I assume it would be false to say that Spark here intends to inform the reader about her experience, and a fortiori that she is offering testimony about it. For one thing, that near-identical events in the guesthouse happened to her at all is not something she could expect the reader of the story to work out very easily. It is only revealed via private correspondence and her biography (Stannard 2009: 216).

In other cases, in contrast, the right sort of intention—to inform the reader about empirical facts and so add to her beliefs—clearly appears to be present. We have seen some examples in the last chapter. Yet now a possible worry arises: that owing to the presence of surrounding false content, which is not supposed to be believed, or to some other factor, testimony-in-fiction cannot function properly, as testimony does in other ordinary conversational contexts. The worry is that, *even if it happens to be true*, it too easily could have been false, so that any beliefs that arise in the reader as a consequence are not 'safe'. I shall now consider this possibility, in order ultimately to dismiss it.

A. Might the reader easily have done something different?

Let's call the beliefs one forms as a result of hearing or reading testimony, testimony-based beliefs, or TBBs for short. Recently Stacie Friend has provided a series of powerful-looking arguments to suggest that in the context of fiction, the 'safety' of the process of forming TBBs is threatened (2014). The epistemic notion of safety is supposed to be one way of explicating the intuition that respectable beliefs could not easily have been false (Friend *ibid.*; Pritchard 2008). Following others, Friend defines 'safety' as follows: a true belief that p is either unsafe if i) in the nearest possible worlds in which the believer believes that p, p is false; or ii) there are nearby possible worlds in which the belief-processes which actually produced the belief that p, produce a false belief that q (Friend 2014: 233). ('Possible worlds' are ways the actual world might have

---

[1] Parts of this section are based on material from Stock (2017a), and reproduced by kind permission of the editors.

been; 'nearby' or 'close' possible worlds are worlds which differ relatively little from the actual world, compared to more 'distant' worlds in which more things are changed, relatively speaking.)

As Friend notes, a familiar way of explaining how a true belief that *p* may be unsafe is via Alvin Goldman's story of fake barns (Goldman 1976: 772–3). In Fake Barn Country, there are lots of fake barns indistinguishable to the observer from real ones. Even if you are standing in front of a real barn, correctly believing 'this is a real barn', there is a close possible world in which you falsely believe 'this is a real barn' because you are standing in front of a fake one. Hence there is a nearby possible world in which you believe that *p* but *p* is false. Your belief is therefore true but unsafe.

Friend effectively suggests that, at least prima facie, TBBs in response to testimony-in-fiction are imperilled in a similar way, owing to the presence in fiction of lots of invented and false content: made-up characters, incidents and places.[2]

> ...the more fake barns there are nearby, the less safe one's beliefs will be, and this explains why it is less likely one has knowledge. Apply the same point to beliefs formed by reading... ([M]ost) authors of fiction typically invent characters, situations, events and so on, and they alter historical, geographical, scientific and other facts when it suits their purposes, to a much greater extent than (most) authors of non-fiction. So it would seem that other things being equal, one is far more likely to go wrong in forming beliefs concerning matters of fact by reading fiction than by reading non-fiction. (Friend 2014: 233)

Initially, this worry looks compelling. Authors of fictions typically spend a lot of their time either heavily embroidering reality or detaching from it altogether, offering pure invention in terms of character, place, and incident. Does the accompanying presence of so much invented false content threaten the safety of any passages of testimony-in-fiction found in a text? Is the reader in something like the position of a person in Fake Barn Country, whose true beliefs about barns are nonetheless rendered unsafe by the presence of so many fake barns all about her? I will now argue that there are at least two ways of interpreting this analogy, neither of which are detrimental to the respectability of TBBs in response to testimony-in-fiction.[3]

One way of reading the point is as saying that the reader cannot reliably distinguish true testimony from other kinds of invented false content also simultaneously present within a fiction.[4] So: when she reads a true piece of testimony and forms a true TBB in response, there is a nearby possible world in which the same belief-forming process would have led to her to believe something else which was false: the world where she read an accompanying invented false piece of content, and believed it instead, or as well.

However, this is not quite right, for it is not the case, in any fiction-specific way, that true testimony cannot be distinguished from other invented/false content for the

---

[2] Her target is 'comprehension-based beliefs', including testimonial ones (2014: 232), about 'ordinary empirical facts' (2014: 227).
[3] For a discussion of the rest of Friend's article, see Stock (2017a).
[4] Invented content is almost always false, though could conceivably accidentally be true.

reader. Or to put the point another way, it is false that the same belief-forming processes typically occur with respect to testimony as to other kinds of content.

What *is* true is that the reader cannot distinguish *true testimony* from *false testimony* simply by reading the text. But of course, this is true of testimony generally. Simply in reading or hearing an ordinary piece of testimony, we have no current independent check on whether it is true or not (this is in the nature of testimony, as originally defined). So there is no fiction-specific reason to undermine the safety of TBBs here.

In order to generate a fiction-specific conclusion, perhaps the assumption should be rather that the reader of fiction cannot distinguish testimony (true *or* false) from non-testimonial (e.g. made-up) utterances within the fiction. However, I submit, this is false. A practised reader can distinguish testimony-in-fiction from other sorts of statement. Identifying a piece of testimony as such is a matter of making reasonable, evidence-based assumptions about the author's intention to induce a belief in her. A number of conventions, grasped by the practised reader, alert her to the presence of this sort of intention.[5] Though I cannot give any precise or extended account of these conventions here, nor say in what number they are sufficient, it seems likely that they include some combination of the following.

First, the utterance should be in the declarative mood, or imply a declarative statement, and should be written in an authoritative tone. Secondly, it should appear to the reader as being likely to concern real existents: perhaps, that the reader has already heard of, or has some other reason to judge as actual (contrast with the passage from Spark's 'Ormolu Clock', which concerns an anonymous, private experience the reader has little reason to think actual, without also reading Spark's biography). Perhaps the utterance appears to complement or extend other information the reader already possesses; it may even (though does not have to) say some things the reader already knows to be true. Truth is good evidence of the relevant intention, since a plausible motive for including true content is that the author wishes the reader to believe that content.

Thirdly, and relatedly, the utterance should be reasonably conceived as containing information that, if true, would be of potential use, interest, or relevance to the reader. Or to put this point another way: the author should conceivably have a reason to want the reader to believe the claim in question. Often this reason will pertain to the didactic theme or point of the larger work in which the (apparent) claim figures. (So in the case of Fowler's *We Are All Completely Beside Ourselves*, introduced in Chapter 3, it is relatively easy to identify truth claims in that text concerning historical instances of

---

[5] Despite denying the safety of TBBs in response to fiction, Friend writes of a reader possibly 'developing a strategy that works very well' for a particular genre, which allows her to 'by and large...believe only what is true' (2014: 244). In that case, the reader forms 'apt' beliefs, i.e. 'true beliefs as a result of exercising...competence in the conditions appropriate to that competence' (*ibid*.). Unlike Friend here, I deny that a practised reader's beliefs are typically unsafe in the first place. Where testimony is concerned, I am also sceptical of the possibility of a strategy, grounded in genre familiarity, which would allow the reader 'by and large...to believe only what is true'. It is more accurate to say, I think, that familiarity with a genre, or even with fiction as a whole, allows us to pick out, defeasibly but on the whole reliably, what is intended to be testimony and what is not.

the mistreatment of higher mammals; among other things, they concern a topic obviously of moral concern to the author in the book as a whole.)

If, on the other hand, we can find a reason within the subject or themes of the text to mistrust any factual-looking claims within it, then this is a reason to withhold the classification of straightforward testimony. Most obviously, this will be the case in any novel whose explicit theme is the playful relation between art and truth; or where the narrator is obviously distinct from the author and unreliable; but there will be other cases too.[6]

Note that at no point am I claiming that one can tell *true* testimony from false, just by reading. Testimony-in-fiction can be undetectably false, just like testimony everywhere. I am claiming rather that one can often tell testimony-in-fiction from other sorts of speech act. If this is right then, just as the presence of ironic statements in a non-fiction text does not threaten the safety of non-ironic assertions within it, assuming we can tell the difference between the two, neither does the presence of non-testimonial invented content in a fiction threaten the safety of testimony within it, given that we can distinguish between the two. Or to put the point in a way which more directly addresses the way the worry was originally introduced: in ordinary cases, the reader's belief-forming process, with respect to passages she identifies as testimony-in-fiction, is not simultaneously operative towards non-testimonial kinds of content, including invented content. So there is no threat of a nearby world in which the same belief-forming process leads her astray.

There is, I think, at least one genre where it is more difficult for the average reader to identify the presence of testimony. Perhaps surprisingly, this is 'information-rich' fiction, heavily inspired by true events. Take, as an example, a historical fiction, most of whose characters are real people, and which describes, at least some of the time, real events, but which also includes invented content about those people and events. Most of the time, it is hard for the average reader without specialist knowledge to distinguish the passages intended to be testimony from those that are not. Take the following passage from Hilary Mantel's *Bring Up The Bodies*:

'Sir, how are you not burned?' Rafe Sadler demands. A redhead like the king, he has turned a mottled, freckled pink, and even his eyes look sore. He, Thomas Cromwell, shrugs; he hangs an arm around Rafe's shoulders as they drift indoors. He went through the whole of Italy—the battlefield as well as the shaded arena of the counting house—without losing his London pallor. His ruffian childhood, the days on the river, the days in the fields: they left him as white as God made him. 'Cromwell has the skin of a lily,' the king pronounces. 'The only particular in which he resembles that or any other blossom.' Teasing him, they amble towards supper.   (Mantel 2012)

---

[6] One might worry: doesn't the reader need to know that she is reading a fiction, before exercising her grasp on the relevant conventions? She does, but this has no bearing on the respectability of any beliefs she gains from testimony-in-fiction, once she knows this. Making assumptions about what sort of discourse or text one is engaging with, before being able to properly assess it for the presence of testimony, is not a special requirement upon interpretation of fiction; it applies generally.

Let's assume that this passage contains some testimony and some invented content. It is very difficult for the reader who does not *already* know the information it genuinely contains to distinguish between the two. All utterances are in an 'authoritative tone'; all refer to known existents and appear to tie in with existing knowledge, for the average reader, at least. All utterances, if true, would be of conceivable use or interest to those generally interested in the period in question. Our best bet for distinguishing testimony from non-testimony here is to work out which utterances refer to 'public' facts about which there might conceivably be some kind of record: presumably, Rafe Sadler's dialogue with Cromwell does not count, whereas his hair being red does (as is confirmed by publicly available portraits of him).

So another feature of the circumstances under which testimony about people, places, and things is most easily identified in the context of fiction is that it should not be accompanied—not by invented content generally, but—by a *lot of invented content concerning the very same people, places, and things*. Here the reader genuinely cannot as easily distinguish testimony from non-testimony; so here, perhaps, there are genuine 'fake barns', for many readers: false utterances that they might easily have believed instead. This looks highly ironic, given the pretensions of information-rich fictions such as historical fictions to educate.

But this does not apply to fiction generally. For many fictions, where true testimony about an object O is offered, there is little invented content also offered about O; or the invented content that is offered is such that it can be easily distinguished from testimony (e.g. where a fiction systematically offers testimony to *general* facts about a city and its people, and invented content about *particular* things that happen to particular people in it).

B. *Might the author easily have done something different?*

In the case where a reader has a true TBB in response to fiction, we have just examined *what she, the reader,* might easily have done instead in a nearby possible world (the claim was that she might have believed a different bit of the accompanying text). But a different worry concerns more directly *what the author* might easily have done. The claim now to be examined is that true testimony in a fiction might easily have been replaced with false utterances by the author, in a way that makes it unsafe as a vehicle for belief.

One way of cashing this out would be to claim that, when a reader reads a true piece of testimony 'p' in a fiction and forms a true TBB in response, there is a nearby possible world in which the author utters the very same sentence 'p', but it is not the case that *p*. This would look properly analogous to Goldman's fake barn scenario: there is a nearby possible world in which appearances, relative to the believer, are identical to those in the actual world, she has a belief with the same content as her actual belief, and yet the belief is false.

However, this is not a pressing worry about testimony-in-fiction; for a world in which an author produces an actually true piece of testimony 'p' in a fiction, but where it is false, would look pretty different from the actual one in several significant ways. Consider again some of Fowler's sentences about the Animal Liberation Front in *We Are All Completely Beside Ourselves*:

Nonhuman animals have gone to court before. Arguably, the first ALF action in the United States was the release of two dolphins in 1977 from the University of Hawaii... (Fowler 2013: 305)

For these very sentences to have been false, facts about non-human animals going to court in the US would have to be different. Additionally, assuming that in the relevant possible world, Fowler still had the right intentions to be producing testimony (albeit false), there would have to be new accompanying facts to explain how Fowler had got things wrong: she had either been mistaken, or deliberately lied. In both cases, we are departing significantly from the actual, in a way that looks non-threatening to the actual true belief.

But say instead that in the relevant possible world Fowler was no longer intending to produce testimony at all, and so not producing it, but rather merely inventing content via these very sentences, intending it to be imagined and not believed, in a way habitual to authors of fiction generally (and let's say that the sentences were accidentally true, unbeknownst to her, leaving aside how improbable this would be). Would this not be a closer possible world than the one just described, in a way that would threaten the safety of our true beliefs as we read those sentences in this world? It would certainly be closer, insofar as there need be no change to the facts about non-human animals going to court, etc., nor explanation of how Fowler could have got things wrong. But it would still be significantly different, in that the history of the production of those sentences would be different, as would Fowler's actual motives in writing them. In the actual world Fowler researched the history of non-human animals going to court in the US, and presumably intentionally included the information as part of a wider artistic purpose: that of building a complex picture of the relation between humans and higher mammals. In the posited possible world, Fowler makes up 'facts' for some other purpose entirely (entertainment? A good yarn?). This looks like a significant difference, and one which might even produce a different work altogether, on some accounts. Equally, one might suggest, there is a possible world in which some set of actually true sentences in a particular work of academic history are invented by their author in a different, fictional work: but that world looks fairly distant, nonetheless, in a way which seems to leave intact the safety of any beliefs produced as a result of reading the actual text.

Friend does not consider this case directly, but later in her essay, considers a related scenario: one where an author offers true assertion 'p' in the context of a fiction, but in a different possible world does not utter 'p' but some different false sentence, 'q'. She makes an analogy between the author of a fiction, and the authors of a particular empirical study who, among other things, randomly distribute true ('Moscow is the capital of Russia') and false claims ('St Petersburg is the capital of Russia) to subjects, in the context of fictional stories. She argues that a participant who gets a true claim, and so believes it, might easily—with 'only a very slight change in the initial conditions'—have got a false claim, and believed it.

Given that the experimenters just seem to be doing what authors of fiction frequently do—namely, changing facts to suit their purposes—their studies imply that empirical beliefs formed in reading fiction more generally are also unsafe. (Friend 2014: 237–8)

But as before, there seems no reason to admit that a world in which an author abstains from producing true testimony, but instead produces invented content for some other purpose, is particularly close to the actual world where she produces true testimony. It certainly does not look as close to the actual world as the one in which experimental subject Joe is told that St Petersburg is the capital of Russia, rather than Moscow. That world is close because very little would have to change for it to obtain: after all, in the actual world, the authors of the empirical study were *already* randomly distributing both true and false sentences to different subjects. Nothing like this is true of the average fictional author.

I conclude that we have seen no good reason to think that true beliefs derived as a result of reading testimony-in-fiction are unsafe. Along the way we have also found confirmation that authors can have genuine intentions that readers believe things as a result of parts of their fictional texts (as well as imagine them).[7] Competent readers can recognize these intentions, and authors can rely upon this competence to promulgate certain beliefs. In the rest of the chapter, I shall use this latter thought, broadly specified, to explain the phenomenon which has come to be known as 'imaginative resistance'.

4.3 The Phenomenon of 'Imaginative Resistance'

Here's a short fiction, entitled 'Death On a Freeway'.[8]

Jack and Jill were arguing again. This was not in itself unusual, but this time they were standing in the fast lane of I-95 having their argument. This was causing traffic to bank up a bit. It wasn't significantly worse than normally happened around Providence, not that you could have told that from the reactions of passing motorists. They were convinced that Jack and Jill, and not the volume of traffic, were the primary causes of the slowdown. They all forgot how bad traffic normally is along there. When Craig saw that the cause of the bank up had been Jack and Jill, he took his gun out of the glovebox and shot them. People then started driving over their bodies, and while the new speed hump caused some people to slow down a bit, mostly traffic returned to its normal speed. So Craig did the right thing, because Jack and Jill should have taken their argument somewhere else where they wouldn't get in anyone's way. (Weatherson 2004: 1)

---

[7] How a reader can both believe and imagine something at the same time will be discussed in Chapter 5.
[8] Some of this material is reproduced, with the kind permission of the editor, from Stock (2017b). Additional material on imaginative resistance is included there.

Looking more closely, we see there is a lot packed into the final sentence of this story. In conjunction with the rest, it apparently implies three fictional truths: i) *Craig did the right thing in killing Jack and Jill because they were holding up traffic*; ii) *Jack and Jill did the wrong thing in holding up traffic just to have an argument* (they 'should have taken their argument somewhere else'); and iii) *Jack and Jill deserved to be killed in this way* (Craig did the right thing 'because' Jack and Jill should have taken their argument elsewhere). In order to simplify matters, I'll follow others, including the author himself, in focusing only on i). Let's call i) 'R'.

It has seemed to many philosophers that, relative to a certain value set, many readers will experience some sort of change in their experience when it comes to reading R. Usually this is characterized as 'resistance'—the reader 'resists' imagining R. Put thus, this is ambiguous, possibly saying that the reader cannot imagine R, or that she does not want to, or that she simply has some difficulty but manages in the end. This is as it should be: for it simply is not clear what the nature of the phenomenon is, just from this example. But given this ambiguity, we need to be careful to avoid initially characterizing the phenomenon in ways that prejudice some particular analysis of it. So let's just vaguely say at this stage that 'imaginative resistance' involves (allegedly) 'having a problem imagining' something.[9]

Resistance to R apparently involves resistance to the *moral* evaluation it apparently makes about fictional character Craig's action, and his reasons for it. An interesting feature of the literature on imaginative resistance is that while philosophers spend a great deal of time discussing resistance to moral evaluation,[10] they almost always discuss examples they have made up themselves.[11] 'Death On a Freeway' was itself made up by Brian Weatherson, a philosopher, in the context of an article on imaginative resistance. But in fact it seems that *professional* fiction-writers rarely include in their works moral evaluations which attract resistance in precisely the way that 'Death On a Freeway' does. A good explanation should account for this fact.

As has been noted by many, resistance would have diminished, had 'Death On a Freeway' been different in certain ways. For instance, had R been: 'Craig *believed that he did the right thing because Jack and Jill should have taken their argument somewhere else where they wouldn't get in anyone's way*'—that is, had it been made explicit that the problematic moral evaluation in question was that of a fictional character— then it seems likely that the reader would have been less inclined to treat the sentence as different to those preceding it (Gendler 2000: 64). Or: had the fiction included the context that, for instance, *an evil monster has hacked into the computerized transport system, so that if it slows down for more than an hour, all the primary schools get blown*

---

[9] Put this broadly, there are apparently many other cases of imaginative resistance too. For instance, there is resistance to viscerally disgusting descriptions in fictions, such as those in Easton Ellis's *American Psycho* which dispassionately detail the torture and killing of women and the desecration of their corpses. Though I have no space to discuss, this looks like a more straightforward phenomenon: owing to its relatively primitive, basic nature, disgust operates on both real and fictional descriptions alike (Korsmeyer 2011: 53–5).

[10] Though not exclusively, as we will see.   [11] A noble exception is Matravers (2014).

up, again *R* would not have been resisted (Stock 2005, Levin 2011). A good explanation of resistance should be compatible with these facts. However, as Weatherson notes, readers are not in fact permitted to supplement the text with any such additional imaginings, unintended by the author, in order to mitigate the resistance they feel (2004: 20). Previous chapters have provided a rationale for this claim, which might otherwise have looked somewhat ad hoc: namely, intentionalism is a good theory of fictional content.

According to Weatherson, *R* is not just resisted imaginatively by readers; it is not even counted by them as a fictional truth. He writes: 'Intuitively, it is not true, even in the story, that Craig's murder was morally justified' (2004: 1).[12] He then seeks to give a principled account of this supposed fact. However, in arguing thus, he is apparently making two odd assumptions: that readers' intuitions about whether *R* counts as fictionally true or not a) will converge and b) will determine *R*'s fictional status, or at least are a reliable guide to it. Yet, actually, there are no clear trends in readers' judgements about the fictionality of *R*, I suspect, since, as pointed out, it is a highly unusual case, relative to professionally produced fiction. Readers are bound to have different responses here, depending on their background beliefs about the nature of fictional truth (see Nanay 2010: 587). Often they will not know what to say. It is not clear how any single theory could fit all such intuitions. And in any case, as I have stressed in my Introduction, theories of fiction aimed at explanation do not have to slavishly aim to fit within ordinary usage. Indeed, ordinary usage might already be infected by bad theories.

We already have a theory of fictional content on the table which has many explanatory benefits. It has it that an utterance expresses a proposition which is fictionally true if and only if it is intended to be reflexively imagined, in the manner spelled out in earlier chapters. Now, it is true that if an author *believes* that *p* cannot be imagined, she cannot seriously intend that *p* be imagined by readers, and so *p* cannot be fictionally true in any text she produces. So if an author believes that *R* is unimaginable *tout court*, it cannot be a fictional truth in her work. But not everyone will judge *R* unimaginable. Indeed, as will shortly become clear, I do not. So it remains possible that this utterance counts as fictional, dependent on a certain story about its genesis. I propose that we treat it as seriously intended to be imagined, and move on. The point at issue is not whether *R* is fictional, but whether it is imaginable.

4.4 'Counterfactual' Explanations

A popular trend in philosophers' responses to imaginative resistance is to say that readers must morally evaluate fictional descriptions of situations as they *would* do in real life, were they confronted with an identical description of a real situation, other things being equal. I will call this a 'counterfactual' approach to resistance, since it

[12] See also Liao et al (2014: 342, fn. 8).

says that resistance is grounded in the way we would counterfactually respond to a non-fictional but otherwise identical description.

See, for instance, Walton (1994), who writes, speaking for readers generally:

I judge characters by the moral standards I myself use in real life.   (1994: 37)

His explanation for this is that moral principles supervene in exactly the same way on natural facts, whether described in a fiction or described in reality (1994: 45). On Stephen Yablo's view too, whether or not a thinker's moral concept *right* applies to a situation is determined by whether she *would judge that situation right*, were she to encounter it as described (2008). Moral concepts are 'response-enabled', Yablo argues (2008: 125–7). Whether a situation counts as *right* or not, as described, is determined by how one would respond to that situation in reality. Weatherson, meanwhile, presupposes that, relative to individual conceptual schemes, some facts are taken to hold 'in virtue of other facts'.[13] *Rightness*, where it obtains, is a 'higher level fact' which holds *in virtue of* 'lower level facts'.[14] The reader cannot imagine R because, in actuality, were it the case that Craig (or anyone else, for that matter) killed two people only because they were holding up traffic, she *would not* class it as right, given the presence of the relevant lower-level facts as described in the text (2004: 24).[15] Driver treats the connections between moral concepts and lower-level facts as psychologically necessary and so non-negotiable even in fictional situations (2008: 304).[16] Though she possesses different background arguments, Mahtani also argues that we resist sentences such as 'R' partly because all and only the moral principles we hold true generally, we 'import' into any given fictional world (2012: 426–7).

Here, in broad outline, is this counterfactual approach (I'll call it COUNT), applied to 'Death On a Freeway':

A) In making R fictionally true, the author intends the reader to imagine that R is true.
B) To imagine that R is true, the reader must generally believe that any real person in a relevantly similar situation to Craig would be doing the right thing.
C) The reader can't believe that any real person in a relevantly similar situation to Craig would be doing the right thing. Hence:
D) The reader can't imagine that R is true.

Yet there is an obvious problem with COUNT. As has often been noted, an author's choice of genre sometimes seems to influence whether resistance is present or not, in a

---

[13] Weatherson is clear that imaginative resistance is a function of 'what we take' the moral and conceptual truths to be, and not a function of what they are (2004: 21).

[14] This position is accepted, with some qualifications, by Levin (2011).

[15] A distracting side issue here is Weatherson's claim that to imagine that S is the case one has to imagine a specific instance of S (that is, in terms already introduced, that imagining must be *objectual*). As I have argued already in Chapter 1, many fictive utterances do not require objectual imagining, yet still require imagining. Weatherson does not need this claim to make his point about 'Death On a Freeway'.

[16] For another view which analyses resistance in terms of conceptual incoherence, see Levy (2005).

way the counterfactual approach can't explain (see e.g. Gendler 2000: 75; Liao et al 2014). Consider, for instance, the following variation on 'Death On a Freeway', and its final sentence (call it 'R2'):

Mayhem in Toontown
Daffy and Bugs were arguing again, in the middle of the freeway, halting traffic and making everyone cross. When Elmer Fudd, feeling particularly grumpy, saw that the cause of the jam was Daffy and Bugs, he took his gun out of the glovebox and shot 'em: BANG. They fell, rigid, mid-argument—Bugs still with a righteous paw pointing in the air, Daffy with an indignant look on his beak. Mickey, Tom, and Butch then drove their bubble cars right over them; while the new speed hump caused some cars to slow down a bit, mostly traffic returned to its normal speed. So Elmer did the right thing, because Daffy and Bugs should have taken their argument somewhere else where they wouldn't get in anyone's way.

Given the (admittedly ineptly!) humorous intent of this piece, I take it that many readers here won't find 'R2' quite as problematic as they found 'R'. We want a principled explanation of why this is so: why resistance occurs in some contexts, but not to the same extent in other apparently similar circumstances, and how genre use interacts with it. COUNT cannot explain this.

I suppose someone might reply that, in response to this, the reader of 'Mayhem in Toontown' does not *really* imagine that 'R2' is true. But on what grounds might one insist that no propositional imagining occurs here? One cannot appeal to the fact that no mental image could adequately convey this scenario; for first, arguably no mental image could convey the 'rightness' of *any* situation, as 'rightness' isn't a thing that is imageable. In any case, as we saw in Chapter 1, there are many fictional sentences more generally that cannot be adequately captured in mental images but yet which obviously can be propositionally imagined. Consider the many sentences in 19th-century novels about the intentional objects of the characters' complex mental lives, for instance. There is no reason to deny that we imagine such sentences are true, even though very often we cannot picture anything much relevantly corresponding to them.

Instead, I suppose that our objector might say that no fictional situation she can (propositionally) think of, when fully fleshed out in its particular details, could count as *verifying* the thought that 'R2' expresses: as entailing that the sentence would be true. (Something like this is imposed as a condition on *idealized* imagining by Chalmers 2002.) Yet we do not standardly require of imagining in relation to fiction that it be accompanied by any such ability. Fictions regularly contain sentences which ask us to imagine things we cannot fully understand in this way. Consider again the following opening line of Murakami's short story, first introduced in Chapter 2:

Katagiri found a giant frog waiting for him in his apartment. It was powerfully built, standing over six feet tall on its hind legs. A skinny little man no more than five foot three, Katagiri was overwhelmed by the frog's imposing bulk. "Call me 'Frog,'" said the frog in a clear, strong voice. (2002: 1)

The reader of such sentences, occurring as they do at the beginning of the story, need have no clear idea what circumstances would have to occur, in detail, to make the sentences true; but it seems that she does not need one in order to do what we normally unproblematically would take to count as imagining their truth. Nor need she be assuming that later parts of the fiction may provide some explanatory context, in order to imagine. Some fictions never explain themselves.

In short, well-functioning or idealized imagining may (for all that has been said) include the capacity to work out details of the imagined scenario in a coherent way, but it would be too demanding to make this a necessary condition of imagining *at all*. When we add to this the fact that, I assume, the reader experiences no phenomenological resistance to 'R2' (or at least, nothing like the degree of felt resistance to 'R') I see no reason to deny that what is happening with respect to that sentence is propositional imagining, akin to that which (we happily accept) happens to other fictional sentences.

A further objection, related to the last about genre membership, is as follows. COUNT predicts that if moral concept M (e.g. *is right*) would *not* have been applied by a reader to a description of a situation S, were S actual, then, where S is described in a fiction, other things being equal, and M is described as applying to S, she will experience resistance. Presumably the underlying explanation here, in at least a lot of cases, is supposed to be that the reader *would* apply *some other* moral concept $M2$ to S as described, incompatible with M (e.g. in 'Death On a Freeway', she would judge it *wrong* to kill people because they were holding up traffic, so cannot judge it *right*). So a further assumption seems to be that if moral concept $M2$ would have been applied by a reader to a description of a situation S, were S actual, then, where S is described in a fiction, other things being equal, she will imagine S as $M2$. Yet there seems to be a range of genre-based counterexamples to this: cases where we do not apply any moral concept in imagination in response to a fictional description, even where *we would have done, had the situation been actual* (a point also noted by Gendler 2000: 75).

For instance, in the 'story-within-a-story' of Angela Carter's 'The Notorious Amours of Lady Purple the Shameless Oriental Venus', the opening lines read as follows:

When she was only a few days old, her mother wrapped her in a tattered blanket and abandoned her on the doorstep of a prosperous merchant and his barren wife. These respectable bourgeois were to become the siren's first dupes. They lavished upon her all the attentions which love and money could devise and yet they reared a flower which, although perfumed, was carnivorous. At the age of twelve, she seduced her foster father. Utterly besotted with her, he trusted to her the key of the safe where he kept all his money and she immediately robbed it of every farthing…Packing his treasure in a laundry basket together with the clothes and jewellery he had already given her, she then stabbed her first love and his wife, her foster mother, in their bellies with a knife used in the kitchen to slice fish. (Carter 1996: 45)

I take it that the competent reader familiar with the genre does not respond with moral revulsion, even though she probably would, were she (admittedly improbably) to read the same sentences in a piece of investigative journalism. Instead she understands that she is reading a subversive gothic fairy tale where morality is partly suspended. We might equally look to erotic fiction and the description of otherwise morally questionable statements and acts:

"I'm a sadist, Ana. I like to whip little brown-haired girls like you because you all look like the crack whore—my birth mother…" He runs a hand through his hair and almost smiles but instead sighs ruefully. "I'm talking about the heavy shit, Anastasia. You should see what I can do with a cane or a cat." (James 2012: 61)

There is also the genre of horror fiction:

The man in red spoke. His voice was water running uphill, birds falling into the sky, sand eroding into rock. *Where is Rafe Baburn?* he asked. The children glanced at one-another. One of the girls offered a nervous smile. Later, Kosar would swear that the man never even gave them time to reply…He grabbed the smiling girl by her long hair, pulled his hand from within the red robes and sliced her throat. His knife seemed to lengthen into a sword, as if gorging on the fresh blood smearing its blade, and he swung it through the air. Three other children clutched at fatal wounds, shrieking as they disappeared from Kosar's view behind the parapet. The two remaining boys turned to run and the hooded man caught them, seemingly without moving. He beheaded them both with a flick of his wrist…Kosar fell to his knees, the breath sucked from him, and rolled sideways into the irrigation ditch. He cringed at the splash, but the hooded man strode across the bridge and into the village without pause. Kosar peered above the edge of the trench and watched through brown reeds as the man approached the first building. (Lebbon 2006: 6)

And equally, consider certain jokes:

As an airplane is about to crash, a female passenger jumps up frantically and announces, "If I'm going to die, I want to die feeling like a woman." She removes all her clothing and asks, "Is there someone on this plane who is man enough to make me feel like a woman?" A man stands up, removes his shirt and says, "Here, iron this!"

In such cases, I suggest, many readers will not automatically make the judgements or evaluations they would make, were these situations real. A reader can find the joke I just recounted funny, even if she would not find a similar situation funny 'in real life' (indeed, this reader does). She can read the horror story, perhaps with moderate excitement but no real or deep feelings of revulsion, even as it describes the murder of children, and without strongly excoriating the perpetrator. And in the realm of the erotic, clearly people can find arousing situations they would find morally repellent and so, presumably, a turn-off in real life. Such facts stand in need of explanation (and the explanation is not, evidently, that such readers are moral monsters). Meanwhile, they sit uneasily with the counterfactual approach.

4.5 An Explanation From the Invitation To Believe

In order to reach a better explanation, we should recall something that has been emphasized in previous chapters: namely, that authors write fictions with a range of intentions, and the competent reader is able to discern them via a grasp of pragmatic context. Now, as just argued, some fictions or parts of fictions are genuinely intended to get readers to believe certain things as well as imagine things. We have seen instances of this in the earlier part of the chapter, when I discussed beliefs intentionally and safely conveyed in fictions, via testimony. But testimony is not the only way in which authors of fictions can intentionally convey beliefs via their texts. One means of doing so, which I have explored elsewhere, is the provision of psychological insight into human beings and their desires (for a detailed defence, see Stock 2007a). Equally though, authors of fictions can intentionally imply the appropriateness of *counterfactual beliefs* about what would be the case, were some initial scenario (or 'premises') the case. Where they do this, they do it by inviting the reader to engage in a certain kind of imagining about the scenario in question: what I'll call 'counterfactual imagining'.

Counterfactual imagining, generally speaking, is imagining with a particular goal. It is aimed at arriving at some counterfactual; some belief about what would be the case, if such-and-such were the case. I take it that we engage in counterfactual imagining very often; and indeed, that it would be inefficient and risky to act without it. It is typically done for the purposes of planning, or for working out what one would feel or think or want or do in a given case: what else would be the case if such-and-such happened? What would I feel? (etc.) As such, its content can be expressed in the conditional tense: I imagine that p, and then imagine that q *would be* the case, given p. In counterfactual imagining there is an initially imagined 'premise' or 'premises', and then various 'consequences' or 'implications' imagined as a result of the initial premise(s), where one's further aim is to work out whether one believes that those consequences or implications would follow from the initial premise(s).

As such, counterfactual imagining is subject to epistemic constraints. If counterfactual imagining is one's goal, for some cognitive purpose, then one cannot just imagine what one likes. It is constrained at least partly by relevant existing beliefs already possessed by the thinker. If for instance, I try to imagine what would happen if Labour were to win the next general election, I bring to bear my existing beliefs about what tends to happen when there is a change of government, among others. I take it, moreover, that the following constraint is operative upon counterfactual imagining: in order to be able to counterfactually imagine that situation S *would have aspect A*, I must not already believe that instances of S, if actualized exactly as described, would *not* have aspect A; nor, perhaps, even have significant doubts that they would. For effectively, counterfactually imagining that S *would have* A requires an openness to the belief that S, thus described, would have A. (Of course, I can *imaginatively stipulate* that S has aspect A, without being open to any such belief; my claim is only that such openness is required for me to imagine that S *would have* A in the context of *counterfactually imagining* S and assessing whether A might follow from it.)[17]

---

[17] In Chapter 6, I argue for a redescription of imaginative stipulation as 'supposition'.

Now, often, we use counterfactual imagining to ascertain what would be the case *morally*, were some prior situation the case: for instance, we imagine an initial scenario in order to work out whether it would be *morally right* or not. Here too the constraint just described operates. So if, for instance, I already believe that action *x* in context *C* would not be right/have serious doubts that it would be right, I will not be able to counterfactually imagine that action *x* in context *C* would be right, because I am not sufficiently open to the belief that it would be.

How does this help explain imaginative resistance? In some fictions—for instance, certain thought experiments in philosophical ethics—an author might convey that she intends readers to imagine a certain situation, intending readers to work out on their own what moral beliefs they would themselves reach in those situations, were they in them. But morally didactic fictions go further. Their authors do not just imply that a certain fictional situation is to be imagined, leaving it open how the reader exactly imagines it, in terms of its moral aspect; they imply that the reader should counterfactually imagine it a particular way, *including* that it possesses some moral aspect. That is, they indicate that the reader should not only imagine the situation that way, but believe that it would be that specific way, were it actualized (or at least, seriously consider that belief as a possibility). These are the cases in which resistance arises, according to me. Resistance arises where the reader detects, via pragmatic context, that she is supposed a) to imagine a given described situation *S* as possessing a given moral aspect *M*, but *also* b) to believe that, were it to occur exactly as described, *S* would be *M* (that is, she is supposed to 'counterfactually imagine' *S* as *M*, as I have introduced the term). However, she cannot do this, because she is not sufficiently open to the belief that *S*, if actualized as described, would be *M*. Either she already believes that actual instances of *S*, thus described, are not or would not be *M*, or she at least has significant doubts that they are or would.

One obvious motive an author might have for intending readers to counterfactually imagine a particular fictional situation *S* as having moral aspect *M* is to get readers to arrive at a new belief (that is, new to the reader): a belief that *S*, if actualized, would be *M*. Morally didactic fictions such as *Uncle Tom's Cabin*, *To Kill a Mockingbird*, or Dickens's *Hard Times* explicitly have the aim of inculcating certain moral beliefs in this way (roughly: if *this*—indicating some scenario—was real, it would be wrong).[18] Where one already rejects the beliefs in question, resistance will follow. Something like this also looks to be the case for the author Phillip Pullman with respect to C.S. Lewis's *Narnia* series. For Pullman, perception of Lewis's moral vision seems to have dominated and disrupted his imaginative experience of the work:

I realised that what he was up to was propaganda in the cause of the religion he believed in ...It is monumentally disparaging of girls and women. It is blatantly racist. One girl was sent to hell because she was getting interested in clothes and boys.   (Pullman, quoted in Ezard 2002)

---

[18] In correspondence Dickens wrote of *Hard Times* and the real-life mill-workers it indirectly describes, 'I mean to strike the heaviest blow in my power for these unfortunate creatures' (Schlicke 2011: 268).

It seems clear that Pullman's rejection of the counterfactual beliefs he perceives as expressed in the text has inhibited his imaginative engagement with it.

In a different sort of case, an author might intend a reader to counterfactually imagine S as M, partly because, she assumes, the reader *already* takes it as uncontroversial that actual instances of S are M. Rather than gain a new belief, she intends her to consciously access an existing belief. Consider again, for instance, the following extract from Conan Doyle's Sherlock Holmes story 'The Adventure of the Three Gables', already encountered in Chapter 3. It is narrated by Dr Watson, conveying a racist contempt for a fellow character (where I take it that this is a kind of moral judgement, broadly construed):

The door had flown open and a huge negro had burst into the room....His broad face and flattened nose were thrust forward, as his sullen dark eyes, with a smouldering gleam of malice in them, turned from one of us to the other. "Which of you gen'l'men is Masser Holmes?" he asked....He swung a huge knotted lump of a fist under my friend's nose. Holmes examined it closely with an air of great interest..."I've wanted to meet you for some time," said Holmes. "I won't ask you to sit down, for I don't like the smell of you, but aren't you Steve Dixie, the bruiser?" "That's my name, Masser Holmes, and you'll get put through it for sure if you give me any lip."

"It is certainly the last thing you need," said Holmes, staring at our visitor's hideous mouth.   (Conan Doyle 1960: 1023)

Here it looks clear from pragmatic context that Conan Doyle himself endorses the racist beliefs and attitudes fictionally exhibited by Holmes and Watson to Steve Dixie; and that Conan Doyle expects his readers to share them already. In this case, Conan Doyle seems to intend readers only to consciously access their (to our mind) racist beliefs, and not particularly to acquire new ones. Equally, it has been argued that in *The Way We Live Now* Anthony Trollope implies a set of beliefs and attitudes concerning male violence and its relation to the social position of women (Smith 1996: 14–17), which the reader is expected to already share.

Putting my explanation a bit more formally, it explains resistance to 'R' in 'Death On a Freeway' as follows:

A) In making R fictionally 'true', the author makes it clear, via discernible pragmatic markers, that she intends the reader to *counterfactually imagine* that R is true (that is, imagine that R is true with a view to developing or accessing the existing belief that Craig would be doing the right thing in acting as he did, were the context as described).
B) To counterfactually imagine that R is true, the reader must not already believe that, given the initial scenario, Craig would be wrong in acting as he did.
C) The reader already believes that, given the initial scenario, Craig would be wrong in acting as he did.
D) The reader cannot counterfactually imagine that R is true.

What are the pragmatic markers mentioned in A)? The way 'R' is phrased in 'Death On a Freeway' pragmatically indicates, via the use of 'so' and 'because', that the author intends the reader to engage in counterfactual imagining. Effectively, by the use of 'so' and 'because', 'R' is presented as an implication from the originally-described scenario: an implication that the reader is supposed to accept. These inclusions suggest that the material occurring before them is supposed to be taken as some sort of justification for the pronouncement that Craig did the right thing, and by implication that killing in his circumstances would be the right thing to do. Of course, 'Death On a Freeway', including 'R', was originally invented by Weatherson, a philosopher, for the purposes of an article, which complicates the story about authorial intention. However, the point still applies to the fictional version of the story we are implicitly encouraged by Weatherson to consider: the imaginary case where we come across 'Death On a Freeway', assuming it to be by an unknown author, and written for some purpose other than as part of a thought experiment.

How does my explanation differ from COUNT? COUNT makes a *general* claim about epistemic constraints operating on imagining with ethical content. But this looks suspect: why should imagining generally be subject to such constraints? It is well understood why there should be epistemic constraints, relating to standards of intelligibility, justification, and evidence, on what we can appropriately *believe*, given that the cost of false belief can be high; but it looks odd to pose parallel constraints on imagining (which is effectively what is being suggested). According to my explanation, epistemic constraints understandably affect *counterfactual* imagining—imagining in the service of working out what would be the case—but not imagining generally. For not all imagining is counterfactual imagining. That is, as we have already seen extensively in earlier chapters, not all imagining is aimed at beliefs about what would be the case. As we have seen, many fictions, and therefore many imaginings, are directed at aims other than the exploration of counterfactual belief: for instance, sexual arousal, horror, thrill, fantasy, and so on.[19]

According to my explanation, then, the reader *could in other circumstances* imagine that sentences with the content of 'R' and even those in the Conan Doyle extract are true. She could easily imaginatively engage with them if she did not take herself to be intended to counterfactually imagine them, but rather took herself to imagine them in order to achieve some non-cognitive goal. Authors unconcerned with exploring counterfactuals can happily 'authoritatively' tell or imply to readers that certain outlandish values operate in their fictional worlds; and readers can accept this, because there is little cognitive cost to their doing so. In contrast, where a fiction makes clear that it has ambitions to change or reinforce ideas about moral matters in the actual world, resistance may well be experienced, depending on the outlandishness of the perspective being displayed. So my view also has a more sophisticated account of fiction than COUNT does: it acknowledges, yet again, that fiction as a medium can be used for

[19] This point shall be defended further in Chapter 6.

different goals. Sometimes the goal is to get the reader to think about the relation between the fictional world and the actual one; but not always. Take for instance *The Man Who Was Thursday*, which the author has described as follows:

> The book...was not intended to describe the real world as it was, or as I thought it was, even when my thoughts were considerably less settled than they are now. It was intended to describe the world of wild doubt and despair which the pessimists were generally describing at that date; with just a gleam of hope in some double meaning of the doubt, which even the pessimists felt in some fitful fashion. (Extract from an article by G.K. Chesterton, published in the *Illustrated London News*, 13 June 1936)

Once she has read this statement and been reassured as to Chesterton's ambitions with respect to his work, even a reader resoundingly optimistic by temperament will then find little problem in engaging with the 'wild doubt and despair' depicted in the book's moral vision, I suggest.

If my view is right, then we have a nice explanation of the interaction between resistance and some fictional genres, as already noted, which COUNT apparently lacks as it stands. That is: an author's intentional use of a certain fictional genre and its associated conventions of interpretation can make it pragmatically clear to a reader that, *even though* a moral judgement-inclusive sentence appears in the fiction, she is not supposed to *counterfactually imagine* whatever situation is being described, but only to imagine it. Some uses of comic, erotic, and horror genres can be like this. In those cases, it is often as if both authors and readers have signed up to a convention which says that what happens in the fiction does not have any or much relevance to what should be taken to be the case in actuality. This is not to say that this convention cannot be overridden in many cases by other deliberately employed cues of interpretation, of course. As usual, everything will depend on a complete specification of the context. However, very often, the purposes of such genres are not to explore what would be the case in reality, but rather to give the reader some fun or a thrill.

It should be noted, however, that the use of such genres is not inevitably a means of conveying distance between an author and some apparently objectionable evaluative principle. Many comedies have deadly serious things to say about the real world. Jokes can fail to be funny as soon as the hearer detects some intended evaluation for real-life situations which they would reject. And despite his use of the fantasy genre, many have balked at Tolkien's description of the men of the East and South as 'black men like half-trolls with white eyes and red tongues' (1955: 828), associating them with Sauron. Insofar as non-racist readers perceive an intended belief about people of African origin, which they reject, they will find this problematic.

We can see some of the effects of genre perception in action by looking at a further example, which I now deliberately introduce without any context.

> The two men...were stripped naked, held down by husky and willing farm hands and their ears and genitals cut off with jackknives...Some wag sewed their ears to their backs and

un...[but were immediately brought down with revolvers by the uproarious laughter of the congregation...[Still living, the two were at a stake while] little boys and girls gaily gathered excelsior, scrap and small branches, while their proud parents fetched logs, boxes, kero- [Reverend McPhule said a prayer, the flames were lit, the victims screamed, and the] crowd whooped with glee and Reverend McPhule beamed with satisfaction...The odor of cooking meat permeated the clear, country air and many a nostril was guiltily distended...When the roasting was over, the more adventurous members of Rev. McPhule's flock rushed to the stake and groped in the two bodies for skeletal souvenirs such as forefingers, toes and teeth. Proudly their pastor looked on...   (Schuyler 2013: 217–18)

Now I assume that, shorn of actual knowledge of context, where a reader suspects that the author of this text intentionally endorses, with respect to the actual world as well as the fictional one, the sentiments of the preacher and others being described, she will strongly resist imagining this passage, taken on its own. But in fact the passage is from a satire: *Black No More: Being an Account of the Strange and Wonderful Workings of Science in the Land of the Free, A. D. 1933–1940*. It was written by George Schuyler, an African-American. The text describes the story of two black men who are changed voluntarily by a new scientific method into white men, and what follows; including, eventually, a lynching. Once it becomes clear that Schuyler does not endorse the moral perspective which may seem to be fictionally operative in the story, and in fact intends to satirize it, I suggest that for many, resistance will somewhat decrease. Any residual resistance will come from a presumably different source: disgust, which seems to trigger independently of understanding of intentional context.

Relatedly, now we can see why, in the case of stories or myths originating a long time ago or in a culture very different to the current reader's own, resistance may be reduced (see Liao et al. 2014): because the reader is simply unable to interpret pragmatically whether she is supposed to counterfactually imagine or not, with respect to them. Understanding of pragmatics breaks down as temporal or cultural distance widens. (In the case of myths, the notion of a single originating author is itself often inapplicable in any case.)

Another virtue of my view is that, in broad outline, it can be extended to non-moral cases (see also Gendler 2006: 161). Weatherson cites a range of (once again contrived, deliberately invented for the purpose) examples of non-moral resistance, including the sentences 'Although shape-shifting aliens did not exist, and until that moment Sam had no evidence that they did, this was a rational belief. False, but rational' (Weatherson 2004: 3), and Yablo's story of a 'five-fingered leaf' which was also an 'oval' (2008: 143). According to me, these sentences evoke resistance on the assumption that the reader takes herself to be invited to counterfactually imagine their truth, but yet she possesses beliefs or doubts incompatible with doing so (about whether uncorroborated beliefs are rational, or five-fingered things are oval).

Actually, it seems to me that if these rather unusual examples had actually turned up in real fictions—for instance, in the work of Terry Pratchett, or some other author deemed likely to write fantastical scenarios, fully aware of their fantastical nature—the reader would not have experienced resistance to them at all, because it would have been clear that counterfactual imagining was not an appropriate response to them. It is only because these are contrived cases, of which the reader is supposed to imagine that she came across them in some context other than a philosophy article, but does not know what context that is exactly, that resistance gets a grip at all, if indeed it does for her. Even so, non-moral cases are still likely to arise where there is some matter of genuine controversy about which people are likely to differ, including authors and their readers. For instance, imagine the following sentence found in a fiction:

> The ice sheets were melting, but it wasn't because the world was getting warmer. There was no such thing as global warming.[20]

Presumably, if the reader of this passage assumed she was thereby being asked to counterfactually imagine it, and she was not already a climate change sceptic, to some extent she would resist. If, on the other hand, she did not assume this, but took the utterance merely to be asking her to imagine it for some other goal (pleasure or humour or the exploration of alternate realities, say), she would not. COUNT cannot easily explain this.

Equally, consider:

> Jeremy wears pink trousers and likes reading. He's gay.

If the reader thinks this utterance is implying a claim about a general causal relationship in the actual world which she would not endorse, she will resist to some extent, I suggest. If not, because the wider fictional context reveals that, for instance, the claim is about two independent and coincidentally occurring properties in the fictional scenario; or that in the world of the fiction, but not ours, these properties are generally causally associated for some particular reason; or because she realizes that she is being introduced to a 'stock character' as a shorthand only for intentionally implying certain fictional content, based on her understanding of such a convention (as discussed in Chapter 2), then she will not resist. Once more, we see that to fail to pay attention to nuances of pragmatics in fictional works is to miss out on a plausible explanation of resistance across various contexts.

Equally, my view can also explain how the mere inclusion of a fictional narrator or a 'he thought...' is sometimes, but not always, enough to automatically deflect resistance to a description of a fictional situation S as having a particular moral aspect M (Gendler 2000: 64). The inclusion of a fictional narrator deflects resistance where it is clear from pragmatic context that the author does not intend or expect the reader to counterfactually imagine that S is M, but only to imagine that *the fictional narrator*

---

[20] The case is not entirely hypothetical: though not this explicit in the message, Michael Crichton has written a novel, *State of Fear*, in which it is strongly implied that global warming is not a genuine phenomenon. Thanks to Stacie Friend for the tip.

believes that S is M. It is insufficient to deter resistance, when it is clear, as in the Conan Doyle case, that the author shares the fictional narrator's perspective on actual events, and still expects the reader to counterfactually imagine it that way.

There is a further complication to be noted. Philosophers' examples of texts which provoke imaginative resistance tend to either present the 'resisted' sentences on their own, without any context (see e.g. Walton 1994), or, as in 'Death On a Freeway', present them at the very end of a short (bad) fiction. Yet in cases of published texts evoking resistance, such as the Conan Doyle case, resisted passages tend to come in the middle of other material. In these cases, the reader may well decide to ignore the invitation to counterfactually imagine/believe something, and instead treat the passage as inviting her only to imagine something, without any accompanying belief. Of course, I am not suggesting that the reader always explicitly calculates whether it is worth her while to imagine what a fiction asks her to imagine in a particular case. Sometimes, she might, presumably: as when—to introduce a fresh example—the viewer of *The Merchant of Venice* who judges the play to be anti-Semitic deliberates about what reason she might have to imaginatively engage, nonetheless. But generally, it seems true that readers engage imaginatively with fiction because they assume there is or will emerge a good reason for them to do so. We pick up and embark upon stories, hoping to be informed, diverted, thrilled, moved, or challenged, for instance. Usually one is to some extent rewarded. On the other hand, once it becomes obvious that none of these things will in fact happen—so that there is no real point, on a reader's own terms, in imaginatively engaging—that reader will not be motivated to continue. The same is true of bad fiction generally (which we also tend to resist imagining!). It is certainly true of the last sentence in 'Death On a Freeway', which, occurring last, is not a bridge to any further content and offers the reader no reason to imagine it, once the invitation to believe that R would be true has been declined.

Earlier I remarked that it was hard to find any non-contrived instances in published fiction of moral evaluations which unambiguously provoked resistance in the way that R does. Effectively, we have just noted one reason: that unlike the case of R, for resisted passages in non-contrived fictions, the reader will at least sometimes find some reason to imaginatively engage with the utterances in question after all. At the very least, the passage typically will provide a bridge to further fictional content which may have its own merits; and it also may fulfil other valuable goals in its own right. But a second reason is that in most cases where fictive utterances intentionally invite belief as well as imagining from a certain readership, and where that belief is unlikely to be one the readership will easily accept, the author will likely know this, and so take care to present it in a way that undermines resistance: perhaps via supplementary argument, or perhaps via the filling in of fictional context such that the claim in question becomes more plausible (Stock 2005). 'Death On a Freeway' is once again anomalous in this respect, for no actual author of a fiction, whose aim was to get her readers to believe the implied general moral claims, would put things so baldly. Having a minimal understanding of human psychology and her readers' likely value systems, she would know that the claims in question were not ones readers would be likely to endorse.[21]

4.6 Comparison to Other Views

I now move to a comparison between my view and others.[22]

A. Nanay's pragmatic approach

We should make a contrast between my view and a rival explanation, grounded like mine in pragmatics: that of Bence Nanay (2010). According to Nanay, resistance arises towards *R* because the reader does not know what the author means or could have meant. The author appears to the reader to be violating something 'reminiscent' of the Gricean 'Cooperative Principle' in conversation (2010: 591). As a result, the reader ceases to be imaginatively engaged with the fictional world and starts to become consciously concerned with reconstructing the author's motivations in writing. This is the source of resistance.

Now, it is an unashamed feature of my variety of intentionalism that the reader is fairly regularly consciously concerned with reconstructing the author's motivations, goals, and intentions, in writing. Working out what one is intended to imagine is responsive not just to features of the text in front of one, but also to knowledge about the author's moral and political views, cultural context, expressed opinions, wider oeuvre, genre preferences, and more. So it cannot be that this in itself is a source of resistance or other imaginative disruption in a startling way. In any case, there are further questions to be raised about Nanay's explanation, even independently of background assumptions about intentionalism.

Readers will recall from the discussion in Chapter 1 that Grice is mainly concerned with speaker meaning in ordinary conversational contexts, and the intentions and goals which tend to be prevalent in it. He thinks that conversational participants typically assume that other participants will cooperate with them in shared conversational goals, such as: being informative but not more than is required, avoiding saying what one believes to be false, avoiding making claims for which there is no evidence, avoiding obscurity and ambiguity, and seeking brevity (Grice 1975). Now, as observed earlier, it is implausible to think that all or even most of these maxims govern fictive utterance. Nanay admits that fictive utterances need not be believed true by their utterers, nor evidenced (2010: 595); but seems to think the other maxims apply. Yet it is not clear how, for instance, 'making your contribution informative' is itself an internal

---

[21] As a text ages, however, the moral values of the current readership of a text may not coincide with those of the originally intended readership, deviating from them in unanticipated ways, in which case any implicit moral evaluations in the text will be more likely to jar with current readers and increase the chance of resistance.

[22] For a more complete round-up of other views, see Stock (2017b).

goal of fictive utterance or fiction-making, qua practice. On most understandings of *information*, many fictive utterances do not *deliberately* supply *any* information about the world, which is surely the point at issue. They are made-up and knowingly false. Equally it is no internal goal of fictive utterance qua practice to be brief, or non-obscure (think of James Joyce!).

The upshot here is that, as long as we try to construe 'something reminiscent of the Cooperative Principle' in terms Grice would recognize as related to conversational goals, it is not clear what principles or maxims the author of a fictive utterance which provokes imaginative resistance is supposed to have violated. Most fictive utterances violate at least some Gricean conversational maxims, without any resistance resulting. (A further troubling aspect of Nanay's view is that he says that some genres but not others are governed by the cooperative principle, but does not explain why.)

Later in the paper, Nanay apparently abandons the firm connection with Grice on conversation and falls back on a 'minimal version of the Cooperative Principle in the case of fictional discourse' as follows: 'we expect the author to make her...contribution such as is required for the reader to be able to understand and follow the story' (2010: 595). Of course this seems right, but is silent on precisely what it takes to 'understand and follow the story'. On the view I am offering, the general and essential goal of the author of a fiction is to instruct the reader to have certain imaginings, and to get her to recognize that she is so instructed. This is what understanding and following the story consist in. The trouble is, now, that there seems no reason to say that we do not understand and follow 'Death On a Freeway' in this sense. We understand what we are intended to (counterfactually) imagine; we just (on my view, anyway) experience difficulty in doing it.

B. *Gendler's approach*

A comparison is also apt with Tamar Gendler's original discussion of imaginative resistance (2000) as well as a later paper (2006). Her original explanation goes like this. Gendler distinguishes between 'nondistorting' or 'realistic' fictions and 'distorting' fictions. In the former, the author has 'imported' a large number of truths from the actual world (about physical laws, psychological generalizations, and historical facts, for instance). (This looks like a selective application of the Lewisian model of implied fictional content which was discussed in Chapter 2.) The fact that in a realistic fiction 'there will be a tremendous number of things which are true in the fiction which are also true in the actual world' (2000: 76) means that in these fictions it is *also* appropriate for the reader to 'export' large numbers of fictional truths from the story to the world (which, in other words, apparently means to believe them). In contrast, 'distorting' fictions represent worlds obviously very unlike our actual one, so that the reader is not free to 'export' to the same extent. Imaginative resistance occurs, Gendler tells us, only with respect to realistic fiction. It occurs when a) the reader encounters a deviant moral evaluation in such a fiction, and assumes she is supposed to 'export it' as a truth to the actual world (i.e. believe it); but where b) she 'does not wish to add' it to her 'conceptual repertoire' (2000: 77); that is, she does not want to (or presumably better, cannot) believe it.

My preferred explanation has obvious similarities to Gendler's.[23] It is worth therefore bringing out the differences. An initial minor amendment I propose to Gendler's position is that she apparently assumes that in cases of resistance, the author (or at least, the fiction—it is not clear to what extent Gendler is an intentionalist) must be inviting the reader to acquire a new belief. On my view, there is also space for an alternative motive: the author might be inviting the reader to counterfactually imagine a scenario in order to consciously access a belief which, she assumes, they already have (as in the Conan Doyle case).

Meanwhile, a disagreement is as follows. Given my brand of intentionalism, I take it that the reader is at liberty to 'export' a given fictional truth (i.e. believe it) only where she takes it she has the specific permission of the author, indicated pragmatically. Or at least, it is not the mere fact that a certain kind of 'realistic' fiction is at stake which allows this. At times Gendler goes further, seeming to argue that once real-world material is incorporated 'into' a text, the reader standardly gets licence to believe *any* of the fictional truths in that text (though 'with numerous exceptions' 2000: 76), but clearly this is false. Equally, even 'distorting' fictions can make clear from context that 'exportation' of beliefs is appropriate and intended by the author. Gendler talks as if the appropriateness or otherwise of exportation is an all-or-nothing affair; it is not. Fictions may be significantly distorting in Gendler's sense yet pragmatically indicate via certain utterances that certain things are to be believed as well as imagined, as we saw in the case of Tolkien's implicit promulgation of racial stereotypes within a fantasy about hobbits and elves.

As it stands, however, the biggest differences between my view and Gendler's original view are as follows. First, in her original paper she explains resistance in terms of an agent's not *wanting* to believe something. In contrast, on my view, it is because she *cannot* accept the implied counterfactual belief, not because she does not want to (whether or not she does want to). I take it that being unable to believe something is to do with lack of reasons or evidence that strikes one as compelling, and not to do with one's desires, particularly. Secondly, in her original paper Gendler does not convincingly explain why rejecting the belief that *Craig would be doing the right thing* (etc.) might constrain one's ability to imagine that *R* is true, as she thinks it generally does. As noted, at one point she says that the reader resists imagining because 'she doesn't wish to add' the moral evaluation in question 'to her conceptual repertoire'. It is unexplained why merely *imagining* that, for instance, Craig did the right thing, or even imagining that *killing people only because they are holding up traffic is the right thing to do* would be a way of adding anything to one's conceptual repertoire: that is (I assume), why it

---

[23] Notwithstanding that in the past I have rejected her view (e.g. Stock 2005). As should be obvious, I have since changed my own position.

should change one's moral concepts. This is especially unclear when one considers that Gendler effectively allows, via her discussion about 'distorting' fictions, that a reader might freely imagine both of these utterances with respect to a 'distorting' fiction (like 'Mayhem in Toontown', for instance). Given that this connection between imagining and concepts is unclear (in fact, does not seem to hold), it is even more unclear why perception of the putative connection should standardly enter into a reader's motivational set, and cause her to desire not to imagine the utterance in question.

Towards the end of her original paper, and again in her later paper, Gendler suggests that imagining generally requires a kind of 'participation' that mere supposing something true does not: that in imagining something, we take our thought to be partly about the actual world and not 'merely restricted to the hypothetical', as supposing is (2000: 80). This is obviously closer to the view I am arguing for, but on my view, is an implausible account of imagining *generally*. As we have seen, imagining can be directed towards non-cognitive goals such as fantasizing for pleasure, or imagining for entertainment or arousal, and in such cases, there is no need to think of imagining as implying any commitments towards actual-world facts. Better to distinguish, amongst cases of imagining, between the kind of imagining directed at finding out what would be the case, counterfactually, and those other kinds of imagining that are not. (These points shall be pursued further in my final chapter.)

In her 2006 paper, Gendler characterizes some cases of resistance as issuing

a simultaneous invitation to imagine and to believe—and we reject the invitation to believe. And I suggest that it is at least in part because we are unable to disentangle the invitations that we reject the invitation to imagine.   (2006: 160)

Again we have a very similar-looking claim to the one I am making. But it is set in a rather different context. Simplifying that context somewhat for our purposes, and focusing again on 'R' from 'Death On a Freeway', Gendler additionally cites as explanatorily relevant a) that the reader first allegedly rejects 'R' as not counting as a genuine fictional truth for that story ('the truth-in-fiction principles that [the reader]...has been tacitly taking to govern the generation of fictional truths in the story prohibit it from following that, in so doing, Craig did the right thing' 2006: 165) and that b) 'R' contains an 'appraisal', so that as a result 'the reader's attention turns towards the actual world'; '[r]ecognizing the falsity of what she takes to be the actual world analogue of *p*—that if someone had done something like what Craig did, he would have done the right thing—the reader experiences resistance'(*ibid.*). So: first she discounts 'R' from being a fictional truth at all, and so presumably does not imagine it; and secondly, recognizing that, given that it contains an appraisal, she is being invited to believe some consequence of 'R', she declines that invitation.

This is problematic on a few counts. For one, I see no reason to admit that a) is true; i.e. that generally, readers will reject 'R' from counting as a fictional truth. As noted before with respect to Weatherson's identical claim, I take it that in fact, reader responses here will be mixed and depend on background theories or intuitions about fictional truth. Gendler adds that, for instance, the 'imaginative impropriety' and moral revulsion which the reader feels in viewing Craig's action as right 'ends up constraining the set of truth-in-fiction principles' she is 'ready to entertain' (2006: 169). But this seems to me speculative. Fictions such as *American Psycho* contain many propositions which evoke moral revulsion as they are imagined, but do not seem to be discounted as fictional truths for that reason. Moreover, once we add in a plausible theory of fictional truth—namely, extreme intentionalism— there is no reason to agree that making a morally revolting utterance is incompatible with constructing a fictional truth.

This leaves us with b) as the remaining explanation of resistance on the table. But we have already seen that there are cases of genre fiction where sentences very similar to 'R' are incorporated without *either* a) *or* b) looking plausible as an account of the typical reader's experience with respect to them (recall 'R2' in 'Mayhem in Toontown'). In the case of 'R2', it would be strange to reject it as a fictional truth, nor (I suggest) does one typically take it to be or imply that a belief should be adopted towards the actual world either. In other words, not all appraisals in fictions imply counterfactual beliefs. Only some do: namely, those where pragmatic context indicates that the author intends such beliefs to be disseminated to readers.

In conclusion: imaginative resistance, I suggest, is a phenomenon which arises in a very particular pragmatic context, where readers are being asked in certain passages not just to imagine certain things, but to believe, or at least consider for belief, certain counterfactuals, which they cannot in fact believe. In earlier chapters, my defence of extreme intentionalism emphasized the multiplicity of purposes with which fictions are written. Not all fictions are intended to explore counterfactuals; far from it. Hence, given my explanation, we should expect to find that not all fictions describing morally deviant scenarios arouse resistance. This is, in fact, what we have found when we looked at some instances of genre fiction. More generalist explanations of resistance, such as COUNT or that offered by Gendler, cannot accommodate this finding.

4.7 Imagining and the Impossible

The stance I have taken here towards so-called imaginative resistance carries the assumption that in every case discussed so far, one *could* imagine what one is asked to, if one did not take oneself to be invited to *counterfactually* imagine it, in the sense I have introduced. Perhaps this will not be so controversial, given the particular range of cases discussed. But one might well wonder: are there some utterances which, if found in a fiction, one *could not* imagine under any description, and which so constitute a different sort of imaginative resistance? Many have thought so. Many agree with Yablo, for instance, when he says that we would be unable to imagine a fiction which had it that *a five-fingered leaf was oval-shaped* (2008: 142). I myself have suggested in the past that one cannot imagine $7 + 5 = 13$ (Stock 2003). Yet I now think that one can propositionally imagine such things: one can propositionally imagine even what one recognizes as blatant conceptual impossibilities, let alone apparently conceptually coherent scenarios which apparently imply some objectionable moral evaluation. I will conclude this chapter with some defence of this claim.[24] It should be noted throughout that I am no longer referring to what I have called counterfactual imagining, but to imagining with other goals.

It seems that one can propositionally imagine that anything is the case, at least as long as one also imagines that there is some (good) explanation for it. To do the latter does not require having to imagine any details about what that explanation might look like. We can see this with respect to 'magical' or surreal or science fiction, which often instructs us to imagine scenarios where (at least) we have no idea of under what circumstances they could be instantiated; or even where we are certain that they could not be instantiated under any circumstances (see also Kung 2014: 98). Broomsticks fly, a stone turns lead to gold, the dead are resurrected, a man turns into a giant insect, holes are ripped in the space-time continuum and possible worlds traversed, a time-traveller colludes in the romance of his own parents, people sprout wings, aliens imperceptibly replace the living, playing cards play croquet, unbodied ghosts intervene in the physical world, two people inhabit one body, and so on. Some of these are physically impossible; some are metaphysically impossible. We should not downplay the frequency of such cases nor their fundamentality to what many tend to like and enjoy about fiction. What the reader does in such cases, I suggest, is imagine what she is asked to, additionally imagining with respect to the scenario in question that there is some good explanation—whatever it is—for whatever else it is she imagines. A reader may imagine this despite any present conviction that what she imagines is physically or even metaphysically impossible. We can do this because even where we are fairly certain of a fact, we can imagine that circumstances obtain such that we might also be wrong about it (even if we cannot imagine *how* we might be wrong about it, given we are so convinced we are right). It follows from my view that epistemic conviction does not preclude imagining oneself being wrong.

Moreover, I suggest, to imagine that such-and-such happens and that there is a good explanation for it (whatever that is) can be a way of obeying the instruction to imagine such-and-such, *even where there is no explicit instruction in the fiction to imagine that there is a good explanation available.* In Chapter 3 we saw that imagining that *Hamlet has an Oedipus complex*—which is not something, I assumed, which Shakespeare could have intended his audience to imagine—could nonetheless count as a means of fulfilling the instruction to comply with Shakespeare's genuine intention (I assume) that the audience imagines that Hamlet suffers from excessive grief at the loss of his father; jealousy of his mother's new lover; anger at his mother's fast remarriage, and so forth. Analogously, I suggest, imagining that *p* and that there is a good explanation for whatever 'p' describes is a way of imagining that *p*.

Despite the prevalence of such cases in fiction and our apparent ease with their presence, some may however still balk at extending this approach to what look like

---

[24] Meanwhile, the relation between imagining and supposition will be discussed in Chapter 6.

blatant conceptual impossibilities, such as the examples we started with. I however see no reason not to insist that it does so extend, once we disambiguate my claim from a couple of others.

I am not claiming that one could *sensorily* imagine—that is, imagine via a *mental image*—a five-fingered leaf which was also simultaneously oval-shaped; or a mental image of 7 + 5 = 13; or whatever the supposedly problematic example is. The claim extends only to propositional imagining. We have established that propositional imagining can occur without mental imagery in Chapter 1, via consideration of cases from fiction which require only the former, but not the latter, and for which the latter would even be inappropriate or irrelevant. Equally, I am not claiming that one can 'objectually' imagine an impossibility, in the sense introduced by Yablo (1993: 27; see also Chapter 1). In fact I leave this matter open (for arguments that one can objectually imagine the impossible, see Kung 2010 and 2014; they will appear in the next chapter). In objectual imagining, one's imagining is of the form 'imagining an O', rather than the propositional 'imagining that there is an O'.[25] Objectual imagining can be more or less accurate, whereas what one propositionally imagines, strictly speaking, can neither be accurate nor inaccurate, though it can be true or false, I have assumed. So objectual imagining looks as if it requires a representation of at least some instantiated detail, as part of what is imagined, in a way that propositional imagining does not.

Nor, a fortiori, am I claiming that one can 'coherently' objectually imagine such scenarios, in the sense in which 'it is possible to fill in arbitrary details in the imagined situation such that no contradiction reveals itself' to the imaginer as she does so (Chalmers 2002: 15). Nothing like this close level of attention to detail need be present in propositional imagining generally, in order for imagining to count as having taken place. In propositionally imagining utterances in relation to fiction, the reader does not stop to work out the details of the scenario she is imagining, and especially not such that no contradiction reveals itself. Propositional imagining that p and q involves (being disposed to) thinking of p and q as true together; as true with respect to the same scenario. This looks different from *thinking of how p and q could or would be true*—that is, of thinking of a concrete scenario in which, by one's own lights fully spelled out and with all possible incoherencies or gaps addressed, p and q would count as true.

Fictions sometimes do instruct us to propositionally imagine blatant conceptual impossibilities. One prominent sort of case, to be discussed in Chapter 5, is where it is fictional (that is, we are required to imagine) that a fictional character as such appears in the real world, and interacts with real non-fictional people and things. The trope is by now fairly common: one example is Miguel de Unamuno's *Mist: A Tragicomic Novel* (1914) in which a character, as such, has a dialogue with the author, as such, in which it is explained to him that he cannot kill himself because he is not real. Other well-known examples include Flann O'Brien's *At-Swim-Two-Birds* and Tom

---

[25] Normally objectual imagining will involve mental imagery and so count as experiential, in fact. I have left it open whether there can be objectual imagining which does not involve this.

Robbins's *Even Cowgirls Get the Blues*. These are not books that readers cannot engage with; they do not throw them away in confusion, simply on the basis that they are to imagine that (from within the fictional perspective) a fictional character is conversing and otherwise causally interacting with a real one. The passages which describe such things do not appear to lapse into gibberish. It is surely preferable to take such responses at face value than to deny that readers really imagine here what they are asked to imagine (Kung 2014). After all, it has been the approach of this book so far to take seriously the sort of mental attitude or act called for and apparently readily produced by fiction, and then to see what else we can find out about it.

Why, then, do people still tend to insist that one cannot imagine what one believes to be impossible? In the case of fiction, where a reader comes across a blatant conceptual impossibility expressed via utterance 'x' and finds herself 'unable' to imagine it, this may be for a couple of reasons. It might be as with the earlier cases of resistance to moral evaluation: because the reader (presumably erroneously) has pragmatically interpreted the utterance as requiring not just that she imagine that x occurs, as described, but that she counterfactually imagine that it does; where this involves believing, or at least being open to the belief, that x as described would be the case.[26] Alternatively, it might be because she (mis)interprets the request as a request to sensorily imagine, or to otherwise coherently objectually imagine x, and cannot: in the first case, because nothing 'imageable' corresponds to x, and in the second, because there is no scenario whose details which, when all filled in coherently, she would accept as corresponding to an instantiation of x.

A similar explanation can be given of the presumably more common case, relatively speaking, where a thinker tries to *autonomously* imagine (that is, without the help of a prop such as a fiction to guide her thought) some conceptual impossibility, 'x', which she would recognize as such, and fails. In that case, I suggest, any resulting failure is likely to be either the result of a) (as in earlier cases) trying to imagine that x *and* believe that x would occur (which is typically bound to fail, given that, precisely, the thinker does not believe x possible); b) trying to sensorily imagine x and failing; or c) trying to coherently objectually imagine x and failing.

Staying away from written fictional works for a minute, a further relevant point is that instructions to 'imagine that...' are not always heard as instructions to propositionally rather than objectually imagine something, since ordinary usage is not clear on the difference. In fact, it looks likely that a thinker will often hear a single, context-free instruction to 'imagine (that) x'—whether self-issued, or from another speaker—as a request to sensorily or otherwise objectually imagine x, rather than as a request to propositionally imagine that x *is the case*. Instructions tend to be heard this way because, generally, propositional imagining that p, as we have seen, tends to be purpose

---

[26] I suggest, however, that in practice, such resistance occurs rarely; because in competently written fictions, it is usually perfectly clear that the presence of an acknowledged conceptual impossibility is not supposed to imply any particular belief in its possibility on the part of the reader.

driven. Where the purpose is not apparent, as, often, in the case of a single, context-free instruction to imagine something, the hearer may reasonably conclude that sensory imagining is an appropriate response to that instruction.

Perhaps there still are those reading who nonetheless will insist on asking, sceptically: what *would it be* to propositionally imagine that a conceptual impossibility was the case, if my points here were true? What would it be to 'think of x and y as true together', or 'to think of x and y as occurring with respect to the same scenario' if one simultaneously believed their combination impossible? How could this even count as *thinking*? Yet clearly, to imagine that *a fictional character meets a real one and there is some good explanation for this*; or that *someone time travels back to help in their parents' courtship and there is some good explanation for this*, or even that, as in Carroll's *Through the Looking Glass*, there is *'jam tomorrow, jam yesterday, but never jam today'* (2009: 65) *and there is some good explanation for this*, is not just to engage in mental gibberish. As I have stressed, when a fiction asks us to imagine what we know to be impossible, it appears that we can comply in a way which satisfies the instruction without lapsing into nonsense-thought. The implication of this is that we should just accept that propositional imagining x and y are true together—whatever that turns out to be—is not constrained by beliefs about the possibility of the combination of x and y.[27]

4.8 Summary

In the first half of this chapter, I defended the claim, relied upon in Chapter 3, that in writing a fiction, an author can intentionally convey beliefs to readers in an epistemically respectable way. I then went on to implicate the fact that authors can intentionally convey beliefs in an explanation for imaginative resistance. The right account of this phenomenon, I have argued, should cite the reader's perception of an intention that she believe, or at least be open to believing, a counterfactual which she cannot in fact believe, and so rejects. I also criticized rival accounts for proposing too-general explanations of resistance, which do not sufficiently take into account the fact that authors of fictions can have various purposes in writing fiction, of which exploring a counterfactual is only one.

I have also argued that, contrary to many people's intuitions, other things being equal, there is no reason to deny that readers can propositionally imagine blatant 'conceptual impossibilities'. Imaginative resistance does not occur in relation to certain contents, whatever the pragmatic context; rather it occurs in relation to a perception of a request to engage in a certain kind of imagining with a distinctive purpose: the sort of imagining involved in arriving at counterfactual beliefs.

---

[27] For those unable to accept this, however, the foregoing explanation of resistance to moral evaluation need not be threatened; for none of the cases discussed there involve the reader being intended to imagine what she believes to be blatantly impossible.

5
The Nature of Fiction

5.1 Introduction

Continuing to build upon work done in the first half of this book, I turn now to a new question. What is a fiction? This will be the main business of the chapter. We all know one when we see it, perhaps—but can we find a theory which explains (most of) those identifications? Many agree that there is a close relationship between fictions and the activity of imagining. The account of fiction for which I will argue respects this relationship in a simple and straightforward way. We have already seen that, according to extreme intentionalism, what determines fictional content in a particular case is the intentions of the author who creates that content: reflexive intentions to get readers to imagine certain things. The author instructs the reader to imagine certain things, and the intentions which inform those instructions determine fictional content. It is a simple step from there to say that fictions just *are* collections of intentional instructions to imagine certain things. Or so I shall argue.

Arguing thus sets me against fellow theorists in a number of ways. On the one hand, it sets me against those (for instance, Gregory Currie, Peter Lamarque and Stein Olsen, and David Davies) who agree with me that creating a fiction *necessarily* involves having reflexive intentions that readers imagine things, but deny that this is *sufficient*. Additionally these philosophers require—roughly—that fiction (or more specifically, the kind of utterance, the presence of which makes something a fiction) be non-truth-tracking, or something close to this. On the other hand, it sets me against those (for instance, Kendall Walton, Harry Deutsch, Manuel Garcia-Carpintero, Stacie Friend, and Derek Matravers) who deny that creating a fiction even *necessarily* involves having reflexive intentions that readers imagine things. I will argue that my view is superior to these other views in terms of explanatory power and simplicity. One sign of these virtues is already apparent: it fits neatly with a plausible account of fictional content. Others will be made apparent along the way.

5.2 F-imagining and One's Belief Set

Before we get there, I need to remind the reader of some basics about imagining, as well as to introduce a new claim. In Chapter 1, I stipulatively labelled the sort of imagining which is appropriate as a response to fiction 'F-imagining' and introduced certain features of it. First, F-imagining is propositional: it takes propositions as its content. Secondly, F-imagining is 'quasi-factual': F-imagining that *p*, where *p* is a proposition, necessarily involves thinking that *p* is the case (though not, of course, believing it). Thirdly, F-imagining is potentially conjunctive: if one imagines that *p* in response to page 10 of a given fiction, and one imagines that *q* in response to page 20, then normally (excluding cases of unreliable narration, etc.) one will also imagine *p and q* with respect to the same scenario (or be disposed to).

I will now defend a further claim about F-imagining, and indeed about propositional imagining generally. In contrast to the approach taken in Chapter 1, it is not so much that this feature is revealed by direct scrutiny of basic features of fiction; it is more that there are independent arguments for this feature, and that understanding it will stand us in good stead to build a more powerful theory of fiction later.

The claim is this: when propositionally imagining that *p*, a reader can also simultaneously believe that *p*. However she cannot imagine *only* what she also believes. In other words, the content of a thinker's propositional imagining cannot coincide wholly in content with the content of her current beliefs, though it may coincide with some subset of them.

The point can be illustrated by an example. I currently believe that *I'm typing on my computer now*. I can also imagine that *I'm typing on my computer now* if I imaginatively conjoin, or am at least disposed to conjoin, my thought *I'm typing on my computer now* with further content, which I do not simultaneously believe. For instance, if I imagine that *I'm typing on my computer now and my office is on the moon*, then this is a way of imagining something that I also (partly) believe. I cannot, however, simply imagine that *I'm typing on my computer now* without also conjoining this, or at least being disposed to conjoin it, with further imaginings whose content I do not also believe.

In more detail the claim is as follows. (To 'conjoin in thought' is to think of as occurring with respect to the same scenario.)

> If *K* propositionally imagines that *p* at time *t*, then either i) *K* doesn't believe that *p* at time *t*; or ii) *K* believes that *p* at time *t* but occurrently conjoins in thought *p* and some further proposition *q*, or is disposed to do so, where *q* is not the content of any belief of hers at time *t*.

One reason for thinking this true is that it nicely complements a commonly referenced story about the general possibility of imagining what one believes, first found in Leslie (1994). A child (taken by those who make use of this example to be representative of imaginers generally) might be instructed by an adult to play a game in which she pretends that the teacup in front of her is 'full' and then, after the cup has been upturned, 'empty', notwithstanding that it was manifestly empty all along. In that case, assuming that pretence of this nature implies, among other things, imagining that *the cup is empty*, and assuming that the child also believes that *the cup is empty*, it appears that at the time of so imagining, the child has a belief and an imagining with the same content. Here it seems reasonable to say that, for this to be the case, the child must also be disposed to conjoin her present imagining that *the cup is empty* with other thoughts whose content does *not* replicate any simultaneous belief of hers: for instance, that *the cup was full a minute ago, before it was upturned.*

I take it that no one will reject disjunct i) of my claim above (that is, no one will deny that one can propositionally imagine that *p* without believing that *p*). One might reject disjunct ii) in two ways. First, one might deny that one can propositionally imagine that *p* whilst believing that *p*. This is the option taken by Gibson (2007: 166–7). He just flat out denies that one can imagine (or 'make-believe') what one simultaneously believes (see also Denham 2000: 202–3). However this looks inconsistent with the plausible thought that there is such a thing as what, in Chapter 4, I called 'counterfactual imagining'; that is, imagining directed towards the goal of acquiring counterfactual beliefs (Williamson 2007). Counterfactual imagining arguably involves imagining something one does not believe (call it 'p') together with other things one *does* believe, in order to further imagine and so come to a belief about what else might or would be the case, were *p* true.

A second way to object to disjunct ii) would be to agree that one can propositionally imagine that *p* whilst believing that *p*, but claim that in doing so, one may conjoin the thought of *p*, or be disposed to, *only with* propositions which she also believes to be true. A problem with this is that it sits awkwardly with a dispositionalist account of belief many would endorse.

That account says that to have a belief is for a thinker to stand in actual or dispositional relations to certain 'outputs'. According to Schwitzgebel (2002), for instance, there are three main kinds of dispositions typically associated with the having of a belief: phenomenal (e.g. dispositions to have certain conscious experiences, such as inwardly uttered thoughts); cognitive (e.g. 'dispositions to draw conclusions entailed by the belief in question or to acquire new desires or habits consonant with the belief' (2002: 252)); and behavioural dispositions.

The possibility we are contemplating is that, in imagining-whilst-believing that *p*, a thinker might conjoin the thought of *p*, or be disposed to, *only with* propositions which she also believes to be true. This would seem to reduce the chances of believing that *p* on its own, *without* also imagining that *p*, being associated with a distinctive set of dispositions in a way which differentiated it from imagining-whilst-believing that *p*. Phenomenally, believing that *p* and imagining-whilst-believing that *p* look pretty similar: as noted earlier, both necessarily involve a disposition to the inwardly uttered thought that *p*. And if it were true that in imagining-whilst-believing that *p*, a thinker was disposed to conjoin the thought that *p* only with her existing belief contents, then it is hard to see how cognitively, there could be a significant difference, in terms of overall dispositions, between this and merely believing that *p*. The same conclusions would look potentially entailed from each. The burden might then be placed upon there being some inevitable difference in desires associated with believing that *p* but not imagining-whilst-believing that *p*; yet this too looks hard to motivate. It would also be hard to see how there could be an inevitable difference in behaviours characteristically dispositionally associated with, respectively, believing that p on its own and imagining-whilst-believing that p. For if, *ex hypothesi*, the contents of one's imaginings were just a subset of the contents of one's beliefs, then identical behaviours in response to the relevant thoughts would look likely.

Perhaps there are ways to avoid this objection; my point is only that if we endorse my original claim, we do not need to find them. For if it is true that a thinker's propositional imagining cannot coincide wholly in content with the content of her beliefs, though it may coincide with some subset of them, we get a straightforward account of the way in which imagining-whilst-believing may differ dispositionally from belief with the same content.

So disjunct ii) looks reasonably secure. We are also now in a position to see more about how a thinker can imagine that p and believe that p simultaneously. If, as Schwitzgebel (2002) plausibly notes, to have a belief is to be in a dispositional state which can be wholly non-occurrent, it follows that a thinker might be occurrently aware of her imagining that p, whilst holding the belief that p non-occurrently. Hence, during a spell of imagining, some of the contents of which are simultaneously believed by the thinker, there need be no phenomenological disruption in consciousness, as some have worried (e.g. Matravers 2014: 38–9).

5.3 Fiction as a Set of Instructions

In sum: F-imagining exhibits the following basic features, I suggest. It is propositional and 'quasi-factual' in the sense I introduced in Chapter 1: it involves thinking that p. It is potentially conjunctive in the sense I have also indicated. And its content can partly overlap with the contents of one's current belief set, but cannot just replicate a subset of the latter. With these points noted, I am now in a position to introduce and defend in more detail an account of fiction.

In my Introduction, I identified, as an alternative to conceptual analysis, the aim of developing an 'explanatory theory': that is, a theory which characterizes a given phenomenon in a way which has explanatory power, relative to some further end. Such a theory should try to accommodate at least some well-established features of ordinary usage, in order to avoid the sense of talking past the original subject. Yet it may also deviate from ordinary usage if the reward is great enough.

A striking example of an explanatory theory of fiction which deviates from ordinary usage, and a highly influential one, is that of Kendall Walton (1990). Walton's central claim is that x is a fiction (or 'representation', which he appears to regard as synonymous with 'fiction') if and only if *x functions as a prop in a game of imagining* (he calls imagining 'make-believe'). This is a claim to which I am sympathetic in spirit, if not in detail. I too will argue that fictions are essentially connected to the production of imagining. I admire the elegant simplicity of a view which characterizes fiction solely in relation to imagining, and not some further conditions too. Indeed, I will seek to emulate this in my own account. However, there are aspects of Walton's view upon which we can improve.

For Walton, *functioning as a prop in a game of imagining* is to be understood as potentially non-intentional. An object may function as a prop in a game of imagining without being intended by any maker to prompt any particular response (1990: 91). For instance, cracks in a rock spelling out 'words' by chance (1990: 86) conceivably may regularly function for some imaginers in this way and so count as fiction. Photographs also count as fictions (1990: 88), as do 'dolls and toy trucks' (1990: 51) and the constellation Ursa Major (1990: 52). This leaves us with a very wide class indeed, a point exacerbated by Walton's reluctance to characterize imagining in any substantial way (1990: 19–21). It is true that he excludes from the class of fictions/representations '*ad hoc* props pressed into service for a single game of make-believe on a single occasion' (1990: 51). Still included, though, are things that are repeatedly used as props for imagining, yet which are not intended to be so used by their makers.

As emphasized by Friend (2008: 151) Walton's view is reasonably understood as an explanatory theory, not conceptual analysis. Hence it is no complaint against it that it delineates a category considerably wider than the folk concept. However, what the theory gains in scope, it loses in ability to make interesting and theoretically useful distinctions. Things can belong to more than one explanatory category at once. Though it might be interesting to discover that dolls, constellations, and novels appear in the same explanatory category, we presumably *also* want, assuming we can find a suitable account of one, some more fine-grained category into which to put novels, along with some poems, short stories, jokes, and thought experiments, but not dolls or constellations.

We can find one by characterizing fiction (but not imaginative props generally) as essentially intentional. Let's call the relevant kind of utterance, whose presence explains why a representation is a fiction, a 'fictive utterance'. With square brackets to disambiguate the scope of the relevant intentions: an author A's utterance x is a fictive utterance if and only if A utters x intending that

i) [the utterance of x should cause some particular F-imagining in her intended audience B]
ii) [B should recognize this intention] and
iii) [B's recognition of this intention should function as part of B's reason to imagine what she does].

The terminology should be familiar. In effect, I have moved from a Gricean intentionalist claim about the nature of fictional content to identifying a fictive utterance in terms of the very same intention. Wherever there is a reflexive intention to produce imagining in a reader or hearer, there is a) fictional content b) a fictive utterance.

How does this help us understand fiction? Quite simply: a fiction is one or more fictive utterances, in this sense, with the added condition that where there is more than one fictive utterance present, the author must also intend that the reader or hearer F-imagine them conjunctively. In other words, fictions typically offer auditors or readers *instructions* to conjunctively imagine certain concrete things. A fiction should be understood as a collection of utterances of a certain kind: utterances intended by their author to produce conjoined F-imagining in readers or hearers, in the reflexive way indicative of communication according to Grice.[1]

Why have I made it an explicit condition upon fictions that, where one or more fictive utterances are present, their author intends that they be conjoined in imagination, rather than simply folding the property of *being conjunctive* into the nature of F-imagining, along with its being quasi-factual and standing at most in a partially overlapping relation to belief-contents? This is because, as discussion in Chapter 1 revealed, F-imagining/propositional imagining generally is not always conjunctive. I might imagine that p and immediately then imagine that q and yet not imagine that p and q. Indeed, as we will see shortly, authors regularly intentionally make use of this feature of imagining.

I suppose it might be protested that on this view, explicit instructions to imagine things, which contain the word 'imagine' as an imperative—such as 'Imagine that there is a boy on a bicycle!'—themselves must count as fictive utterances, and that this is implausible. In fact I think that they do, and that this is a harmless consequence. It follows from my view that explicit instructions like this are of the same basic kind as fictive utterances found in fictions. All, by their nature, convey instructions to imagine things; but in fictions, the instruction is normally suppressed because it is so well understood, via a grasp of the conventions of reading fiction. There could well be a novel whose every sentence began 'Imagine that...'. It wouldn't be incomprehensible as such, though it undoubtedly would be repetitive.

I've just characterized a fiction. What, then, one might wonder, is a fictional *work*? I do not propose to analyse this more complicated notion here in any depth, but it is clear that the two are not equivalent. A fictional work is something usually carefully constructed; a fiction may not be (it might, for instance, be a couple of throwaway lines uttered at a party). A work is usually either written down for posterity, or performed publicly; a fiction may be uttered only once in conversation with a single interlocutor. A work may contain utterances which are not fictive utterances and so not intended to be imagined—for instance, in the preface or in the introduction—while, on my view, as we will see, a fiction may not. Moreover, as we shall also see in §5.8, a fictional work may contain *more than one fiction*; whereas, tautologically, a fiction may not.

Another preliminary is as follows. Though my focus in what follows will be on texts, it is worth pausing for a minute and seeing how the view might extend to images. Grice is not committed to thinking of communication as necessarily involving speech or writing. While 'the normal vehicles of interpersonal communication are words, this is not exclusively the case; gestures, signs and pictorial items sometimes occur'

---

[1] Single works can have multiple authors: as in *Behind the Screen*, a serial detective fiction written in 1930 by Hugh Walpole, Agatha Christie, Dorothy L. Sayers, Anthony Berkeley, E.C. Bentley, and Ronald Knox; or the detective novels of 'Nicci French', the pseudonym of writing partnership Nicci Gerrard and Sean French. In such cases, it still makes sense to say of individual utterances written by particular members of the group, that they intend them to be F-imagined conjointly with other propositions in the fiction.

(Grice 1989: 354). I might construct a picture, or make a gesture, motivated by the relevant complex intention to produce a response in you based on recognition of my intention. Grice talks of 'utterances' being the vehicles of communication, and I follow him in this; however it is important to remember that 'utterances' is to be understood broadly, as potentially including some pictures and some gestures.

On my proposed taxonomy, only those images intended by their makers to produce propositional imagining in their viewers, and moreover, intended to produce such imagining partly as a result of recognizing this intention, count as fictions. Grice himself argues that only some images are communicative of belief, in his reflexive sense. For instance, even if a photograph of O is produced by a person intending to use it to convey beliefs about the appearance of O, the photo does not inevitably communicate this appearance, because the viewer would have reached those beliefs in looking at the photograph, independently of recognizing this intention (1957: 382–3). The photographer's intention cannot count as a reason for the eventual belief. Whether or not this is right about photos and the production of belief, it seems clear that for many photos and for hand-drawn pictures as well, there is no convention mutually understood by artist and audience, such that the audience is intended to *imagine* that certain things are the case, as a result of looking at the picture, nor a fortiori to recognize that she is intended to do so, so that this would count as a reason for her doing so. Such images will not count as fictions, on the view I am proposing.

For one, many images do not seem as a matter of fact to produce imagining in viewers, nor are they intended to produce a response of imagining: rather they produce, and are intended to produce, a response only of belief. Examples include documentary photographs; court illustrations; many still-lifes; maps; *trompe l'œil* paintings; and graphs. These do not count as fictions, on my proposed taxonomy.

Other images produce imagining, but are not intended to produce that imagining.[2] I might stare at a still life of apples, and imagine that I am biting into one of them. This point is consistent with denying that the picture is thereby a fiction. Even if a picture as a matter of fact produces imagining, this does not yet make it a fiction; it has to be intentionally produced, and moreover, the intention that imagining be produced has to function as a reason for the viewer to imagine what she does.

Other images *do* look intended to produce imagining in viewers, but that intention is not intended to count as a *reason* for the imagining in question. Think of photographic images used by advertisers, of people in (allegedly) desirable situations. Families frolic on the beach; a woman smiles whilst eating yogurt; a man runs powerfully through a desert. In each case, members of some particular viewing demographic are intended to imagine themselves in the relevant situation, in order to increase the likelihood of their buying whatever product is for sale. However, the intention that

---

[2] In Stock 2008, I argued that propositional imagining is a component of much seeing-in to pictures, suggesting that to see object O of appearance x in picture P is often, *inter alia*, to propositionally imagine that an O of appearance x exists (Stock 2008: 365).

they imagine this is not supposed to count as a reason for them to imagine what they do. If it did, arguably the adverts would not work so well. Instead they are supposed to imagine themselves in these situations, simply because they are triggered to do so by having the relevant background desire. These images do not count as fictions either, on my view.

Images which do count as fictions, on my view, are those where there is a mutually understood context such that both image-maker and audience recognize the intention in question. Illustrations to children's stories count as fictions on this view. The inclusion of Tenniel's drawings, accompanying the text of *Alice in Wonderland*, clearly indicates that the reader is to imagine e.g. that *the Duchess has a round head*; or that *the Caterpillar has human-looking hands*; and that a reason for her imagining this should be that she recognizes this intention. More generally, depictions of what are manifestly fictional entities—unicorns, Sherlock Holmes, Mickey Mouse—count as fictions for the same reason. So might mythological paintings, or Renaissance paintings of ancient religious figures in contemporary dress, since it seems that the viewer is intended by the painters to *imagine* that the figures have a particular appearance, rather than believe it; though investigation of the context of production of the images would also be necessary to confirm this.

We are now in a position to revisit our discussion of Walton, and compare findings. On my view, it looks as if there are three explanatorily interesting categories, where Walton would apparently explicitly recognize only one. In the first, Category 1, there are, amongst other things, novels, short stories, many films, most or all pictures, dolls, toy-trucks, cracks in rocks that luckily spell out 'words', and the constellation Ursa Major. This is the category of things which regularly function as imaginative props, no matter whether they are intended to or not by their makers, or whether indeed they have any makers. If Walton wants to insist on calling Category 1 'fictions', this in itself is not problematic; what is more problematic is that he is left with no interesting account of two further categories. In the second category (Category 2) there are, amongst other things, novels, short stories, some photos, pictures and films, dolls and toy-trucks, but not cracks in rocks or constellations. This is the category of things that are deliberately made with the intention that they produce imaginings in readers/viewers/users, whether or not that intention is reflexive in the Gricean fashion. And in the third category (Category 3) there are, amongst other things, novels, short stories, some pictures and some films, but not dolls, toys, cracks in rocks, or constellations. This is the category of things that are deliberately made with the intention that they produce (conjoined) imaginings in readers/viewers/users, and moreover where that intention is reflexive in the Gricean fashion. This is the category that I propose we identify as 'fictions'.

Walton explicitly considers whether fictions must be communicative in a Gricean sense, and rejects the thought:

One may well read a story or contemplate a picture [which is a fiction] without wondering which fictional truths the author or artist meant to generate. Photographers, especially, can easily be unaware of fictional truths generated by their works. Authors and other artists may be surprised at where extrapolation from the fictional truths they intentionally generated leads. (Walton 1990: 88)

Yet these points can be accommodated unproblematically. On the account I have just offered, most photographs are not fictions and do not 'generate fictional truths' at all, though they may be used as imaginative prompts or props. And I have already argued extensively for extreme intentionalism, according to which the fictional truths generated by a fiction coincide with the truths the author intended to generate. This is not to deny that authors may be unaware of what fictional truths are in their words and hence surprised at their discovery, for in Chapter 1 I explicitly acknowledged that authorial intentions might be hidden from their owner. However, this is compatible with such truths being intentionally generated, and fictions being essentially communicative.

5.4 Fiction, Belief, and Truth

I have argued that my account of fiction is preferable to that of Walton. In this section I will argue that it is also preferable to several other prominent accounts. To this end, one of the claims made earlier about F-imagining will be particularly important: the claim that the content of one's propositional imagining can partly overlap with the contents of one's simultaneous belief set, but cannot just replicate a subset of the latter.

I am claiming that being composed of utterances reflexively intended to produce conjoined F-imagining is what explains a thing's counting as a fiction. Several prominent theorists of fiction would agree with me. However, such theorists tend to continue: whatever the relevant explanatory unit is, the presence of which is responsible for something's counting as a fiction, it cannot be characterized *simply* in terms of a reflexive instruction to imagine things. Accordingly, they introduce a second condition upon fictive utterance: that it should stand in some negative relation to truth or truth-telling, or something similar.

A case in point is Currie (1990). Like me, Currie uses the term 'fictive utterance' to refer, necessarily and sufficiently, to an utterance made with a reflexive intention to produce imagining in the relevant Gricean sense. Unlike me, though, he thinks that the 'fiction-making' explanatory unit is not simply a fictive utterance in this sense, but a *fictional statement*, where this is characterized as a fictive utterance *which is false or at most, accidentally true, but certainly not non-accidentally true.*(1990: 46). That is, it must not be the case that, had different events occurred, the content of the utterance would have been correspondingly different; nor that, if the same events had occurred in otherwise different circumstances, the utterance would still have described them (1990: 47). Call this the 'non-non-accidentality condition', or NNA for short.

To avoid confusion over Currie's and my divergent uses of the term 'fictive utterance' and his introduction of the term 'fictional statement', from now on let's simply call whatever the explanatory unit in a fiction is which is responsible for it counting as a fiction, an 'F-unit.' Currie agrees with me that, necessarily, an F-unit is intended by its author to produce imagining in the reader, and moreover is intended to produce this imagining as a result of the reader's recognizing the former intention (that is, the intention is reflexive). However, unlike me, he adds NNA as a further condition upon F-units. Taken together, these two conditions are supposed to be sufficient.

Yet the addition of NNA is rather unfortunate. For as we have seen in Chapters 3 and 4 with the examples of testimony, fictions often contain propositions that are also non-accidentally true, in violation of NNA. Here are some new examples:

When one man has been under very remarkable obligations to another, with whom he subsequently quarrels, a common sense of decency, as it were, makes of the former a much severer enemy than a mere stranger would be. To account for your own hard-heartedness and ingratitude in such a case, you are bound to prove the other party's crime.   (Thackeray 2003: 176)

The city of Singapore was not built up gradually, the way most cities are, by a natural deposit of commerce on the banks of some river or at a traditional confluence of trade routes. It was simply invented one morning early in the nineteenth century by a man looking at a map.

(Farrell 1992: 3)

Let's assume that each of these expresses or implies a proposition which is non-accidentally true. In each case, let's say, the author knowingly observes some fact about the world, and then describes it, with a view to inducing belief in the readership. It seems that we should say that such sentences simultaneously serve two intentions on the part of their author. On the one hand, they are intended to produce imagining in the reader. On the other, they are also intended to produce belief. I have already explained how it is possible to both believe and imagine that p simultaneously. It is also possible to have different, non-competing intentions fulfilled by the same utterance. An utterance in code can be intended to convey two distinct true claims, for instance. Likewise, in principle there seems no impediment to a single utterance's being seriously intended both to say something true and to be recognized as such, *and* seriously intended to be imagined and recognized as such, simultaneously, assuming that the right sort of context can be generated such that the relevant intentions are communicable by the form and context of the utterance. Indeed, I have depended on this possibility in my discussion of testimony in Chapters 3 and 4.

Currie acknowledges this possibility. The consequence swiftly follows that, on his view, not every utterance in a fiction is an F-unit. He admits that a text might well be a 'patchwork' of F-units (fictional statements, in his terminology) and utterances which are not F-units (1990: 49). This is an odd and rather inelegant consequence of the view. Recall that an F-unit is supposed to be whatever explanatory unit it is, the presence of which determines whether something is a fiction. Now it turns out that only some but not other utterances within a fiction are F-units. This leaves an awkward question unanswered: what proportion of F-units is needed to determine that a representation counts as a fiction? (Friend 2012: 186). Currie dismisses the question (1990: 49), but one might well prefer a view where it did not get raised in the first place.

Rival accounts face essentially the same problem. D. Davies (2007) effectively agrees with Currie and with me that necessarily, F-units are reflexively intended to produce imagining³. However, like Currie and unlike me, he thinks that a further condition operates on the F-unit: not NNA, this time, but an 'infidelity condition' (my italics):

> ...what is also crucial is that, whether or not the narrated events are true or known to be true, their having occurred is not relevant to what the author is trying to achieve in writing the narrative. *In other words, what [utterer] U wishes to achieve in having readers make-believe that p does not depend upon p's being true. That proposition's being true is not the reason for its inclusion in the narrative.* (2007: 46)

On this view, the author of an F-unit may desire to be 'faithful' to real-life events, and so present non-accidentally true utterances, but only if some goal other than telling the truth is her main reason for doing so. For instance, an author might non-accidentally tell the truth in order to achieve some thematic or aesthetic end (2007: 47).

However, this too entails that certain passages in fictions do not count as composed of F-units. Consider the case of morally didactic works of fiction. Here it seems reasonable to think that many true propositions are expressed or implied *mainly* in order to tell the truth and convey belief. For instance, in Beecher Stowe's anti-slavery work *Uncle Tom's Cabin* it is surely reasonable to think Beecher Stowe's main reason for the inclusion of the following passage was to tell the truth, rather than this being instrumental to any aesthetic or thematic end:

> Scenes of blood and cruelty are shocking to our ear and heart. What man has nerve to do, man has not nerve to hear. What brother-man and brother-Christian must suffer, can't be told us, even in our secret chamber, it so harrows up the soul! And yet, oh my country! these things are done under the shadow of thy laws! O, Christ! thy church sees them, almost in silence! (Beecher Stowe 2014: 346)

So on Davies's view too, effectively, fictions come out potentially as patchworks of F-units and utterances which are not F-units. Meanwhile, Lamarque and Olsen (1994) also apparently have a view according to which fictions are patchworked. Like all discussed so far in this section, they think that necessarily F-units are reflexively intended to produce imagining (1994: 45).⁴ But they propose a further condition: that in such utterance, there must be

> a disengagement from certain standard speech act commitments, blocking inferences from a fictive utterance back to the speaker or writer, in particular inferences about beliefs. (1994: 46)

That is, the reader should not infer that the author believes what she writes. Nor should she herself believe the content of F-units upon reading them, as she might do, were the sentences asserted normally. The trouble is that both points looks false with respect to

---

³ Davies has since changed his view: see his 2015.
⁴ They add that the reader is intended to imagine that she is being told things; I would deny that this is an inevitable part of the instruction.

the passages from Thackeray, Farrell, and Beecher Stowe quoted just now. At a different point they write:

> Fictional content is such that how things are (in the fiction) is determined by how they are described to be in a fictive utterance. This points up the contrast with truth because how things are (in the world) is not determined by any kind of utterance.   (1994: 51)

Again, this looks false of the passages quoted. How things are in the fiction, in these passages, is at least partly determined by how things are in the world.

In an attempt to avoid this worry, perhaps Lamarque and Olsen acknowledge that there are passages in fiction which are 'factual', but apparently deny that they are genuinely asserted. Rather, they say, they are present in a fiction for non-truth related reasons. Talking of the famous opening lines of *Anna Karenina*, they write

> The literary function of the sentence has little or nothing to do with trying to induce a belief in a reader about happy and unhappy families; it has far more to do with an initial characterization of a theme which gives focus and interest to the fictional content.   (1994: 66)

If this was true, then qua works of literature, fictions would not be patchworked after all: no utterance would be introduced in order to induce belief about some fact of the world, even if, as it happens, it introduced a fact. But there seems no good reason to exclude from literature, as such, an intention to tell the truth or convey true belief. Lamarque and Olsen take seriously an author's intending to produce imagining in her audience; it is therefore strange on their part to ignore or deny the additional possibility of an author intending even in a 'literary' fiction to simultaneously communicate beliefs in her readership, despite many clear cases of it.

Meanwhile, another view denies the intention to produce imagining even as a *necessary* condition of fiction. Harry Deutsch effectively characterizes an F-unit not in terms of an intention that imagining be produced at all, but rather in terms of being 'a token of a type that was made up out of whole cloth' (2000: 167). An utterance 'made up out of whole cloth' is one not intended to track or reflect what is actually true. Lies, intended only to be believed by hearers or readers, but not imagined at all, can be fictions, in his sense. For instance, he explicitly counts as fictional the fraudulent reports for the *Washington Post* of Janet Cooke, who made up certain aspects of her story about a child heroin addict and presented them as true and to be believed (2000: 170). Yet Deutsch acknowledges a fiction may contain 'generous amounts of the fabric of fact woven in as well' (2000: 167). So here too, apparently, we have a view according to which fictions are patchworks of F-units and utterances which are not F-units.

All of these theories of fiction end up with a position according to which only some utterances in a fiction are F-units, while F-units are supposed to be the sort of unit the presence of which explains why a thing counts as a fiction. Why is this undesirable? To repeat, it leaves an explanatory gap. We are left in doubt to what extent, or in what number, F-units must be present for fiction to be present. This is not an advantage, when the goal is explanation.

It is also notable that none of these theories coincides particularly well with ordinary usage. Deutsch is right that the folk might apply 'fiction' to lies, but equally, it seems, they might apply 'fiction' to utterances which are not (wholly) made up, as long as they were also intended to be imagined; something he would presumably downplay. Meanwhile, Currie thinks we need to introduce NNA as a condition upon an F-unit on the basis of four thought experiments. In two, an author deliberately reproduces facts but intends them be imagined. In two others, an author produces a story, intending it to be imagined, where unwittingly the story reflects facts—in one because he does not know his source is reliable, and in another because he has repressed memories of the events he describes (1990: 42–3). In all cases, Currie thinks, we might accept that such utterances are 'products of fictive intent' without counting as fictions; his non-non-accidentality condition is supposed to explain this (1990: 46). Lamarque and Olsen (1994: 50–2) and D. Davies (2007: 44–8) each discuss the same thought experiments and reach different conclusions, presumably based on their prior theories, about whether each counts as involving fiction or not. Yet no compelling pre-theoretical intuitions emerge here about whether fiction is or is not present in such cases. The cases are too marginal and artificial.

In any case, my aim is not conceptual analysis but to characterize a category of explanatory value. It may be, for instance, that in ordinary usage, lies are often counted as 'fictions'; however, my aim is not automatically to attempt to accommodate ordinary usage, assuming one could. Even so, there is still an explanatorily important distinction to be made between, on the one hand, true or false utterances intended only to be believed, and on the other, true or false utterances intended to be imagined, whether or not they are also intended to be believed. The latter is the category I am designating as fiction. (If we called the former 'type-1 fiction' and the latter 'type-2 fiction' I wouldn't mind, as long as the distinction was still recognized.)

To this end, a better way to proceed, I think, is to hold the line: F-units are necessarily and sufficiently, reflexively intended to be (where relevant, conjointly) imagined. On my view, then, there is no further condition to add, negatively relating individual F-units to truth, truth-telling, or the inducing of belief. As long as they are also reflexively intended to produce conjoined imagining, individual F-units can be non-accidentally true, introduced by an author as true and to be believed for that reason, and can be reasonably taken to reflect an author's beliefs. This means that all utterances within a fiction standardly count as F-units. There need be no 'patchwork'.

This does not, as might be feared, leave us without resources to posit a negative relation between fiction and belief. Earlier we noted the following as a feature of propositional imagining: the content of a thinker's propositional imaginings can partly overlap with the contents of her current belief set, but cannot just replicate a subset of the latter. This means effectively that *some* of the F-units which compose a fiction may be believed by the reader, but not *all can be, simultaneously*. A fiction, *taken as a whole*, cannot be believed by the reader. Were a reader, *per impossibile*, to imagine and believe all the propositions of a fiction simultaneously, then effectively the content of what she imagined with respect to this text would simply be a subset of the content of what she believed. But this cannot be the case. This, then, is a better account of how fiction sits at an oblique angle to the truth, as it were. Some of its utterances can be believed by a reader, but not all of them can at once. Yet we do not need to posit this as an *additional* feature of fiction, explicitly. It simply follows from the nature of propositional imagining, in conjunction with the thought that necessarily, fictive utterances are to be imagined.

Some may wonder whether, on my view, a fiction might still be intended by its author to be both wholly imagined and believed, even given the impossibility of a reader's complying. I think that in some strange and highly artificial circumstance, it might.[5] After all, there is no reason to think an author must have access to the arguments I have mounted against the possibility of imagining only what one believes. She might believe in good faith that this is possible, and so have the relevant intention. Even so, the important point to retain is that the reader could not possibly comply.

To repeat: a fiction is, necessarily and sufficiently, a collection of propositions reflexively intended by their author to be conjoined in imagination. These propositions are conveyed via fictive utterances. Were my claim devoid of any detail about what is supposed to be involved in the imagining in question, then it would be unattractive. For, 'imagining' being such a widely and loosely used term, it would then be hostage to those understandings of imagination that falsified it. As has been pointed out by Friend (2008: 154–8) if, for instance, by 'imagining' was meant 'merely having mental images', or 'the mere making of inferences about implicit content from the explicit content of a text', the claim would be easily falsified, since many sets of utterances that have nothing to do with fiction are clearly intended to prompt such activities. Yet such worries should be at least partly assuaged by the account offered so far, in which I have specified, in more detail than is usually given, what is involved. For the same reason, I do not think my view is subject to the objection, made to it by Manuel Garcia-Carpintero, that:

> we embark upon imaginative projects regarding contents which we have no reason to disbelieve; reading biographies or histories...contemplating in imaginative detail a course of action...or recreating in our imagination the landscapes we walked across. (2013: 343)

Of course we talk as if imagination is involved in each of these cases; but even so, this is clearly not the sort of 'imagining' I have in mind.

5.5 Non-fiction

What then is a non-fiction? A worry is expressed by Friend in response to my view: many non-fictional works include instructions to imagine things (2011: 172; see also

---

[5] In Stock (2011) I was not clear about this.

Matravers 2014: 42). Friend cites 'irony, hyperbole, questions, jokes, and so on, as well as quotations of sources who are not taken as reliable', and descriptions of possible future states of affairs or 'alternative pasts' (*ibid.*). She writes:

> If it is the case that a work containing at least one connected component we are not supposed to believe is *ipso facto* constituted entirely, or nearly entirely, by fictive utterances, then presumably it is a work of fiction. But many paradigm works of non-fiction contain at least one such component. Consider an academic history of World War Two in which the author argues that had Hitler been killed in the assassination attempt of 1944, his generals would have negotiated peace. Particularly if this counterfactual possibility is central to the argument of the book, understanding the text will require readers to connect most or all of the rest of what they read—which, let us assume, consists entirely of claims to be believed—to at least one thought they don't believe, namely that Hitler was assassinated in 1944. It will therefore turn out that most or all of the utterances within the text are fictive utterances... and that the text is fiction.   (Friend 2011: 171)

Taking this example as representative of the supposed problem: let's agree that a non-fictional work of history may instruct readers to imagine something they do not also believe, namely that *Hitler was killed in 1944*. This counts as a fictive utterance on my view. Let's also agree that this non-fictional work may instruct its readers to conjoin their imagining that *Hitler was killed in 1944* with other factual propositions in the text, intended to be believed but also, in this context, to be imagined, in order to see what *would have been* the case, had Hitler been killed as described. These factual propositions might include that *the Holocaust has occurred*, that *Stalin has ambitions for political influence in Eastern Europe*, and that *there is a fuel shortage in Germany in 1944*. At the behest of the author, the reader is supposed to conjoin in imagination these propositions with the proposition *Hitler was killed in 1944*, and presumably draw a view about what else would have been the case. (I do find it unlikely that in such a case, as Friend suggests, '*most or all* of the utterances with the text' would be relevantly conjoined with the original imagining, but let that pass.) Let's agree, then, that the non-fictional work *contains a fiction*: a collection of propositions, reflexively intended by the author to be imagined together, though some of them are also to be believed. This, in fact, seems *exactly what we should say*. Non-fictional works can *contain fictions*. (In another familiar case, a non-fictional philosophy work can *contain a fiction* in the form of a thought experiment: a collection of propositions, where what they describe is intended by the author to be conjointly imagined as occurring with respect to the same scenario.)

However, the non-fictional work as described by Friend also instructs the reader to believe many things that she is *not* also intended to simultaneously imagine. For one, it instructs the reader to believe the counterfactual that *had Hitler been killed in 1944, his generals would have negotiated peace*. This conversationally implies a further belief for the reader, which in any case the book presumably otherwise adequately conveys, given its historical brief: namely *Hitler was not in fact killed in 1944*. This is not something she is supposed to imagine. So such a text may *contain* a fiction, but it does not follow that it *is a* fiction. It is not. *As a whole*, it is not a collection of propositions whose content is intended to be imagined as occurring with respect to the same scenario.

The same treatment can be given of cases of (alleged) non-fictions that include invented elements. Friend offers us the examples of the histories of Tacitus, and Edmund Morris's *Dutch*, the 'biography' of Ronald Reagan that contains invented elements such as a 'witness' narrator with no basis in actuality. She treats these as non-fiction, unambiguously, apparently on the basis of claims about ordinary usage. In fact, ordinary usage looks confused about such peripheral cases; even less pressure, then, upon an explanatory theory to fit with relatively tendentious interpretations of them. But in any case, assuming the reader was not/is not intended to believe these invented elements, but only imagine them, they look like passages of fiction in a non-fiction, and can be treated as above. Alternatively, if the reader was supposed to believe them but not imagine them, then they look like deceptive but still non-fictional passages. *Pace* Deutsch, biographies and histories can lie without ceasing to be non-fictional, on my view.

What then is a non-fiction? It is, minimally, any set of utterances *not* wholly reflexively intended by their utterer to be imagined; though some subset of them might be. Beyond this, different conditions will be operative on different kinds of non-fiction. Obviously, this is massively broad; but something as minimal as this is presumably all we can reasonably hope as a general characterization. The substantive class of non-fiction looks huge, comprising work directed at a variety of ends and with various functions. It includes journalism, travel writing, philosophy, history, geography, and literary studies; as well as, perhaps, mathematics and science writing. It would be strange to attempt to offer a single, non-minimal, substantive characterization of non-fiction to cover all of this.

It follows from my view that non-fictional works can be 'patchworks' of fictive utterances and utterances which are not fictive utterances. Is this a problem, given that I denied the desirability of thinking of fiction as a patchwork? No. *It fits the case.* Fictions that instruct the reader to believe that p also instruct her to imagine that p, so that there need be no discontinuity in kind of utterance here: all are to be imagined.[6] Non-fictional works that instruct the reader to imagine that p, as in the case offered by Friend, do not *also* instruct her to believe that p (or, at least, do not instruct her to believe all of what she imagines). There *is* discontinuity in kinds of utterance here. Hence the appropriateness of positing a 'patchwork' of different kinds of utterance, requiring different treatment.

---

[6] Arguably an exception is a work such as *War and Peace*, which contains disquisitions on history, humanity and war, in a way which arguably indicates that such passages are not to be conjoined imaginatively with others in the text and are only to be believed (or at least considered for belief) and not imagined. If this is right, then this fiction contains a non-fiction, and as such is a patchwork. But this is a rare case. I'm grateful to Robert Stecker for pressing me on this.

5.6 Fictions as Normatively Constituted

A different approach to the nature of fiction is argued for by Manuel Garcia-Carpintero (2013). He denies that fictions (or fictive utterances, or 'F-units', as I have designated them) need to be accompanied by the sort of reflexive intention that I say is necessary to them. Instead, whilst agreeing that to make a fiction is to engage in a certain sort of speech act, he takes a view of speech acts according to which they generally are constituted, not in terms of psychological intentions to induce certain mental events in others, but instead by being subject to certain social norms. For instance, he suggests, the speech act of assertion in ordinary conversation is constituted by being subject to a norm along the following lines (opinions vary): either that it should be true, or that it should be reasonable to believe it, or that the speaker should know it.[7] The claim is that an utterance is not an assertion if it is not subject to one of these norms. The utterer of an assertion need not reflexively intend hearers to believe anything as a result, à la Grice, so long as they are committed to what they say being true/know it is true. Assertions can be criticized if they fail to meet the relevant standards.

Relatedly, Garcia-Carpintero proposes that a fiction is constituted as such by being subject to one of the following norms:

(FM_N) For one to fiction-make p is correct if and only if one's audience must imagine p, on the assumption that they have the relevant desires and dispositions. (2013: 350)

(FM'_N) For one to fiction-make p is correct if and only if p is worth imagining for one's audience, on the assumption that they have the relevant desires and dispositions. (2013: 351)

That is, roughly, a fiction is constituted as such by being subject to the norm that it should provide readers with reasons to imaginatively engage with it (i.e. it is the provision of interesting imaginings, relative to the reader's desires and dispositions). Whatever is subject to this norm is a fiction, and all fictions are subject to this norm.

Garcia-Carpintero notes that Gricean-style accounts of fiction like mine, which characterize it in terms of reflexive intentions that readers imagine things, can also readily admit that fictions are subject to norms; only they will treat those norms as 'regulative' rather than as constitutive. My own account has confirmed that fiction can be written for a variety of purposes, and to satisfy a range of reader interests, and of course it will be perfectly appropriate to criticize a fiction and its author for not in fact achieving the particular goal it was aimed at. It is likely that if an author of a given fiction intends, for instance, to produce a text which prompts imagining for the purposes of developing counterfactual beliefs; or which prompts imagining for the purpose of thrilling entertainment, she will accept that the text will be deficient if it does not achieve this aim.

What determines, on the view now being considered, whether an utterance is subject to the allegedly constitutive fiction-making norm in question? Garcia-Carpintero

---

[7] Garcia-Carpintero surveys the available options (2013: 344).

says that this happens partly due to an author's 'intention of conforming the product of what [she]…does to a norm' (2013: 351). So in relation to my own preferred account, we can now ask: are there any cases of an F-unit/fiction where it seems that the author does *not* have a reflexive intention that readers imagine certain things, but *does* have the intention that what she produces be subject to the norms $(FM_N)/(FM'_N)$? Garcia-Carpintero thinks so, citing cases where fictional content allegedly is not derived from authorial intention per se, though its presence is 'consistent' with what has been intended (2013: 353–4).

The example he uses is from a film (*Last Year at Marienbad*), a medium already explicitly excluded from the remit of this book, not least owing to the problems with saying that any one person intended its content. Meanwhile, in the case of texts, I have argued at length that there are in fact no cases of fictional content that do not derive from authorial intention. Recall also that my aim is to provide an explanatory theory, and not to do ordinary language philosophy about 'fiction' or 'fictional content': I therefore have renounced any pretensions to covering all case-by-case intuitions in these areas. No theory can realistically hope to fit with all such intuitions. (Indeed, Garcia-Carpintero's theory also clashes with some intuitions: for it seems to entail that children who write stories unaware of the norms governing the practice of fiction-making cannot be making fiction, which will strike many as intuitively implausible.)

In any case I do not think the objection works, even if we were to allow unintended content. Let's assume that (contrary to what I have been arguing) a given set of F-units S, with explicit and thoroughly intended content p, can also have unintended fictional content q. Presumably the background thought of Garcia-Carpintero here, and why he thinks this sort of case counts against a Gricean account of fiction, is that where S has unintended content that q, then S, qua bearer of content q, cannot count as fictional on the basis of any authorial intention that readers imagine that q (for there is no such intention: fictional content 'q' is unintentionally present). That seems right. But even so, for all that has been said there is nothing to stop S counting as fictional on the basis of the accompanying authorial intention, explicitly recognized, that readers imagine that p. What makes S fictional is still a reflexive intention: namely, that readers imagine that p. Hence there is no need yet to invoke the norms $(FM_N)/(FM'_N)$ to explain S's fictional status instead.

Garcia-Carpintero is at least partly motivated to reject a Gricean theory of fiction because of worries about Gricean intentionalism in the field of ordinary conversation: that, for instance, 'the clerk in an information booth uttering "The flight will depart on time"' may lack *any* of the sort of relevant reflexive intentions to have hearers believe things which Griceans would posit as essential (2013: 345). This may be true, but the point does not extend to fictional passages, where even if, as in the example just discussed, an author lacks a *given* intention that readers imagine certain things, she does not in that case (I have argued) lack any intention that readers imagine things at all.

Moreover, had the objection to my account worked, a parallel objection could have been levelled at Garcia-Carpintero's own account. The objection would have gone (with square brackets to disambiguate the content of the intention): where a set of F-units ('S') has unintended fictional content that q, then S cannot count as fictional on the basis of any authorial intention that [S, qua bearer of content q, be subject to norms such as $(FM_N)/(FM'_N)$] (for there is no such intention: after all, fictional content q is unintentionally present). In fact this objection would not work, for reasons analogous to those previously given: for in fact there still would be nothing to stop S counting as fictional on the basis of the authorial intention that S, *qua bearer of content p*, be subject to the relevant norms.

There is perhaps more to say here: but in the meantime, I think we have not yet seen good reason to abandon my account.

5.7 Against Imagining

I turn now to two further accounts that deny that a Gricean-style reflexive intention to imagine something is necessary for an F-unit, and so for fiction.

A. Friend

Stacie Friend agrees that instructing readers to imagine certain things is *often* what fictions do, but denies they do this *necessarily*.[8] Instead, her positive view is as follows. Both fiction and non-fiction are 'super-genres', into which other genres fall (2012: 181). Into the super-genre of fiction, for instance, fall sub-genres such as 'chick-lit', pulp fiction, realism, and modernism. Generally, a genre, super-genres included, is a way of classifying works, where this classification generates 'expectations about the features of a work, and thereby determines appropriate standards of evaluation' (*ibid.*).

To understand this, we have to go back to Walton on categories of art (1970); for a genre is a category of art, and Friend is heavily influenced by Walton in this matter. According to Walton, objects within a category of art can have 'standard' features (features which are normal for members of the category), 'contra-standard' features (features which tempt one to disqualify their possessor from membership of the category), and 'variable' features (features which can vary happily amongst members of the category, and which are not contra-standard). Standard, variable, and contra-standard features of a category are all *contingent*: no particular standard (or contra-standard) feature must be present (or absent) for membership of the category to obtain.

These features also generate appreciative expectations for members of that category in various ways. Variable and contra-standard features are usually what are focused

---

[8] Some of this material is drawn from, or is a modification of, Stock (2016a), which also contains some discussion of further objections by Friend to any account of fiction as necessarily involving instructions to imagine.

upon in appreciation, directly. What is standard for a category is often ignored in appreciation of a work. For instance, in one of Walton's examples (1970: 345), grasping what are standard features of the genre of *Roman busts* allows viewers to appreciate members in a way not hampered by horror at the severance of the depicted subject's arms and lower torso. That is, viewers ignore this standard feature, and do not interpret the bust as a 'perpetually motionless man...severed at the chest' (*ibid.*). So standard features of a category are usually taken for granted as present, and rarely thought of as contributory to value. In contrast, the absence of standard features and/or the presence of contra-standard features are experienced as unsettling.

Along these lines, Friend argues that the presence of standard features of fiction or non-fiction, qua genres, is usually irrelevant to appreciating a work in that genre; but that the absence of standard features and/or the presence of contra-standard ones is experienced as unsettling and may give rise to criticism. For instance, memoirs are standardly expected to be true, and not praised for meeting this expectation, but criticized if false (2012: 179–80; 190). Fictions are standardly invented, or mostly invented, and so are not treated as revelatory, even when based on fact (2012: 179–80; 191). Standardly, fictions are standardly taken to refer to non-existents (2012: 198). Non-fiction, in contrast, is not expected to include invented elements and where it does (e.g. Edmund Morris's *Dutch*), this is treated as controversial (2012: 187). Certain *formal* features are also standard and contra-standard for the genres of fiction and non-fiction respectively: for instance, Nabokov's *Pale Fire* has a form contra-standard for narrative fiction (2012: 190), whilst Capote's *In Cold Blood* uses novelistic techniques contra-standard for non-fiction (2012: 191). Moreover, if we read a given passage as fiction we will expect the presence of formal features such as free indirect discourse and 'inner' reporting of a character's mental life to be standard; if we read it as non-fiction, these will be contra-standard (2012: 197). What counts as standard for fiction can develop over time: sometimes due to the inclusion, within particular works, of (at the time) contra-standard elements, such as digressive narrative (2012: 192) and unreliability (2012: 191), but sometimes due to other factors too (2012: 192–3).

Noting all this does not yet give us the conditions under which a work counts as a fiction—as belonging to that (alleged) genre. According to Friend, there are no substantive necessary and sufficient conditions for a fiction. Rather, we are told that an author must intend to write in a tradition that is publicly recognized as fiction at the time; or at least, is recognized by some recipients as writing in such a tradition (2012: 193–4); and that the work must satisfy some unspecified number of conditions standard for the genre (2012: 188). That is, Friend identifies the changing features of the ordinary concept of *fiction* across time as features of a stable, permanent social practice: one whose varying spatio-temporal conditions are a permanent feature.

This looks like an 'institutional' account of fiction: roughly, what counts as fiction is what the dominant institutions call fiction.[9] Friend explicitly distances her account

---

[9] A famous institutional theory of art is offered by Dickie (1983).

from an institutional reading, arguing that '[t]he role of standard and contra-standard features in genre classification' entails that hers is not an institutional theory; in an institutional theory of art, for instance, 'art status is conferred by relevant members of the "artworld" with no internal constraint on the type of thing that qualifies' (2012: 193, fn.18). This attempted distancing is unconvincing: in an institutional theory of art, there needs to be room for time-indexed, non-permanent but publicly recognized features that guide classification as art. That is, at a given time and in a given cultural context, there must be features which count as standard for art, as well as those which count as contra-standard and 'variable'. To deny this would be to suggest that art classification is wholly arbitrary and individualistic, something no institutional theorist could plausibly assert, so long as they thought of *art* as a coherent practice.

Friend isn't engaged in conceptual analysis; like me, she seems to be offering an explanatory theory of fiction. If so, one possible issue here is that, perhaps like institutional theories generally, her account provides no informative non-circular substantive conditions, under which a fiction counts as such. In terms of substantive features of fiction, it offers only standard non-necessary ones, and moreover, ones explicitly time-indexed to the present context and which may change. Now, Friend cannot simply rejoinder that this is because there are not any necessary and sufficient conditions according to the folk concept *fiction*. That this is so is compatible with an explanatory theory positing some, since an explanatory theory aims to clean up and in some cases redraw categories, not simply to uncover them. Moreover, an explanatory theory that does not posit any such conditions, or offers only circular ones, risks being rather unsatisfying, relative to what was originally wanted.

Despite this, Friend would, I think, protest that her theory still does valuable explanatory work. Namely, it accounts for the sort of appreciative expectations about fiction and non-fiction that I described earlier. But really, what kind of explanation is being offered here? The general form of the putative explanation seems to be this. If fiction and non-fiction were super-genres, then this would explain why some features are standard and contra-standard for fiction/non-fiction, respectively. And if some features were standard and contra-standard for fiction/non-fiction, respectively, then this would explain certain aspects of our appreciative practice of each, e.g. the fact that if *x* is a feature standard for fiction, readers do not notice *x* when it is present in fiction, but are disturbed by its presence in non-fiction.

There are two critical points to note here. The first is that the proposed explanation is not very deep. As Friend acknowledges, the features standard for fiction change over time and are not, on her view, what make a fiction a fiction. Rather what makes something a fiction is (roughly) that it is intended to be part of a particular social practice. So it is not that a fiction being a super-genre explains why *some features in particular* are standard for fiction, or why *some appreciative practice in particular exists*. For instance, fiction counting as a super-genre, as Friend claims, cannot explain why *standardly, fictions include invented content*. Rather fiction counting as a super-genre can 'explain' only why *some features, whatever they are*, are standard for fiction; namely, because genres, by definition, have standard features. Because fiction counting as a super-genre cannot explain why in particular it is that fictions include invented content, it also cannot explain why, in particular, the reader tends to expect fictions to include invented content, and non-fictions not to, so that they are confused or disturbed when these expectations are not realized. For instance, on Friend's view, we are entitled to criticize a contemporary historian who includes a lot of invented content only because he goes against what is currently contingently considered to be a standard feature, and for no deeper reason. Had he lived in Roman times, where this was not a standard feature, we would not have been entitled to criticize him.[10] This is rather anti-climactic, especially given the emphasis Friend places on her account's being able to explain features of our evaluative practice. In fact, on Friend's view, any concrete explanation of why some feature in particular is standard for fiction will apparently have to be a historical one. She discusses a few historical influences on what has counted as standard and contra-standard in fiction and non-fiction, though only in passing (2012: 192).

The second point to make is that, leaving aside her objections to my view, Friend's positive view is not obviously a rival to mine, except in a couple of details. My view proposes a certain condition as necessary and sufficient for fictive utterance—being a set of reflexive instructions to conjointly imagine. Saying this is perfectly compatible with allowing that certain contingent features are standard for fiction generally; that these may change over time, and that they have the appreciative consequence Friend outlines. We *should* allow this. Indeed, if this is all that is essentially meant by fiction counting as a super-genre, I admit this too. The main disagreement between Friend and me here seems to be about one feature in particular—namely, whether or not intentionally inviting imagining from hearers or readers, via one's utterances, is a defining characteristic of fiction, or merely a contingent and possibly impermanent standard feature.

I am arguing that there are many explanatory benefits to treating this feature as the former, not the latter. Friend apparently disagrees. But for instance, both she and I can still agree that *standardly, fiction possesses invented content*. In fact, arguably my view can explain why this is so, at least as satisfyingly as her view can, and perhaps more so. As I have argued, she seems to be saying that *standardly, fiction possesses invented content* either i) because *fiction is a genre and has standard features, generally*; or ii) because of some local historical explanation, not explicitly given by her. i) is relatively unsatisfying, relative to what we want; because of the lack of detail offered, so is ii). On my view, the relevant explanation is more detailed: that i) (roughly) necessarily and sufficiently, fictions instruct readers to imagine things and ii) normally anyway, to instruct a reader to imagine that *p* is to instruct her to imagine something (directly or indirectly) which she does not simultaneously

---

[10] I am grateful to Manuel Garcia-Carpintero for illuminating discussion of this point.

believe. *Often, one way of achieving this is by including manifestly invented content in one's work.*

To sum up: as a theory with explanatory ambition, Friend's theory faces difficulties on at least two counts. First, perhaps frustratingly, it does not tell us in a non-circular way under what circumstances, exactly, something counts as a fiction or as a non-fiction. Secondly, it does not offer a particularly deep explanation of features of our appreciative practice, as it pretends to. For these reasons, I continue to think that my own view is preferable, especially since my view is compatible with agreeing with Friend that fiction and non-fiction, respectively, contingently have many standard and contrastandard features which can explain our appreciative practice.

B. Matravers

As we have just seen, Friend does not deny that much of fiction standardly calls for an attitude—imagining—that is not called for by much non-fiction. Rather, what she denies is that fiction can be defined in terms of this attitude. Derek Matravers (2014) takes a more radical position—there is simply no difference in the attitudes prescribed, even standardly, by fiction and by non-fiction. It is false that fiction prescribes imagining but non-fiction does not.

Matravers claims that the distinction between fiction and non-fiction does no explanatory work; we should abandon it. Instead, he introduces a 'more fundamental' distinction between 'confrontations' and 'representations' (2014: 53). This has the form of an explanatory theory par excellence (2014: 7–8), seeking to redraw categories in a more enlightened way than mere deference to ordinary usage would permit. A 'confrontation' is a situation in one's egocentric space to which one is directly perceptually related (2014: 50). What we currently think of as fictions *and* non-fictions are representations, as opposed to confrontations: they prompt thoughts of objects that are not currently perceptually present and towards which no direct action is possible.

Matravers often talks as if the distinction between 'confrontation' and 'representation' were a rival to that of the distinction between 'fiction' and 'non-fiction'. But fictions and non-fictions could still both count as representations in Matravers's technical sense, whilst there would remain an interesting difference between them that did explanatory work. Matravers denies that there is any such difference. In particular, he denies the claim that the relevant difference concerns imagining.

He considers at least two possible values for 'imagining' here. According to one, 'imagining' is interpreted as a kind of taking on of someone's perspective, in a vivacious or lively way (2014: 16–17). He correctly argues that both fiction and non-fiction can prescribe this: autobiographies, for instance, can obviously do so. He also considers imagining as 'offline simulation' (Currie 1995b). On this view, an imagining that p is negatively distinguished from a belief that p, in terms of typically having different perceptual causes, causal connections to accompanying mental states, and causal connections to behavioural outputs (2014: 26–7).[11] Yet, Matravers argues, the mental states which fiction makes appropriate do not differ in any of these three ways from those made appropriate by non-fiction. In particular: A) there is no difference in kind in the perceptual inputs typically caused by fictions versus non-fictions; B) there is no difference in kind in the behavioural outputs typically caused by fictions versus non-fictions; C) there is no difference in the kinds of accompanying mental states typically caused by fictions versus non-fictions. In other words, fictions and non-fictions function exactly alike in the mental states they make appropriate, characterized in terms of inputs and outputs.

A) looks true: all are of texts. B) is not strictly true, since possibilities of action exist towards actual particulars described in non-fiction that have no typical analogy in fiction. One could read a report about a homeless person, find her and help her, for instance; whereas usually, at most, a fiction might prompt a generalized desire to help homeless people (2014: 28).[12] What *is* true is that the possibilities of action towards i) *invented* particulars characterized in fictions and ii) *past* historical particulars, described in non-fiction but no longer existent, look similarly obstructed (though for different reasons), and hence we cannot easily distinguish fiction from non-fiction in terms of this factor alone.

The real trouble lies with C). Why should we accept that there is no difference in the kinds of accompanying mental states typically caused by fictions versus non-fictions? Matravers considers various possible accompanying states typically shared by responses to fictions and non-fictions (2014: 30–5), ignoring the possibility I have been arguing for: the total content of a fiction is stored as imagining in the mind of the reader (whether or not parts of it are also stored as beliefs), whereas the total content of a non-fiction is not stored as imagining (though parts of it may be). Moreover, when stored as imaginings, as we have seen, the relevant mental items tend to be excluded from indiscriminate conjunction with further stored beliefs in a way that beliefs themselves are not.

Matravers in fact implicitly acknowledges this, advocating a 'two stage' model of engaging with representations generally. He writes: 'the first stage is neutral between non-fictional and fictional representations generally'; the 'mental model' created in response to the work is 'compartmentalized' from 'pre-existing structures of belief' (2014: 90). However, in the 'second stage', in response to non-fiction, 'the content of the mental model' is 'integrated' into those structures, whereas in response to fiction, this occurs markedly less frequently with the utterances contained therein (2014: 95). Why deny that this integration, which takes place in one case but not the other (whether at a 'second stage' or not) can form a basis, suitably adapted, for a distinction between fiction and non-fiction? To do so looks ad hoc, and Matravers himself seems

---

[11] Effectively I agree with this negative characterization, though I disagree with further statements which simulation theorists tend to make—see Chapter 6 for details.

[12] An exception would be if the fiction contained non-accidental truths about an actual homeless person.

explicitly worried by this accusation (2014: 95). There is no apparent reason not to include the inferences to which one is disposed, in reading a text, as part of the mental state appropriate to that sort of text. At least on the whole, fictions and non-fictions make different sorts of inference appropriate. So there is still room for a meaningful distinction here between fiction and non-fiction; and moreover, it looks to be cashed out in terms of the former but not the latter, making imagining, as I have characterized it, appropriate.

5.8 Non-conjoined Fictions

I conclude this chapter by considering a possible objection. Essentially I have claimed that a fiction is, fairly simply, one or more utterances reflexively intended by an author to be conjoined (at least, where more than one is present) in imagination. What they describe is intended to be thought of as occurring 'with respect to the same scenario' by readers/hearers. Yet there are some works commonly classified as fictions which apparently do not satisfy this description, because they contain utterances which, though intended to be imagined, are not intended to be conjoined in this sense.

Let's start with an example. In Lionel Shriver's *The Post-Birthday World*, after a certain point the reader is presented with two distinct scenarios: one where the heroine has an affair and leaves her partner, and one where she resists and stays with her partner. The book explores the consequences of these decisions in parallel, using identical actual historical events to measure the action in each case. There are two Chapter 2s, two Chapter 3s, and so on. Though it is clear that the reader is supposed to *compare* the two scenarios to each other, it is also clear that she is not supposed to conjoin the whole in imagination. What should we say about this sort of case?

Given my view, it follows that we should not treat this work as a single fiction, since the whole is not intended by Shriver to be imagined by the reader conjunctively (she does not intend of the whole that the reader be disposed to conjoin all of its propositions in thought, etc.). Rather, in this work there are two separate sets of instructions, each containing utterances which pertain to a distinct scenario. Generally, I am treating a single fiction as possibly giving rise to at most one scenario: one set of fictive utterances, the content of which is to be imagined together, conjunctively. Effectively, 'fiction' is equivalent to 'fictional scenario'. It follows that *The Post-Birthday World* is not a single fiction. To some ears this may perhaps sound jarring; but recall that my aim is not to square with ordinary usage at all costs. I prefer to invent a term of art for a work such as Shriver's: it is a 'multiple fiction'. That is, it is exclusively composed of fictive utterances, *and* contains more than one fiction (more than one set of fictive utterances conveying what is to be imaginatively conjoined by the reader). The important point is that we here have an interestingly different case from the standard or simple case, and we now have some vocabulary to mark it (Shriver 2007).

In a different case, a work can present the reader with two alternatives as to what is happening or has happened. Here is a simple example from *Alice in Wonderland*, describing Alice as she falls down the rabbit-hole:

> Either the well was very deep, or she fell very slowly, for she had plenty of time as she went down to look about her, and to wonder what was going to happen next. (Carroll 1928: 3)

Let's assume that Carroll intends us to imaginatively entertain each of these events consecutively, and to be disposed to conjoin each respectively in imagination with the rest of the plot, but not the two with each other. (Of course, if this is not true of Carroll in this example, then we simply need to find a better example; the interesting question remains.) In a more complicated but essentially similar case, a work can present us with much more extensive ambiguity, as in James's *The Turn of the Screw*, described in Chapter 3. In such cases we apparently have two scenarios, each intended to be imagined and conjoined with other propositions in the story, but not conjointly. Here too, I suggest, we should say that we have a 'multiple fiction', containing more than one fiction. Again, I am not particularly concerned that this might sound odd, relative to ordinary ways of talking. The point is to gain a theoretically useful set of concepts with which to discuss the full range of possible cases.

One reasonably might be wondering in what relation the notion of a 'narrative' stands to my notion of 'fiction'. The short answer is that they look non-identical, since, most obviously, wholly non-fictional works can have narratives as well as fictional ones. Moreover, I take it as plausible that a fictional text can have a single narrative even where it contains (in my terms) multiple fictions/scenarios. For instance, as we shall see shortly, an unreliably narrated text on my view contains two or more fictions, but usually will be counted as having only one narrative.

Of course, whether or not this is right ultimately will depend on one's theory of narrative, but it fits with leading contenders. For instance, according to Noel Carroll, very roughly, a narrative is 'a characterization of a sequence of events' which displays an unspecified sufficient number of 'narrative connections' between those events, and where the relevant sort of connection is that of causal necessity (2007: 11). So on this view, presumably, though *The Post-Birthday World* would count as containing two narratives (because the events in each respectively are not causally connected to one another) *The Turn of the Screw* would count as having only one. On Velleman's view, meanwhile, a narrative is identified as such by its 'emotional cadence', 'from an essentially initiatory emotion to an essentially conclusory one' (2003: 15). I am unsure whether he would count *The Post-Birthday World* as one narrative or two, but it seems clear at least that here *The Turn of the Screw* would again count as one.

Leaving this interesting issue aside, I turn now to what colloquially are often called 'fictions within fictions'. Here in fact what we have, at least in a straightforward case, is, once again, a fictional work (as just described) containing two independent fictions: two distinct sets of instructions, again differentiated from each other by what propositions are to be conjoined, and what conjunctions are to be excluded. For instance, in *The Brothers Karamazov*, the story of 'The Grand Inquisitor' is told by fictional character Ivan. The story Ivan tells concerns Christ's return to earth during the Spanish Inquisition and an interview with the eponymous inquisitor. On the one hand, at this stage in the narrative Dostoevsky intends us to imaginatively engage with the scenario in which the brothers, their extended family and acquaintances, exist, and where Ivan recounts the story; and to conjoin in imagination the thought of this event (the telling) with other imaginings concerning the brothers, their father, and so on. This, then, is one fiction within the work. On the other hand, Dostoevsky also intends readers to imaginatively engage with the scenario relayed in 'The Grand Inquisitor': to conjoin in imagination the events described there, but to *exclude* them from conjunction with utterances about Ivan and his brothers. So the Grand Inquisitor figures as a fictional character in the former fiction, but as a real human being in the latter; Ivan figures as the teller of a story in the former but does not figure in the latter at all. Strictly speaking, then, in this sort of case, we have two fictions, each within a larger fictional work.

In a more complex case, however, there is permitted imaginative interaction between (what looks like) one fiction and another within a work. For instance, in 'The Loves of Lady Purple' by Angela Carter, we are told of 'The Asiatic Professor' and his puppet troupe, who regularly perform, with the help of the Professor's favourite marionette, a play called 'The Notorious Amours of Lady Purple', which is then told as a story (see Chapter 4 for an extract). This *mise en abyme* concerns the evolution of a murderous, sexually rapacious young woman. Later in the work, after the description of the play has concluded, in a witty reversal of many a fairy tale the marionette used in the play is awakened by a kiss from the Professor: she becomes flesh, kisses him back, and vampirically drains him of his blood. Moreover, we are apparently intended to think of this marionette-made-human as one with the character she played in 'The Notorious Amours…'. Here, then, what is, on one level, explicitly a fictional character in a play also becomes an existent alongside the Professor, occupying the same ontological plane, as it were. Arguably, readers are intended to conjoin thoughts of her qua actual living murderer of the Professor, with thoughts of her qua fictional character in one of the Professor's plays.

Now, there are several questions here. One obvious one is whether in fact the reader can imagine what she is ostensibly intended to in such a case (a positive answer in principle was indicated in Chapter 4). But here I wish to focus on the separate issue of how many fictions such a work contains. I think we should treat it, effectively, as an extension of unreliable narration. For that reason I will first move to discussion of unreliable narration, returning to an example originally discussed in Chapter 2.

Recall that in Sarah Waters' *The Little Stranger*, the following passage is uttered by the narrator, Faraday, at a point in the book before most readers suspect he is unreliable. It concerns events which fictionally take place on one Wednesday 7th April sometime in the 1940s:

My first sight of Mrs Ayres's swollen, darkened face made me shudder, but worse was to come, for when I opened up her nightgown in order to examine her body, I found a score of little cuts and bruises, apparently all over her torso and limbs. Some were new, some almost faded. Most were simple scratches and nips. But one or two, I saw with horror, had the appearance almost of bites. (Waters 2009: 396)

It will turn out later in the text (arguably anyway) that in fact Faraday inflicted these injuries on Mrs Ayres. Nonetheless, the reader at *this* prior point of reading is still intended to conjoin the imagining that (roughly) *on Wednesday 7th April Faraday was having his first sight of Mrs Ayres's injuries* with other imaginings had in response to the text thus far, and which she also takes as reliable. Later in her experience of the text, given further plot revelations, she is intended to retract that particular conjunction, as it were, and instead conjoin the thought that *on Wednesday 7th April Faraday was **not** having his first sight of Mrs Ayres's injuries* with other imagined content now licensed by the text.

I suggest that once again what we have in this case, effectively, is a multiple fiction: two scenarios, and so two fictions, within a single work. According to one of them, Faraday did not injure Mrs Ayres, and saw her injuries for the first time on Wednesday 7th April; according to the other, ultimately more authoritative, one, he did injure her, and so has seen the injuries before. Each of these sets of propositions, or something very like them, are intended, at particular points in the reader's experience of the work, to be imaginatively conjoined with other content at that point; but they are not intended to be conjoined with each other. Yet the fact that there are two fictions, not one, is hidden to the reader till late in the work. At the point in the narrative in which the sentences quoted are offered, she takes them to be reliable, and so takes herself to be intended to imaginatively conjoin their content with other propositions which she also takes as reliable. It is only later that she is deliberately made aware by Waters of the narrator's unreliability in this matter.

Simplifying the case for the purposes of explanation, let's call the (relatively late) point at which the reader is made aware of Faraday's identity as murderer 'point N' in the text. Before getting to N, the reader is intended to conjoin '*on Wednesday 7th April Faraday was having his first sight of Mrs Ayres's injuries*' with all other propositions up until point N. This is one fiction, then. The second fiction includes the propositions *Faraday is the murderer*, and *on Wednesday 7th April Faraday was not having his first sight of Mrs Ayres's injuries* plus many other propositions prior to N, though not all of them (for others will need to be adjusted in the light of the revelation too).

This interacts rather neatly with the discussion in Chapter 2 of fictional content/fictional truth as it relates to unreliable narration. There I adapted extreme intentionalism to accommodate unreliable narration as follows:

> An author *Au*'s utterance *x* (or set of utterances *S*) in fiction *F* has fictional content that *p*, if and only if *Au* utters *x* (or *S*) intending that, once *x* (or *S*) is read for the first time: i) *x* (or *S*) *persistently* should (be disposed to) cause propositional imagining that *p* in her intended readership *R*, for as long as she is thinking of *F* at all; ii) *R* should recognize this intention; and iii) *R*'s recognition of this intention should function as part of *R*'s reason to propositionally imagine that *p*.

Let's call the part of the text before Faraday is revealed as a murderer the 'Faraday-is-innocent-fiction'; and the larger fiction (which includes propositions such as *Faraday is the murderer,* and *on Wednesday 7th April Faraday was not having his first sight of Mrs Ayres's injuries*) the 'Faraday-is-a-murderer-fiction'. Then '*on Wednesday 7th April Faraday was having his first sight of Mrs Ayres's injuries*' counts, on the account just given, as a fictional truth for the 'Faraday-is-innocent-fiction', since once read, it is intended to be imagined persistently with respect to that fiction, for as long as the fiction is being thought about at all. However it does not count as a fictional truth for the 'Faraday-is-a-murderer-fiction', since it is intended to be imagined only *temporarily* with respect to that fiction, not *persistently*.

In unreliable narration, what looks apparently like a single fiction at a point before the end of the work turns out later to have been two (or more) all along. The author's intention in this respect gets revealed late in the work. Turning back to cases such as the Carter short story, here too, I suggest, we have a multiple fiction, with a fiction revealed late in the text. This time, call 'point N' the point in the text at which Lady Purple, the eponymous heroine of 'The Notorious Amours of Lady Purple', transgresses fictional boundaries as it were, and interacts with the Professor, enactor of her drama with his puppets. Now, one fiction in the text is the embedded one prior to point N, entitled 'The Notorious Amours of Lady Purple', which concerns Lady Purple as a flesh-and-blood murderous young girl, and her development into a terrifying adult. As one reads the text, one is not *at that stage in the text* intended by Carter to conjoin thoughts prompted by its content with those concerning the Professor and his troupe. One is intended to think of this story as a discrete fiction, and to interact with it as such, excluding it from thoughts of those who tell the story as such, just as in the earlier *Brothers Karamazov* case. Correspondingly, a second fiction in the text, prior to point N, is that which concerns the Professor and his marionettes and assistants, but not Lady Purple qua murderous girl, before the boundary-trangression occurs. Here the reader is intended to conjoin imaginings about the Professor and about Lady Purple qua fictional character, but exclude them from imaginings about Lady Purple qua girl. And a *third* fiction emerges at point N, when the reader realizes she is intended to conjoin imaginings about the Professor with imaginings about Lady Purple qua girl *and* Lady Purple qua fictional character.

Why not treat this case as the inverse of unreliable narration: what apparently *looks* like two distinct fictions, at a point in the reader's experience before the end of the text, turns out later to have been a single one all along? It does not count as a single fiction, on my terms, because of Carter's manifest intention, at various points in the narrative prior to N, that the reader treat a certain set of propositions within the text—concerning Lady Purple qua girl—as excluded from interaction with others. To treat the work as a single fiction throughout would obscure this important fact, which is, after all, partly responsible for the 'shock' of the boundary-transgression later. Moreover, as the reader reaches the end of the work, it is not that she is no longer intended (at any point) to exclude the thought that *Lady Purple is a murderous girl* (etc.) from conjunction with thoughts of the Professor. It is more accurate to say that it has emerged that she is not intended to do this at *this point in her experience of the work*. However it remains true, even as she reaches the end of the work, that earlier in the work, and so now too, she remains intended to exclude the thought that *Lady Purple is a murderous girl* (etc.) from conjunction with thoughts of the Professor.

5.9 Summary

In this chapter, I have taken what I hope are some relatively minimal claims about the sort of imagining called for by fiction, and used them to develop a theory of fiction. Baldly stated, a fiction is a set of instructions from authors to readers or hearers, instructing them to imagine various things as part of a single scenario. I have shown how, with a proper understanding of the relation between a thinker's imaginings and her contemporaneous belief set, we do not need any further condition upon fiction citing some negative relation to belief or truth. I have also defended my view against those who would argue that there is no necessary connection between fiction and the intention to produce imagining. I have finished by applying my view to a range of cases: split narratives; 'ambiguous fictions', 'fictions within fictions', unreliable narration, and cases where a fictional character appears as such in a fiction.

In my next and final chapter, I conclude my project of extending my theory of fictional content to adjacent philosophical matters by considering what my discussion so far can tell us about the propositional imagination.

6

Back to the Imagination

6.1 Introduction

A remaining commitment of this book is to reach a point at which we can more interestingly characterize the nature of the imagination, or at least, the sort of imagination called for by fictions (which earlier I stipulatively called 'F-imagining'); and see what follows for questions about the imagination more generally. Imagination is a hot topic in academic philosophy at the moment, but as we saw in my Introduction, relatively little is agreed about its nature.

In particular, I will focus upon two relatively popular approaches to propositional imagining generally, each of which is problematic. One tends to treat it as significantly 'belief-like' in a certain sense: namely, it construes the typical development of an imaginative episode as constrained in a way very similar to how belief is constrained. A different approach construes imagining as highly unconstrained and stipulative, and worries about the consequences for our ability to connect imagining to certain kinds of knowledge or justified belief, including knowledge of counterfactuals and possibility. In what follows, I will argue that both tendencies are misleading, insofar as they purport to capture something about propositional imagining generally. In some contexts, propositional imagining is belief-like in the relevant sense, and in some contexts it is highly unconstrained and stipulative. We can allow this once the goal-driven, intentional nature of propositional imagining is properly acknowledged.

A further vexed issue in the literature is the nature of supposition and its relation to propositional imagining. Towards the end of this chapter, I will offer a new account of supposition, again drawing upon earlier lessons of the book. Generally, we will be left with an enriched picture of the propositional imagination, which, since it has been grounded in close inspection of a context in which such imagining is uncontroversially present—fiction—is not ad hoc and contains new insight.

6.2 The Generation of Imaginative Content

In this section, I will identify a popular assumption about the propositional imagination, and then show how it is not true of F-imagining. If it is not true of F-imagining, then it cannot be true of propositional imagination generally.

I start with the notion of imaginative content-generation. Forget fiction for a minute. We are all familiar, generally speaking, with the idea of an imaginative episode's extending and developing over time. In exploring a certain scenario from an initial starting point, one's imagining is taken in a particular direction. How does this happen? Here is a certain *general* picture prevalent in some quarters of how an episode of propositional imagination develops for a thinker. It is often presented as a claim about the characteristic or typical case. The idea is roughly this: that a thinker starts with certain imaginative 'premises'. What she imagines next corresponds in content to *what she would believe, if she believed those premises, in conjunction with further 'background' beliefs of hers*.

Properly unpacked, there are two elements to this picture. The first is the assumption that (where the contents of a 'belief that p' might in fact be a compound proposition involving logical connectives, e.g. *if q then r*; or *q or r*), the following principle applies to propositional imagining, generally:

> [INF] As a default it is true that, had you believed that p, q, and r and from this inferred and so believed s; then so too will it be true that, if you imagine that p, q, and r, from this you will infer and so imagine s, *ceteris paribus*.

The following authors all presuppose something close to [INF]:

Imagining that you are famous is belief-like partly because it mirrors the inferential role of the belief that you are...imagination preserves the inferential patterns of belief.
(Currie and Ravenscroft 2002: 12)

[B]y and large, if the belief system takes input from or produces output to a cognitive mechanism, then the imagination system does as well (and vice versa). For example, the belief system drives various inferential mechanisms, and the imagination system does too...the imagination interacts with our ordinary inferential systems in much the same way as does the belief system. (Weinberg and Meskin 2006: 178–80; see also Weinberg 2008: 204)

[C]onstructive imagination uses beliefs by default to infer new imaginings from imaginings that have already occurred...imagination does proceed as described by the Belief Governance Thesis unless special circumstances arise. (Van Leeuwen 2013: 226)

Although the imagination is flexible in some ways, it's fairly rigid and predictable in other ways. In particular, when people engage in imaginative activities, they often follow orderly inference chains. When I read that Wilbur is a pig, I infer (in imagination) that Wilbur is a mammal. When I hear that Hamlet is a prince, I infer (in imagination) that he isn't a member of the hoi polloi. These inferences track the kinds of inferences that I would have if I really believed that Wilbur was a pig and Hamlet a prince. (Nichols 2006: 7)

Meanwhile, a second element in this picture of content-generation concerns what further background content imaginative premises may inferentially interact with, in order to produce new imaginative content. It comes in two strengths. The first and strongest is:

> [ALL] *All* of a thinker's current beliefs are available for potential inference from imaginative premises, save those which are inconsistent with the primary 'premises'.

See, for instance, Stich and Nichols's hypothesis that (where, roughly, they use 'what is in the possible world box' for 'imaginative content'):

> Everything in the pretender's store of beliefs gets thrown into the possible world box except if it has been filtered out (i.e. altered or eliminated) by the UpDater.   (Stich and Nichols 2000: 124–5)

On their picture, the 'UpDater' is responsible for the elimination of beliefs incompatible with 'the pretense premises' (*ibid.*)—by which they mean the initially imagined scenario. *This makes the unfolding of imaginative content look very like the way in which implied fictional content is supposedly generated according to David Lewis's Analysis 1* (explored in Chapter 2). In developing an imaginative scenario, on this view, one is interested in working out would be the case in reality, were what one imagines (or is explicitly told to imagine) true.

On a weaker version, the content of only *some* of a thinker's current beliefs is available in generating the relevant imaginative content. For instance, according to what is known as 'Simulation Theory', imaginative episodes can be a guide to understanding another person, and/or trying to predict what they will do or think next (see e.g. Gordon 1992: 21). In this case, a thinker starts with imaginative premises, and then makes available for inference with those premises *only those beliefs which, she believes, are shared by the other person whose thoughts or actions are her predictive target*. Obviously the target's beliefs may differ in other ways from the thinker's own. More generally, the weaker claim is:

> [NOTALL] Some more limited subset than that described by [ALL] is available for potential inference from imaginative premises e.g. only those beliefs of a thinker *T*'s, which *T* believes some other person *R* shares.

This makes the unfolding of imaginative content, in this case, less like Lewis's Analysis 1 and more like his Analysis 2, or Currie's theory of fictional truth (see Chapter 2 again). In the latter two models, imaginative content is effectively extended via the imaginative simulation of another's perspective—the intended reader, or the fictional author—and the inferences she would make.[1]

The conjunction of [INF] and either [ALL] or [NOTALL] results in thinking of the generation of imaginative content proceeding as one would formulate a counterfactual: one starts with a certain scenario, and then, relative to a more or less restricted set of background beliefs about the world, works out what else would be true, were that scenario the case. The central problem with such views is that, as we have seen in Chapter 2 with respect to the discussion of Lewis and Currie, in the case of imaginative engagement with fiction, the generation of implied fictional content, and so the imaginative path of the reader, do not necessarily proceed like this. That is, they do

---

[1] In what follows, I shall call allegiance to [INF] and either [ALL] or [NOTALL] the view that imagining is 'belief-like', and reject it; but it should be understood that I am concerned with this alleged feature of imagining in particular, rather than other more harmless ways in which propositional imagining is 'belief-like'. (For one, as acknowledged, they are both propositional; for another, they are both quasi-factual.)

not inevitably proceed via the sorts of inferences we would make with respect to beliefs with the same content.

We saw in Chapter 2 that neither Lewis's nor Currie's views of implied fictional truth can accommodate certain important features of the competent reader's experience. They cannot, for instance, account for those implied fictional truths that follow as a result of understanding genre; or symbols. Lewis's view also implausibly predicts that 'silly questions' (such as why Bertie Wooster is not dying of alcohol poisoning) should routinely trouble the reader. It populates a fiction with millions of fictional truths irrelevant to its interpretation. And it also predicts the wrong experience for the reader, both at the beginning and the end of a fictional work. Extreme intentionalism suffers from none of these defects, I have argued, and offers a more convincing account of implied fictional truth.

In contrast to these views, it follows from extreme intentionalism that, in reading fiction, a reader's imaginative content should be directed by her perception and comprehension of fictive utterances. Her goal is to try and work out what the author intended to imply by her words, and to imaginatively engage with that content. Now, as we also saw in Chapter 2, working out, relative to some background set of beliefs about the world, what would be the case given some initial imaginative premise, *may* be a defeasible route to a theory of what an author intends to imply in some cases. However, equally, the process might operate via a different route: for instance, working out what a given symbol was intended by the author to mean with respect to fictional content; or her use of a stock character, or some playful metafictional reference, or some innovative but meaningful use of language. That is, imagining in these cases is not exclusively aimed at what would be the case in the world, were some explicit sentences true; nor does the generation of such imagining draw exclusively on background beliefs about the world, or not in the same way. It draws equally or even more heavily upon background beliefs about fiction and language: for instance, about the author and her characteristic technique; about conventions governing fictional reference, or genre, or symbolism, or words, and so on; and about how those might be adopted or playfully adapted.

It is true, I suppose, that working out an author's intentions as to what is to be imagined in these latter ways may *loosely* be counted as a kind of 'inference' 'drawing upon' beliefs e.g. beliefs about authors, fiction, genre, history, language, etc. (see for instance the word choice of Weinberg and Meskin 2006: 179). But, crucially, the contents of these beliefs are not entering into inferences *directly* with imaginative content *as such*, as, allegedly, the contents of beliefs do according to the model I am criticizing. To take an example already mentioned in various places: say that I read *Jane Eyre* and so imagine that (effectively) *Jane is locked in a red room*. In interpreting what else is made fictional in the light of this fact, I can permissibly draw upon a belief that *the use of a red room is intended by Brontë to symbolize a womb, and so imply, in conjunction with other content, that Jane is much affected by the loss of her mother*. I may then on the basis of these two thoughts derive the imagining that *Jane is much affected by the loss of her mother*. However, I do not conjoin these thoughts *directly*, in the sense of thinking both their contents true *with respect to the same scenario*. The imagining that *Jane is locked in a red room* concerns Jane qua orphan girl, former inhabitant of Lowood, and future wife of Rochester: as a flesh-and-blood girl with an existence independent of Brontë's pen. The belief that *the use of a red room is intended by Brontë....* (etc.) concerns the events of the book qua fictional constructs and elements of a novel composed by Brontë *as such*. There is little obvious sense in which these two kinds of thought, one imaginative and one a belief, come into *direct* inferential content: for they take different scenarios as objects (the imaginary scenario of the novel, and the actual world, respectively). The point generalizes to the interaction of imaginings about other fictional truths with beliefs about the fiction and its history, qua fiction.

In short, as I argued in Chapter 2, making inferences from fictional content as to what to imagine is not inevitably or even *often* like counterfactual thinking. Yet [INF] plus either [ALL] or [NOTALL] implies that *generally* propositional imagining is 'by and large' like, or even a form of, counterfactual thinking. To that extent, these views seem wrong as general claims about propositional imagining.

What of the empirical evidence sometimes cited that [INF] is near universally true? When authors cite evidence for [INF] they often cite Alan Leslie's so-called 'tea party experiment' (Leslie 1994), already introduced in Chapter 5, where a child is told to pretend, of an empty cup, first that it is full, then that it has been turned upside down.[2] This involves a child moving from imagining 'the teacup is full' and then 'the teacup has been turned upside down' to imagining 'the teacup is empty', via an inference which also draws on 'background' imaginings, themselves derivative in content upon existing beliefs about what tends to happen to liquid-filled receptacles when they are tipped. Here the inference performed looks identical to one which would have been performed had the child started with the beliefs that 'the teacup was full' and 'the teacup was turned upside down', and made an inference as to what must have happened next. But this evidence is wholly consistent with *the child's taking her instruction to be to imagine what would be the case, were her teacup full and then turned upside down*: that is, of having as an explicit goal of imagining, counterfactual knowledge. So the evidence does not yet support a generalized claim to imagining which does not have this goal.

Also cited as evidence for [INF] is the following piece of research, as reported by Van Leeuwen (2013: 226), and discussed earlier in Chapter 2:

[P]sychologists Deena Skolnick Weisberg and Joshua Goodstein (2009) provide direct evidence that individuals following a story import elements of what they take to be reality (in other words, their beliefs) into their understanding of what happens in the story. They had subjects read stories and then simply asked them questions about what else would be true "in the story." They found subjects held that mathematical, scientific, conventional (about social norms), and contingent facts were true in the stories, even though these were not given by the text. (Van Leeuwen 2013: 227)

---

[2] Currie (1995b: 151); Stich and Nichols (2000: 122); Currie and Ravenscroft (2002: 13); Weinberg and Meskin (2006: 178–9); Nichols (2006: 460); Van Leeuwen (2013: 227).

Yet as I argued in Chapter 2, it is plausible that what subjects are doing in this study is not, in fact, straightforwardly applying [INF] but rather, anticipating what, they believe, they are intended to imagine.

According to the position apparently taken by those I am criticizing, imagining in general is characteristically driven by the aim of working out what else would be true/ would be believed, were an initial scenario true/believed, *because that is its basic nature*. On my view, imagining in response to fiction is *sometimes but by no means always* driven by that aim, *contingently, because of a further aim*: that of working out what one is intended to imagine. Sometimes, contingently, it is a reasonable assumption that the author intended the reader to work out what else would be true, were an initial scenario true (that is, to explore a counterfactual and inculcate beliefs about it in the reader). However, this is not inevitably the goal of an author. Alternatively, as I have emphasized, her goal might be to create suspense, to explore a given theme, to prompt laughter, to capture the phenomenology of a particular experience, to create propaganda, to make a popular work that makes lots of money, to write in a particular genre, and so on. None of these need involve exploring counterfactuals. Hence recovering fictional content driven by these goals need not involve exploring counterfactuals either.

Here one might object that the picture I am offering is true of imagining directed by fiction; but that no moral should be drawn for other imagining which is not similarly directed. What we might call 'autonomous' imagining—that is, self-directed imagining uninfluenced by any external object or prop such as a fiction—might be thought to proceed as [INF] describes. However, a bit of further reflection will show that this is not true either.

Consider the *author* of a fiction, who creatively and autonomously imagines a certain plot for a story, and writes it down; not because she is following someone else's instructions, but under her own steam, as it were. I am assuming that active propositional imagining on the author's part occurs with respect to at least some of the plot she creates. This assumption looks natural enough, and looks supported by evidence about the phenomenon known as 'the illusion of independent agency'. This 'occurs when a fictional character is experienced by the person who created it as having independent thoughts, words, and/or actions' (Taylor, Hodges, and Koháynyi 2003: 361). In a study of 50 contributors to *Inkspot*, a website for writers, 92 per cent were reported as having experienced this illusion at some time (*ibid.*). Another author reports:

When describing their experiences in the writing-realm, writers tended to speak in the first person: "I wanted to..." "I saw that..." When describing writing that had gone well, though, they no longer spoke of themselves as active agents. Rather, they described their experience in much more passive terms, as if the fiction-world were acting on them, even possessing them. (Doyle 1998: 32)

This seems to provide good reason to implicate propositional imagining in at least some creative writing of fiction. There is a feeling of 'flow'; of being lost in imagination in the events the author is describing. However, it should not be assumed from such feelings of relative automaticity and flow that the imagining is no longer autonomous. Although there is an illusion of independent agency in such cases, it is still just that: an illusion. The author is nonetheless responsible for what is included in her work via her acts of imagining, and it seems likely that it will still be influenced and shaped by her conscious goals in writing what she does. Other 'automatic' fast processes such as answering a direct question in conversation may still be intentional and responsive to certain speaker goals, after all.

Now, as acknowledged, amongst the goals an author of a fiction might have, *one* of these is that of counterfactual imagining: exploring what would happen or have happened or been the case, if some particular scenario had happened. We saw this in the discussion of imaginative resistance in Chapter 4. In that case, as with counterfactual thinking generally, the author's imagining may be guided by principles such as [INF] plus [ALL] or [NOTALL]. But equally, as we have just seen, her imagining may well be guided by other purposes altogether. Whatever the authorial goal, this is likely to give rise to consequences for the author's decisions about what to imagine with respect to the plot, characterization, structure, and so forth. If an author wants to create suspense, she will include certain plot elements to that end; if she wants to sell lots of books, equally she will include certain plot elements to that end; and so forth. Hence in these cases, what the author imagines may and often will explicitly clash with what, she would judge according to her background belief set, would be the case 'in the real world', were her initial scenario to be the case. In real life, most virgins walking into creepy old houses are not about to get killed, yet this is a norm for horror genres; most people who fall in love at first sight do not experience happy endings, yet this is a norm for romantic fiction; and so on.

Again, one might protest: this is a special sort of case. *Other* kinds of autonomous imagining, wholly unrelated to either reading or creating fiction, respect [INF] much more inevitably. But this is not true either. Consider autonomous (non-prop driven) *fantasizing*. As I have argued elsewhere, fantasy is a pleasurable imagining which represents a situation for which one has a hedonically-motivated desire (Stock 2009). Thus the unfolding of its content is arguably guided by what thoughts the fantasist finds *pleasurable*; and this may have little to do with her beliefs about what would really be the case, were the situation as initially described true. In fact this surely seems likely: sadly, life and what one believes about it are not like one's fantasies. Moreover, arguably, fantasizing can sometimes involve actively *excluding* from inferential transaction with one's fantasy beliefs about what would be the case which would inhibit one's pleasure as one fantasizes (Stock 2009: 362–9). Or consider catastrophizing: morbidly picturing terrible outcomes, even where one rationally acknowledges they are highly unlikely to come about. This does not look as if it is constrained by one's beliefs as counterfactual imagining is, either.

In short: [INF] plus [ALL] or [NOTALL] describe the generation of imaginative content, only relative to two *particular* available *goals* of propositional imagining:

working out what would be the case, were certain other things the case; or, alternatively, what would be believed by a different version of oneself or some other person to be the case, were certain other things the case. This is by no means the whole of propositional imagining. It is only a part of it, as our examination of engagement with fiction has demonstrated.

6.3 Imagining and the Role of Intention in Cognitive Architecture

Now, of course, philosophers cannot really be ignorant of cases where propositional imagining fails to generate content in the way outlined by [INF] plus [ALL] or [NOTALL], and indeed they are not. So, for instance, we find Stich and Nichols noting that imagining (or 'pretense')

> is full of choices that are not dictated by the pretense premise, or by the scripts and background knowledge that the pretender brings to the pretense episode. (Stich and Nichols 2000: 127)

Accordingly, these authors add to their 'cognitive architecture' of the imagination a 'Script Elaborator' 'whose job it is to fill in those details of a pretense that can't be inferred from the pretense premise, the filtered contents of the Belief Box and the pretender's knowledge of what has happened earlier on in the pretense' (2000: 127; see also Weinberg and Meskin 2006: 182). As such, this looks a bit like a placeholder for a good explanation rather than a satisfying explanation in itself (see Peter Langland-Hassan 2016: 73 for a similar point). But what is also mysterious is the extent to which such authors ignore how these facts, which lead to the positing of the Script Elaborator, interfere with their initial generalization that propositional imagining *generally* respects the inferential orderliness of belief. In fact, as just noted, it seems much more accurate that imagining *relative to the particular goal of counterfactual belief* exhibits such orderliness; where that is only one goal the propositional imagining might have.

An account of Script Elaboration which effectively promises to largely preserve the picture provided by [INF] has recently been offered by Langland-Hassan, apparently with respect to propositional imagining generally (2016). He claims that the role of Script Elaborator is performed by a thinker's intention to introduce some new 'premises' or additional element. In what he considers to be the central case of propositional imagining, a thinker intentionally chooses to imagine that a scenario S occurs.[3] Content-generation from this point on proceeds by way of representing what would have happened, were S the case, in conjunction with background beliefs about the world and what would/could happen in it—that is, as imagining in pursuit of counterfactual knowledge—*except where* some new aspect of S is intentionally introduced later by the thinker (which may occur often). So content-generation occurs *either* by

---

[3] He calls this 'Guiding Chosen' imagining.

what he calls the 'top-down' intentional introduction of new content, *or* by the application of the inference mechanisms and background beliefs used in belief generation from an initial set of premises. In the former capacity it is freely chosen; in the latter capacity it is 'laterally constrained'. Langland-Hassan writes:

[I]magining, in its more freewheeling instances, then becomes a kind of cyclical activity, during which new and sometimes unusual premises are "fed" to a lateral algorithm at varying intervals. The output of the lateral "inferential" activity can then, at different intervals, be recombined with a novel element contributed by one's intentions to begin the lateral processing anew (it is because of this recombination that I am calling the process "cyclical"). This allows the imaginative episode, as a whole, to both be constrained (by the lateral algorithm) and to freely diverge from anything one would have inferred from the initial premise alone. (Langland-Hassan 2016: 75)

Langland-Hassan goes on to argue that all or nearly all propositional imaginings can be understood along similar lines. Even imagining which is relatively fantastical is so guided, he argues:

I imagine that I drop a glass and that, as it hits the floor, it shatters; the shards then meld together into the shape of a bird, which flies away. Fantastical though it is, most of the imagining is tightly constrained: the way the glass both falls and breaks, and the way the bird is shaped and flies are all determined by lateral constraints that are grounded in background beliefs about the relevant kinds of objects. What about the moment where the glass shards turn into a bird? This moment in the imaginative project can be accounted for by a top-down intervention by a new intention in action—specifically, an intention to imagine what would happen if the glass shards turned into a birdlike creature. (Langland-Hassan 2016: 79)

So to sum up: on this view, the basic architecture of imaginative content-generation is as follows. On the one hand, there is 'top-down' intention to insert some new 'imaginative premises' or additional embellishment, at least (normally) at the beginning of the episode and perhaps during it too; on the other hand, there is a non-intentional, 'laterally constrained' belief-like inferential process, calling upon background belief content about the world to create further content. Effectively, Langland-Hassan analyses the sources of imaginative content as either a) constrained, rational, and inferential (i.e. involving belief-like processing of content); or b) intentional and goal-directed (or as he puts it in another paper, driven by one's 'desires and interests'; 2012: 172). Yet, on closer inspection, things are more complicated than this would suggest.

Certain relevant complications are as follows. We first need to distinguish between two different kinds of intention possessed by anyone who imagines something: i) 'initiating' intentions; that is, those intentions that initiate an imaginative episode in the light of a certain goal, and sustain its production; ii) 'content-controlling intentions'; that is, those intentions that control (or fail to control) content in the light of that goal. Content-controlling intentions are constrained by initiating intentions: they will be influenced by whatever the associated goal-directed intentions are aimed at. Moreover, we should also note that during any goal-directed imaginative episode, it is likely that various possible scenarios will come to mind relatively automatically and spontaneously: some will be 'assented to' as a genuine fulfilment of the imaginative brief, and others will be rejected. It is reasonable to think that content-controlling intentions influence— at least to some extent—the production of what comes to consciousness automatically as potentially relevant to one's imaginative project, in the light of one's goal. It is also plausible that they wholly influence the acceptance or rejection of that material. So for instance, if I am an author and my aim is to imagine a scenario that will thrill readers, what comes to consciousness will naturally be somewhat shaped by this goal, but at the same time, it is not automatic that I must accept every thought that comes to consciousness as relevant to my goal. Some potential scenarios which occur to me may be dismissed as not thrilling enough, even so. The same sort of point might be made with suitable adjustments for fantasizing: sometimes what occurs to a person engaged in fantasizing about a particular scenario can be dismissed as not sufficiently pleasurable after all, on reflection, and replaced with something more conducive to that aim. Indeed, it might also be made for counterfactual imagining: in doing so, I might consider one possible scenario and then dismiss it as not in fact what would be the case. In fact, I assume, for every imaginative project, there will be a potential distinction between what comes to consciousness immediately, and what is assented to or rejected as appropriate or relevant. Sometimes what comes to consciousness will immediately seem right, given one's aims, so that there may be limited awareness of having a choice as to whether to 'accept' it; but nonetheless the acceptance is intentional.

Now, one relevant point for Langland-Hassan's picture is that even counterfactual imagining (that is, imagining aimed at the establishment of counterfactual beliefs) is sustained both by initiating intentions and by content-controlling intentions. It would be a simplification to think that the only point at which intention is relevant to the process of counterfactual imagining is in the matter of voluntary 'insertion of content'. For the number of belief contents one might conceivably reflect upon or involve in a counterfactual inference, given a certain starting premise, is huge, and it seems obvious that here too goal-related influences play a role. Say that I imagine that I am sailing in a boat in the North Sea. Do I next imagine that *the boat is surrounded by a mixture of water and salt,* or that *the wind is propelling the sails,* or that *underneath the boat are cod and haddock and mackerel,* or that *the landmasses around the boat include Scotland, Norway, and Denmark*? All of these reflect extant beliefs of mine. It is likely that here too what I actually imagine will be affected by my intentions and goals in engaging in the counterfactual imagining in question. What exactly do I want to find out about? My content-controlling intentions will influence both what comes to mind in the service of my goal (at least to some extent), and (more importantly) what conscious productions of my intellect I 'assent' to, as relevant to my project, and what I reject as irrelevant. Here too, some of the thoughts which automatically occur to a thinker engaged in a particular project of counterfactual imagining may be rejected on further consideration as not actually relevant.

A second complication of Langland-Hassan's picture is suggested by comments made already. As emphasized, there are imaginative episodes which do not proceed, in terms of content-generation, as beliefs with the same initial content would. Moreover, we cannot explain their deviance from belief-like scenarios simply in terms of the 'top-down' intentional insertion of new content. Here too, given a certain imaginative goal, there are relevant 'lateral' constraints, even if these are not generated by inferential constraints which would operate on beliefs with the same content. The constraints in question depend on the particular instance and what the imaginative goal is, but might include: (in the case of writing fiction) beliefs or suspicions about what is funny, what is suspenseful, what is emotionally powerful, what is titillating (etc.); or (in the case of fantasizing) what causes the thinker pleasure. (This point is effectively acknowledged by Langland-Hassan when he writes of an actor imagining that he is riding a pterodactyl because 'he wanted to shift the pretense to something more surprising, funny, and unusual—to something that would suit his goals, *qua* improvisational comedian' 2016: 75. The example originally comes from Van Leeuwen 2011.) Better then, I think, to posit imagining as potentially 'laterally constrained' *either* by certain beliefs about what would be the case if certain other things were the case *or* by beliefs or suspicions about what counts as funny *or* terrifying *or* titillating *or* by what the thinker would find pleasurable (etc.), depending on the imagining's ultimate aim in a particular case. There is no reason to count one of these sets in particular as privileged, and a fortiori no need to count counterfactual imagining as the central case.

Despite this, it is sometimes insisted that imagining is belief-like in the way indicated by [INF] (perhaps with the additional intentional insertion of premises at various points) 'by default' (see for instance Van Leeuwen 2013: 226). What might it mean to say this? One thing it might mean is that propositional imagining is *normally* or *most frequently* driven by counterfactual aims (see Weinberg and Meskin's use of 'by and large', and Nichols's use of 'often' in the passages quoted above). This is an empirical claim and hard to establish; certainly, those who claim imagining is belief-like as a default have not done the research required to establish its frequency. What does seem true is that thinkers may fall back upon belief-like imagining when prompted to try in the course of philosophical discussion, partly because they do not have a clear idea of the purpose of the task. However, this hardly shows us something about propositional imagining in its native and less artificial habitat. It may also be easier to engage in belief-like imagining than other kinds of imagining because it takes less mental effort to reproduce familiar combinations of events in imagination than otherwise.

The following point also seems relevant. I have just distinguished between what is automatically delivered to consciousness as one pursues an imaginative goal, and what content is deliberately assented to as germane, or rejected as irrelevant, to that goal. Not all of what comes to mind will be judged as relevant to the task in hand. Now, it is true that for many of us, no matter what the imaginative project, *much* of what spontaneously comes to mind will be informed by background beliefs about the world. To put it baldly, if I imagine that there is a cat, what comes to mind is likely to be informed by basic beliefs about cats. This is the case whether I am fantasizing or creating fiction or pursuing counterfactual knowledge about cats. But whether or not I *assent* to a particular belief-informed representation of cats as germane to my project depends on the project, and does not automatically follow from the fact that it initially comes to mind. I might, for instance, be trying to imagine a highly unusual cat, very unlike others. Moreover, *even where my goal is counterfactual imagining*, it is not obvious that the automatic, spontaneous deliverances to my consciousness necessarily will be *exclusively* informed by background belief. Rogue fantastical elements may creep in, which I have to reject as not suitable for the task. So in short, even if often (though not always) the basic deliverances of consciousness during imaginative episodes are informed and constrained by beliefs, it does not follow that the trajectory of the episodes themselves, taken overall, is so constrained.[4] Hence, taken overall, imagining is not belief-like 'by default' here either.

An alternative possible version of the claim that imagining is belief-like (in the relevant way) 'by default' is that, if there is or had been no intentional insertion of content along the way, a given imaginative episode is or would have been wholly driven by belief-like inferences (etc.). Langland-Hassan seems to think this. Given the variety of sorts of fiction we have looked at, we have seen reason to doubt this, however. Additionally, there is some imagining where there is apparently no intentional insertion of content at all, but yet the process is not driven by belief-like inferences. For instance, there are compulsive, repetitive fantasies or obsessive non-voluntary catastrophizing.[5]

A different interpretation of the claim (at a push) might be that the only *useful* function of the imagination is to plan and/or engage in counterfactual thinking. However, this depends on a very narrow conception of usefulness. Other kinds of imagining clearly also have psychic pay-offs: pleasure, relaxation, understanding the phenomenology of the states of mind of others, and so on.

Finally, by claiming that imagining is belief-like 'by default' perhaps the claim (again, at a push) is that it is *the function* of the imagination to engage in planning/counterfactual thinking, in the sense that engaging in planning/counterfactual thinking is why it is there at all (see Wright 1973: 156 for this notion of function). That is, the counterfactual imagination was selected for: other imaginative functions (e.g. imagining for the purposes of creating fictions to be enjoyed by others, fantasizing for pleasure) are spandrels ('secondary epiphenomenon representing a fruitful use of available parts, not a cause of the entire system': Gould and Lewontin 1979). Obviously, to say this is to assume that the imagination is itself a genuine unit and not (say) itself a spandrel of some other process, or a composite of parts which are spandrels of other systems. But assuming the former, it still does not follow that 'by default' or 'normally' imagining is

---

[4] I'm grateful to Neil Van Leeuwen for pressing me on this point.
[5] Perhaps for this reason, Langland-Hassan tentatively seeks to exclude unbidden 'imagining' which is non-belief-like from the class of imagining proper, though this looks to me rather ad hoc (2016: 78).

belief-like or directed at counterfactual thought in any other sense, nor that it should be. We should not confuse a thing's originating function with the highly fruitful and perfectly permissible uses to which it may later be put.

6.4 Imagining and Belief

To sum up where we are: we have seen no reason to accept that propositional imagining *generally* or *normally* is 'belief-like' in the way indicated by [INF]. In fact, the trajectory of propositional imagining can be significantly influenced by constraints other than those operative upon beliefs with the same contents: constraints connected to the particular goal of the imaginative episode, and the reasons of the thinker for undertaking it. A fortiori, the view that imagining is in fact a *species* of belief—'imagining that *p* amounts to making judgments about what would likely happen if *p*, from retrieved beliefs in relevant generalizations' (Langland-Hassan 2012: 157)—is also impugned. A sensible alternative to the picture given by [INF] is that *a single kind of propositional imagining with a particular intentional goal*—the gaining of counterfactual knowledge— shares the inferential role of beliefs with the same contents.

In the rest of this section I shall consider three further interesting respects in which propositional imagining differs from belief. As we shall see, all of them relate to propositional imagining's goal-driven, intentional nature, something that I have been emphasizing throughout this book.

A. Propositional imagining, belief, and truth

A propositional imagining can be had 'because' it is true, in the following sense: a thinker can choose to imagine what she believes to be true, because she believes it to be true. She can do this where, for instance, she wants to gain counterfactual knowledge. She wishes to work out what would be the case, were some proposition that she does not believe true, true; and she does this by imagining that proposition as true, in conjunction with *other propositions she already believes are true*, in order to see what would follow. Or to change the example: she imagines a scenario, the concrete details of which she believes false, which nonetheless intentionally exemplifies some general claim she believes true (as where an author creates a fiction about made-up characters exemplifying some general moral point she believes true).

There is an obvious connection here to earlier discussion of fictive utterance, in Chapter 5. There we rejected theories of fictive utterance which claimed that fictive utterances could at most be accidentally true (Currie 1990: 46) or that the reasons for their utterance were independent of their truth (D. Davies 2007: 46). We acknowledged that fictive utterances might be included in a fiction because they were believed to be true by the author. In an analogous sense, an imagining during a private imaginative episode can be 'non-accidentally true'—non-accidentally related to what the thinker believes to be true, insofar as she has chosen to incorporate what she believes to be true into her imaginative episode, for that very reason.

Therefore it is not true, as is sometimes said (e.g. by Velleman 2000: 250) that in imagining, necessarily one imagines what one does irrespective of whether it is true or not. In fact, imagining can even be responsive to new evidence, just as belief is. Say that I want to know what would happen if my house burnt down and I commit myself to imagining whatever true circumstances will contribute to this goal. I cannot remember whether or not my house is insured; I actually search for and find my insurance certificate. Then on the basis of this information, in line with my governing intention, I imagine that my house burns down and I am insured. The imagining that I am insured is evidence-responsive, at least in a sense.

However, even so, there is clearly a different and more direct sense in which a belief is held 'because it is true'. Where truths are deliberately imagined, they are imagined because they are or would be believed true by the thinker. In contrast, beliefs are not believed true because they are or would be believed true; that would be obviously circular (see Railton 2014: 123). Rather, they are believed because the evidence available to the thinker compels her to have them, in a way which is not directly under her control. A belief is not held because it is true in the sense that (some of) her thoughts being true is an explicit current goal of the thinker, which she equally well might not have held, with an ensuing difference in the content of her thoughts. There may be a coherent sense in which either beliefs or believers aim at the truth, or that having true beliefs is a goal of every thinker (see Owens 2003 for discussion) but whatever this sense is, it is not true that believers deliberately set out to have true beliefs in particular cases, where they might as easily set out to have false ones.

B. Propositional imagining is an action; belief is a state

That propositional imagining can—indeed, is usually—goal-oriented hints at a further distinction between belief and imagining: whilst belief is a state, propositional imagining is an action, and not strictly speaking a state at all. We may talk casually of imagining as a mental state; but this is at most loose talk.

Having an imaginative episode, or imagining something as a part of such an episode, satisfies the following criteria typical of actions. First, propositional imagining is normally under intentional control; and even where it is not intentionally initiated, it usually can be stopped at will. To this extent, the latter imagining is like those relatively non-deliberate actions that one may find oneself doing without having deliberately started (e.g. tapping one's foot or chewing a pen) but which can at least be deliberately stopped. Even where such actions are compulsively done in a relatively uncontrollable way, so that they cannot easily be stopped (as in compulsive foot-tapping, or compulsive morbid daydreaming) such activities still count as actions in a loose but recognizable sense, in that they are still less automatic than spasms or itches or sneezes. Moreover, where compulsive instances of a behaviour are relatively rare instances of a general action-type (foot-tapping; imagining), the action-type need not count as any less intentional in virtue of that fact.

A further reason to think of propositional imagining as an action is that, as I have stressed, it is also typically goal-oriented. We have seen this both in the case of imagining in relation to reading fiction and in its creation; as well as propositional imagining aimed at counterfactual knowledge, and fantasizing. Even when it is not consciously or intentionally initiated, it can usually be traced to the satisfaction of some goal, to emerge after reflection: often, in imagining which is not deliberately started, the having of pleasure (as in fantasy, for instance). And as with many goal-oriented actions, an imaginative episode usually passes through various stages, involving change over time. States, in contrast, tend to be homogenous and non-changing over time. This includes belief.

According to some, a further characteristic feature of action is that a person's actions exist in her consciousness in some form at the time of execution, whereas her states need not (O'Shaughnessy 2003: 177–8). This too seems true of imagining: there is no such thing as a merely tacit or dispositional imagining (Currie 1995b). In contrast, beliefs need not be consciously accessed: often, the sorts of circumstance that justify claims about a belief's existence, its persistence over time, or its destruction, are not circumstances about conscious mental events at all. On one plausible account, they are to do with dispositional facts about how a subject *would* think or behave in certain circumstances (Schwitzgebel 2002). While occurrent reflection on the content of a belief looks like an action, the having of the belief itself is not. Generally, the thoughts and behaviour to which one is disposed in having a particular belief, are not themselves to be identified with the belief, at least on one attractive account.

To this, the following question might be raised. I have claimed that generally, in propositional imagining, often one will be disposed to conjoin one's thought with other imaginings. Take, for instance, the case of imagining in response to fiction: as a reader engages with a fiction, at page n of the fiction she will normally be disposed to conjoin in imagination many/most/all of the propositions in a fiction that she has read up until page n (where, usually, she does not believe most of them). One might wonder: should we treat the imaginative thoughts to which the reader is *disposed*, whilst reading a book, but which she may not occurrently be aware of, in a way structurally analogous to the way philosophers tend to treat the various manifestations of belief to which one may be disposed: that is, as symptoms of some deeper dispositional state? That is, should we say that her imagining is a dispositional state, whose manifestations are conscious thoughts?

The answer seems to be no, or at least, not standardly; the reasoning is worth rehearsing for further interesting differences it brings out with belief. The main difference seems to be that to have a belief that p seems associated, necessarily, with a relatively *permanent* disposition to manifest certain thoughts and behaviour, which persists for (roughly) as long as one's memory works and one is not confronted with sufficient evidence to disconfirm the claim that p. Moreover, attribution of this disposition to an agent is not contingent upon the agent's having some other conscious thought in particular, e.g. consciously thinking about some belief which she is disposed to inferentially connect to the belief that p. In contrast, in many an imaginative episode representing a scenario S, the disposition to have certain imaginings representing various aspects of S is relatively short-lived, and moreover, contingent upon some conscious imaginative activity, directed towards S, occurring at all; as soon as this is not the case, so that the thinker ceases to imagine anything about S, there seems to be no reason to attribute the disposition to have any S-related imaginings at all. For this reason, there seems to be no pressing need to countenance imagining generally as a dispositional state, even though having dispositions is often involved. It is true that for *some* imaginings, such as those concerning iconic fictional characters or scenarios very well known by a reader, there may well be a more permanent disposition to imagine certain things about those characters or scenarios, which is not contingent on conscious imaginative activity already occurring about them.[6] Here the disposition looks more deep-seated. However, not all imagining is like this.

C. *Propositional imagining is only potentially conjunctive; belief is necessarily conjunctive*

A further feature of propositional imagining can be highlighted more briefly, as follows. I have stressed that propositional imagining nearly always has a goal, more or less conscious; for instance, to engage with a particular fiction for some further end; to create a work of fiction which will arouse excitement/titillation/suspense (etc.); to bring the imaginer pleasure; to work out a counterfactual, and so on. The observation that propositional imagining is nearly always a goal-directed action sheds further light on the initial findings we observed in respect of propositional imagining in relation to fiction, in Chapter 1. There we noted that fiction-directed imagining was potentially but not necessarily conjunctive. That is, I can pick up a novel, read a sentence, and imagine that p in response to it: immediately afterwards I might pick up a different novel, read a sentence, and imagine that q in response to what I read: it does not mean that I either do or should imagine that p and q. In fact this is also true of autonomous imagining too: an author can imagine that she quits her boring day job; immediately afterwards, she can imagine one of her characters falling down the stairs. It does not follow that these two imaginings are part of the same imaginative project. They belong to different ones, between which she has switched.

In contrast, belief is necessarily conjunctive, at least in the case of rational thinkers: if I believe that p, and I believe that q, then I (should) believe that p and q (Evnine 1999). This difference between belief and imagining can be explained in terms of the fact that usually, imagining, unlike belief, is an activity oriented towards the obtaining of particular goals and is sustained by intention. If I pick up a fiction and read one sentence, and then pick up a different fiction and read another one, and am aware that they are different fictions, then insofar as I do not have the goal of melding both sentences together into some single fictional scenario, but intend to treat them both separately,

---

[6] Thanks to Neil Van Leeuwen for this point.

my imaginings—though temporally consecutive—belong to different imaginative scenarios. Equally, where an author fantasizes that she quits her boring day job because this thought gives her pleasure; and then imagines that a character she has invented falls down the stairs, then these do not count as part of the same imaginative scenario for her, because she does not intend to imagine them for the same sort of reasons and so does not intend to conjoin them.[7] In characterizing beliefs, in contrast, there is no possibility of relativizing sets of beliefs to a given goal, since whatever 'goal' there is, if indeed it can be characterized that way, is always the same and is one over which one has no deliberate control: to believe what is true.

In short: the typically goal-driven, intentionally-controlled aspect of propositional imagining is what makes it very different from belief. This goal-driven aspect is responsible for its particular relation to truth and falsehood; its counting as an action, not a state; its being potentially but not always actually conjunctive; and for the fact that its manner of content-generation is only *sometimes*—for instance, relative to a particular goal of gaining counterfactual knowledge—inferentially derived from existing beliefs.

6.5 Propositional Imagining, Possibility, and Knowledge of Counterfactuals

We have just examined, and rejected, a view which would construe propositional imagining generally as, normally or 'by default', heavily constrained by the thinker's background beliefs about the world, so that it counts, in its essential or typical nature, as 'belief-like' itself. I turn now to a different tendency, which is to see propositional imagining as radically unconstrained in all contexts, in a way which apparently threatens its functioning as an effective epistemic tool.

Traditionally, conceivability has been viewed as a reasonable guide to knowledge of what is metaphysically possible. On this view, baldly put, if one can conceive of something as the case, then that thing is at least prima facie possible. Recently, some philosophers have tried to cash out the notion of conceivability in terms of imaginability. For instance, Yablo (1993) has argued that a proposition is conceivable for a person if and only if she can objectually imagine a situation which she takes to 'verify' that proposition, in the sense that, were that situation to be actually the case, she takes it that the proposition would be true (for the notion of 'objectual' imagining, see Chapter 1). Where this occurs, the proposition appears possible to her, with accompanying prima facie though defeasible justification. David Chalmers extends this account (2002). Like Yablo, he claims that it is conceivable that S is the case when one can objectually imagine a situation that verifies S: 'an imagined situation verifies S when reflection on the situation reveals it as one in which S' (2002: 152). But he adds that the imagining must be 'coherent', in the sense introduced in Chapter 4: 'a situation is

---

[7] For more about the relation between the identity of an imaginative scenario and the thinker's purposes, see §6.6.

coherently imagined when it is possible to fill in arbitrary details in the imagined situation such that no contradiction reveals itself' (2002: 153). Coherency comes in prima facie and idealized versions; the former is a defeasible and imperfect guide to possibility; the latter tracks it more reliably (2002: 160).

Against such views are those who argue that imagining cannot be even a somewhat good guide to possibility, on the grounds that imagining generally is largely stipulative and unconstrained. For instance, Peter Kung (2010) argues that anything which is not experienced as certainly false by a thinker is epistemically possible for that thinker (that is, could be true for all she knows); and anything which is epistemically possible, in this sense, can be propositionally imagined by way of its being objectually imagined; including that which is metaphysically impossible.

In more detail, Kung argues as follows. Like Yablo and Chalmers, Kung assumes that objectual imagining, and more particularly, sensory imagining—imagining via mental images—can be a way of propositionally imagining that p. (In Chapter 1 I argued that wherever there is objectual imagining of *an O*, there is propositional imagining that *there is an O*.) Kung distinguishes between two types of content mental images can have. On the one hand, there is the 'basic qualitative content' of the image—roughly, what is represented in a 'direct and immediate way', such as colours and shapes (2010: 623), and which it could not fail to represent, to count as the image it is. On the other there are 'assigned contents'—roughly, anything represented which goes beyond basic qualitative content. This is, or at least can be, expressed propositionally, as Kung makes clear. So if, for instance, one had a mental image of *David Cameron in front of the Taj Mahal*, then amongst this imagining's assigned content would be the proposition 'David Cameron is in front of the Taj Mahal'. This content counts as 'assigned' because Kung assumes one could have had an identical mental image without that image being about David Cameron or the Taj Mahal; it could have been about his imaginary twin instead in a visually identical but actually different location (a fake Taj Mahal, as it were). Assigned content may include 'stipulative content': content that 'goes above and beyond that of the mental image' (2010: 625). If, for instance, one's mental image was accompanied by the label *David Cameron is in front of the Taj Mahal thinking about fiscal policy*, that he counted as *thinking about fiscal policy* would be a matter of 'stipulative content', on Kung's taxonomy, since (arguably) this is not something that could be represented by the image itself in any way.

Kung then claims that there is only one constraint upon the content that may be assigned to the 'basic content' of a mental image: certainty that a proposition is false (2010: 634). In that case, one will be unable to imagine it. What Kung is prepared to countenance as 'absolutely certain' is a pretty restricted group of propositions:

[P]lausible examples include that squares have four sides, that bachelors are unmarried, and that modus ponens is a valid inference rule.   (Kung 2010: 630)

According to Kung, as long as one is not already certain that a proposition 'p' is false, one will be able to propositionally imagine that p simply by stipulatively assigning the content 'p' to some appropriate qualitative content. So one might easily imagine impossibilities, so long as one is not certain they are false: for instance, imagining that *I have proven Goldbach's conjecture* via an image of oneself receiving a medal; or imagining that *Mark Twain and Samuel Clemens have a fight* by imagining two identical men fighting whilst stipulatively labelling this 'Mark Twain and Samuel Clemens have a fight'; or imagining that *water is XYZ not H_2O* via an image of clear liquid labelled 'water', with added assigned content 'this liquid, this water, is composed of XYZ' (2010: 628). In each case one has an image but assigns some propositional content stipulatively such that one counts as imagining the (in some cases, impossible) thing in question.

I myself have some doubts concerning Kung's story of how mental image content and 'assigned' content come together. But leaving those aside, even so, in some ways we are not so far apart. I too acknowledge that propositional imagining *can* be unconstrained, though I have not done so via his story of the stipulative assignment of content to mental images. Indeed, I have allowed that one can propositionally imagine even things one is certain are false.[8] However, Kung appears to treat propositional imagining as *always* unconstrained. It is this that grounds his scepticism about the relation between imagining and possibility. Admittedly he has an additional story about how the imagistic, 'qualitative' content of an imagining can in certain circumstances provide evidence of possibility. But as far as the 'assigned', i.e. propositional content of an imagining goes, he is clear that this is useless in providing evidence of possibility, precisely because it is so unconstrained (2010: 645).

For different reasons, Marcello Fiocco (2007) takes an equally pessimistic view of the power of propositional imagining to give us good information about the possible. Like Kung he is concerned to criticize the thought that one can propositionally imagine that *p* by objectually (sensorily) imagining a scenario which exemplifies what 'p' describes (2007: 370). However, the thrust of his objection would look to threaten any claim which said that propositional imagining could be a guide to what was possible, whether via sensory imagining or not. Like Kung, Fiocco thinks of propositional imagination as essentially stipulative: in imaginatively engaging with a proposition, one stipulates a scenario in which that proposition obtains. He rejects the notion implied by Yablo and Chalmers in their discussion, that one might prima facie imagine a proposition by imagining a situation S that verifies it (counts as an instance of it being true), but then *work out on further reflection* that the situation that one has imagined does not in fact verify S, so that one was initially mistaken. Effectively, he objects that it is unclear what could constrain such a process of 'working out', since for any given proposition, and whatever image one took to 'verify' it, that image itself would open to

---

[8] Actually, Kung allows this too. Following Kind (2001) he apparently excludes what I have treated as non-imagistic propositional imagining from counting as a kind of imagining at all, and instead classifies it as 'supposing'. He thinks of supposing as even less constrained than imagining involving imagery (2010: 634): one can suppose anything at all without resistance (2010: 632), presumably including things one is certain are false. For more on supposing, see §6.6.

multiple possible interpretations: some of which would verify the proposition, and some of which would not.

> If Yablo ... [was] ... correct ..., the attempt to ... imagine [by way of a mental image] Humphrey winning the presidency in 1968 would only yield a world according to which someone who appears to be Humphrey wins the election or one according to which headlines report "HUMPHREY DEFEATS NIXON!" But both worlds—and any other characterized in generic, qualitative terms—are compatible with Humphrey himself losing the election. (2007: 372)

Instead, he argues that in imagining a proposition by objectually (sensorily) imagining some scenario, one simply stipulates that the scenario one is imagining counts as verifying that proposition in question. In this way one can, for instance, 'simply stipulate consideration of a possible world in which', for instance, 'transparent iron exists' or 'a computer generates some number that falsifies Goldbach's conjecture' (2007: 376) or any other impossibility, for that matter. Equally, presumably he would say, where one is simply trying to propositionally, but not objectually, imagine in some detail that some scenario obtains (e.g. that transparent iron exists), one can simply stipulate that what one is imagining, in detail, counts as the scenario in question.

One might wonder however if the sort of position taken by Kung and Fiocco establishes too much. For, though it is not a use to which either put their own view, if Kung and Fiocco were right then it looks as though propositional imagining could not readily be a good guide to what was *likely* to be the case either. Say that K, a mother who found the pregnancy and early lives of her two children challenging (she had been ill throughout; they had not slept much and had difficulty gaining weight), is trying to decide whether to use contraception in her relationship, and to that end, tries to imagine *what would happen if she got pregnant and gave birth again*. This is a plausible sort of scenario in which one might seriously engage in counterfactual imagining—where one has to make a serious decision affecting one's future life. If imagining were always as unconstrained as is being made out, in response, K might easily, despite what past experience has taught her, imagine having a healthy pregnancy, culminating in a perfectly docile baby who never cried and slept all night, simply stipulating that this counts as *what would happen if I got pregnant again*. More extremely, she might imagine giving birth to octuplets, or to a four-headed green alien, or a piece of cheese. The point is that, given that imagining is on this picture supposed to be basically stipulative and unconstrained, it will not seem to reliably give K any useful information about what is likely to be the case. Yet this looks obviously unduly pessimistic, since it just seems to be a basic truth that we *do* often usefully get information about counterfactual situations from imagining.

It is true that *in some contexts*, propositional imagining can be stipulative and unconstrained. In Chapter 4, I claimed that one can imagine even blatant impossibilities in some contexts. I have not used the story that Kung has used to establish this; and unlike either Kung or Fiocco, in this book I have not been particularly concerned with propositional imagining which involves sensorily or otherwise objectually imagining a given scenario (i.e. where that imagined scenario is being counted by the thinker as an instance of the proposition in question). But like them, I have conceded that one can imagine that p and q are true together, where one also believes that p and q are an impossible combination.

However, Kung and Fiocco each ignore a further lesson repeated throughout this work in connection with propositional imagining in relation to fiction: that it can have various aims or goals, and be constrained according to those aims in a relatively local way. *If* one's aim is to produce propositional imagining which is a guide to what would be the case, in certain given circumstances, then this imagining is constrained in a particular way that other imagining is not. Namely, it is constrained by relevant beliefs about the world. So where K tries to imagine what would happen if she got pregnant again, she is in fact likely to factor into that imagining, relevant beliefs about: how she felt during her last pregnancy, the cost of pregnancy, her past experience of caring for a newborn, and so on. That she *could*, under certain circumstances, imagine the unlikely event of having a perfect pregnancy followed by giving birth to a baby who never cried and who slept all night; or even that under certain circumstance, she *could* imagine giving birth to a green four-headed alien; are irrelevancies. Those imaginings belong to different imaginative projects, with different aims. *Given her current goal*, of counterfactual imagining in order to work out what would happen were she pregnant, she lets her imagining be guided by relevant beliefs and experiences, in a way which is not just stipulative. She lets relevant beliefs and experience guide what she would count as the relevant scenario.

In a recent article, Kung considers the claim that imagining is sometimes constrained 'under a supposition': for instance, if we suppose that water = the chemical compound XYZ, then we cannot imagine that water contains hydrogen 'under that supposition' (2014: 103). He declares the notion of imagining something 'under a supposition' 'obscure', objecting that it should make no difference to imagining's unconstrained nature: for '[u]sually imagining can depart from actuality; that is its point' (*ibid.*). He then produces a range of thought experiments designed to produce intuitions in the reader that one can imagine pretty much anything, whether 'under a supposition' or not. I will discuss the nature of supposition properly in §6.6; but in the meantime, we can say that Kung seems to be eliding a distinction between a) whether one can imagine something in a given context; b) whether one can imagine it at all, in any context. Were someone to suppose that water = XYZ, presumably in order to see what else might follow, then it seems as if she would be committed to holding this content fixed for the purpose of the imaginative project in hand; under those circumstances, given this goal, and given her extant belief that what is XYZ cannot simultaneously contain hydrogen, then normally she will not be able, in the course of the same project, to imagine that water contains hydrogen, I suggest. On the other hand, if this was not her goal, she could. Discussion in Chapter 5 has revealed the sense in which propositional imagining 'departs from actuality': namely, its content can never wholly coincide with the content of one's current belief set. But that is compatible with much of its content overlapping with one's belief set, and this is what happens when one's aim is to produce imaginings useful in their contribution to information about counterfactuals.

Though I cannot pursue it here at any length, it seems at least prima facie plausible that a similar point might be extended to cover cases where imagining aims at establishing metaphysical possibility too. Here too, so long as imagining is positively aimed at the goal of establishing what is possible in a certain case, relevant background beliefs might readily be brought to bear, such that the imagining could in many cases count as suitably constrained. Take a case discussed by Peter Van Inwagen (1998), that of whether it is possible that *there could be naturally occurring purple cows*. In order to establish this, he writes, we would have to bring to bear beliefs about 'whether there is a chemically possible purple pigment such that the coding for the structures that would be responsible for its production and its proper placement in a cow's coat could be coherently inserted into any cow DNA that was really cow DNA—or even "cow-like-thing-but-for-color-DNA"' (Van Inwagen 1998: 78). Now, most of us do not have any such specialist beliefs and so cannot have reliable imaginings in this direction. But those with the relevant beliefs presumably could. Someone with the relevant background beliefs and a serious intention to establish whether there could be naturally occurring purple cows would be unlikely simply frivolously to picture a purple cow or a headline announcing 'Purple cows discovered in nature!' and call the job done. Rather, she would bring to bear her relevant knowledge, or seek out relevant information, to guide what she imagines.

In fact, once we start thinking of modal imagining—imagining aimed at possibility—as informed by relevant background beliefs or new information, Kung's claim that all but the most basic qualitative components of imagining *must* be 'stipulative' starts to look suspect. Though I do not necessarily claim that this is Kung's intention, on a natural reading of 'stipulative', something is stipulative when it is *voluntarily held fixed* by someone, independent of any subsequent tracking of reality. But beliefs are not things over which one has direct voluntary control, and one is normally not free to hold them fixed in a reality-independent way. Hence the content of our beliefs is not stipulative, and arguably nor are the imaginings we choose to allow as informed by them.

Say that a suitably informed thinker *K*, seriously intent on working out whether there could be naturally occurring purple cows, initially imagines a situation with purple cows in it under circumstances *C*, but then comes to realize that some background belief, or new piece of information, makes the scenario she is imagining incoherent; at the same time, she realizes that some other circumstances *D* would need to be in place for a world with purple cows to obtain. It is important to note that this description does not perniciously resemble Fiocco's objectionable model of a thinker first having an imagining, and only then working out exactly what situation she is imagining (is it a world where *x* is possible, or one where *x* is only apparently possible?). The objection there was that, given the inevitable indeterminacy of imagining, many situations would satisfy whatever it was one explicitly imagined; so that the model must be incoherent. This is absolutely right, for reasons well established by Sartre about mental images and which extend to imaginings generally (for discussion see Stock 2007b). That is, there should be no suggestion that a thinker stands to her imagining as an interpreter of pictures might stand to a painting in a gallery. There is nothing analogous to the picture in the gallery's remaining fixed, whilst the interpreter hypothesizes what it represents. However, this is not the model I am endorsing. It is not that *K*'s imagining has remained fixed whilst her view of what it represents has changed. It is that, though her overall imaginative *project* has stayed the same, the basic content of her imagining has changed on further reflection about the world.

We can see this by returning, yet again, to earlier lessons (this time a point made earlier in this chapter, with respect to 'content-controlling' intentions). Where imagining has a goal, it follows that, at least often, it aims at getting something right, and can fail to achieve this. In such cases it involves a choice between alternatives. A reader, working out what to imagine in reading a fiction, may ask herself: is this what the author wanted me to imagine, or is that? An author, constructing a fiction, may ask—is this the best way of conceiving of this scenario, relative to my goal of causing suspense in the reader, or is that? A person fantasizing may revise and 'correct' her fantasy at various points to produce one that mentally satisfies her the most. A person wanting to work out whether a co-worker would enjoy a gift of chocolates may first imagine her enjoying them, but then correct this imagining by bringing to bear a memory that she has not got a sweet tooth. And so on. In these cases it looks as if there is a distinction between a) the scenarios, thoughts, images, and so on that first and spontaneously come to mind when trying to imagine something for some end, and b) the choices one makes, and remakes, in the light of one's current goal in imagining. One can mentally assent to what first comes to mind, or one can reject it and imagine something better, relative to the goal one has. We also saw this in discussions of the role of Lewis's Analyses 1 and 2 in working out what is fictionally true: a reader may defeasibly apply something like one of the Analyses in working out implied fictional content, but this may well be subject to revision.

So in the case currently being considered, *K*'s overall goal remains constant: to imagine, or fail to imagine—and so work out either way—whether it is possible for there to be naturally occurring purple cows. In the service of this project, she makes various attempts at imagining the scenario in question. In our current scenario, her first attempt, she concludes on reflection, is unsuccessful; the second, apparently more successful. At no point in this process does she fail to know, or have to try to work out, what she is imagining in the sense of a). However, in the sense of b), she may at times have to work out whether she has really succeeded in imagining what she intended to, bringing to bear background beliefs or new information. This does not imply the model of a thinker's relation to her imaginings to which Fiocco rightly objects.

None of this is intended to conclusively establish that imagining is in any circumstances a good guide to what is possible; that would be too ambitious an aim in this context (for a positive solution and references to other discussion, see Ichikawa and Jarvis 2012). The principal aim of this section rather has been to establish that it is too hasty to treat imagining as unconstrained in all contexts, just because it is in some. Where, I have argued, philosophers such as Stich and Nichols err in relating imagining too closely to belief, Kung and Fiocco err in effectively downplaying too strongly the importance of the relations between imagining and belief in the context of particular uses of the imagination.

In §6.6, I pursue a further live question in the philosophy of imagination, by considering the relation between propositional imagining and supposition, which once again we are now in a more informed position to consider.

6.6 Imagining and Supposition

a) What is supposition?

Philosophers working on supposition have enumerated certain alleged features of it, based on assessment of the contexts in which the associated ordinary language concept tends to be applied. In no particular order, three features frequently claimed for supposition are that:

a) Supposition is wholly unconstrained. There is no equivalent to imaginative resistance for the activity of supposition (Gendler 2000: 80; Weinberg and Meskin 2006: 193). In support, it is often noted that we can suppose an impossibility in the course of a *reductio ad absurdum*.
b) Whereas, allegedly, imagination is fine-grained and detailed, supposition is not, at least in paradigmatic cases (Weatherson 2004: 20 fn.9; Weinberg and Meskin 2006: 192). Relatedly, imagining but not supposition tends to involve embellishment 'in arbitrary ways' (Weinberg and Meskin 2006: 193).[9]
c) Relatively speaking, in comparison with imagining the same content, supposing tends not to be accompanied by emotion (Moran 1994: 104–5 *et passim*; Weinberg and Meskin 2006: 194). For instance, one can suppose even horrifying situations to be true, without feeling horrified.

Because (as with my treatment of *imagining* generally) my aim is not simply to reconstruct the ordinary language concept, but instead to provide something of explanatory value, it is not essential that my view can accommodate each of these features. On the other hand, if nonetheless I can at least explain in a plausible way why they tend to be attributed to supposition, I take it that this will add to the view's attractiveness. I shall turn to this later; but first, I shall survey some existing accounts.

Various taxonomies relating supposition to imagining (or not) are available. Some (for instance, Casey 2000: 42; Denham 2000: 202–8)[10] apparently treat supposition

---

[9] These authors explain this in terms of the absence of use of the 'Script Elaborator' in supposition but not imagining (see §6.3).
[10] It seems however that for these thinkers, this may just be a convenient way of talking, so that it is perhaps unfair to commit them to the view.

as straightforwardly *identical to* imagining, or at least to propositional imagining (imagining-that); or as a 'belief-like' variant of propositional imagining (Currie and Ravenscroft 2002: 33–8). An apparent problem with this view is that, without further explanation, it would look unable to account for the features of supposition just specified. If the whole story was just that supposing was propositional imagining, it could not easily be true that there was often a difference between supposition and imagining in terms of resistance, detail, embellishment, or accompanying emotion. A different tack, meanwhile, is to treat supposition as an importantly different kind of mental activity from imagining, either propositional or sensory (see e.g. Gendler 2000: 80–1).[11] Though this can account for the features just enumerated, it does so in a rather unparsimonious way, multiplying mental kinds, and ignoring basic apparent similarities between supposing and imagining which have led the former thinkers to class them as identical. For instance, supposition is propositional; one can suppose what one does not currently believe; one uses supposition in the working out of counterfactuals; and so on.

White (1990) gives a detailed though ultimately rather elusive defence of the claim that supposition and imagining are different kinds of mental acts. His general strategy is to treat the concept of *supposition* as including not only those instances where one (say) supposes something one does not believe for the sake of argument, but *also* those cases where one is 'supposed to' do something in the sense of there being a requirement that one does (1990: 136); *and* those cases where one supposes that something is true in the apparent sense of suspecting or believing it (*ibid.*). He then offers an account of supposition according to which (as far as I can reconstruct it) to suppose that p is to commit oneself to p 'either for consideration or for implementation' (1990: 146). The attempt to treat all such ordinary uses of the word 'suppose' as revelatory of a unified concept in this way seems to me to have unfortunate consequences. One of these is that White ends up with a rather vague disjunctive account, as above; where the disjunction, one suspects, is a result of running together at least two usages which would, it seems, be more helpfully treated as distinct. Another is that many of his claims about supposition generally seem more persuasive when applied to the (I would argue, separate) sense in which one supposes that p by virtue of believing or suspecting that p. For instance: that there can be unconscious supposing though not unconscious imagining (1990: 145); that one can be 'justified or unjustified' in supposing something (1990: 137); and that we often explain p (directly) 'by supposing that q' (1990: 146).

Still, parts of White's argument point towards something more useful. He is right, in a sense, that to suppose something involves a commitment (1990: 147); though not in the sense of committing oneself to the truth, as in belief, nor in the sense that some other action or state is an expectation or a requirement, as in what we are 'supposed to do'.

---

[11] In a variant of this view (Kind 2001), it is denied that there is any imagining which is not sensory, thereby leaving only sensory imagining and supposing as contrasting mental activities, not of the same kind.

Rather, I suggest, it is a *commitment to propositionally imagining something, for the length of a given imaginative scenario*. That is, supposition is a *kind* of propositional imagining, which plays a particular role in determining the identity of the imaginative scenarios in which it features. One supposes that p if and only if one propositionally imagines that p *stipulatively*, in the sense that, given the thinker's wider purposes in imagining, p counts as 'fixed' for the imaginative scenario she is engaged in. What this means in practice is that, should the thinker then come to imagine that not-p, which is of course possible, it will be natural to think that she has ceased to engage in the original imaginative scenario, and instead moved on to some other one. What is supposed, if anything, determines the identity of the imaginative scenario of which it is a part, for those scenarios that feature supposition.

Not all imagining involves any supposition in this sense. If I propositionally imagine some scenario in the course of fantasizing for fun, then relative to this goal I need not privilege any particular proposition as fixed for the scenario in question.[12] But for goal-driven imaginative episodes, some supposing will normally be present.

As noted by White, one well-identified use of supposition is to pursue counterfactual knowledge, and this can easily be accommodated on my view. Consider the thought experiment in philosophy: offered, at least putatively, for the reader to work out what else would or could be the case, were some initial set of suppositions the case. The initial description of the thought experiment sets out what may not be altered, on pain of failing to satisfy the purposes of the thought experiment. When students try to adapt the initial premises in ingenious ways, teachers tell them that they are fixed and not up for discussion; they must be accepted as such, on pain of not engaging with the relevant scenario. Take, for example, the famous thought experiment by Thomson (1971: 48–9) designed to persuade the reader that abortion is morally permissible:

> You wake up in the morning and find yourself back to back in bed with an unconscious violinist. A famous unconscious violinist. He has been found to have a fatal kidney ailment, and the Society of Music Lovers have canvassed all the available medical records and found that you alone have the right blood type to help. They have therefore kidnapped you, and last night the violinist's circulatory system was plugged into yours, so that your kidneys can be used to extract poisons from his blood as well as your own. The director of the hospital now tells you, 'Look, we're sorry the Society of Music Lovers did this to you—we would never have permitted it if we had known. But still, they did it, and the violinist is now plugged into you. To unplug him would be to kill him. But never mind, it's only for nine months. By then he will have recovered from his ailment, and can safely be unplugged from you.' Is it morally incumbent on you to accede to this situation?

A thinker K's supposing this is compatible with her imagining all sorts of things not explicitly specified by the content of the experiment as written, whilst still counting as

---

[12] The question of what, if anything, determinately determines the identity of other scenarios which do not feature supposition but only non-suppositional propositional or other imagining is not a question I can tackle here.

engaged with this scenario: for instance, that, with an unconscious violinist attached to one, K feels claustrophobic; that she feels angry that her hopes and plans for the next nine months have to be shelved; and so on. However, she is not at liberty to imagine that, for instance, new evidence comes to light that shows that she does not, in fact, have the right blood type to help the violinist. This would be to move to a different scenario altogether, defeating the purpose of the imaginative exercise.

Supposition is also present in terser and more mundane cases of imagining aimed at counterfactual knowledge. Say that I am on holiday, away from home, and read that a storm is coming to my home town. I wish to think about what will happen. I suppose that *it rains torrentially*. This is fixed for the purposes of my imaginative activity. I may then imagine various things which are not fixed for the purposes of the thought: that *my roof leaks*, that *my plants get watered*, that *my bins overflow*, and so on. These parts of my imaginative activity are not supposed, and so not fixed: they can be revised in the light of reflection without rupturing the continuity of the imaginative scenario, given the initial premise plus the purpose of the imaginative project. Or I might try to work out what would have to be the case, in order for some proposition p to be true. In that case, I will suppose that p, stipulatively, and then work out how that might be true. (Arguably this is what happens when, as described above, one attempts to think of a scenario which would 'verify' a proposition p, with the aim of seeing whether p was possible or not.)

To say that the pursuit of counterfactual knowledge in these ways is *one* familiar use of supposition is not to say, however, that it exhausts its use. On my view, one might suppose something, or instruct someone else to suppose something, for a number of purposes, including but not limited to the pursuit of counterfactual knowledge. What is definitive of supposition as such is not its use in counterfactual reasoning but its reasonably counting as stipulative for the purposes and so identity of the scenario one is engaged with.

We can usefully distinguish here between i) 'autonomous' or self-generated supposition, and ii) 'instruction-based' supposition, i.e. supposition in response to an instruction from someone else (as in fiction). Generally in autonomous supposition, what one supposes will be directly responsive to one's *own* purposes in engaging with imagining at all in that case. In the simple example just offered, I want to know what will happen if it rains torrentially in my home town; naturally enough, then, given this aim, this thought will be fixed for the scenario in question. In the case of instruction-based supposition, on the other hand, things are slightly more complicated. Here, what one supposes (i.e. holds stipulatively fixed) is dependent, not directly upon one's own purposes, but rather upon one's perception of what one is intended by the instructor to suppose (which in turn may well be partly dependent on one's perception of the instructor's purposes in issuing the instruction). I will return to this point in the next section.

Often, 'supposition' is taken to describe the *whole* process of imagining leading to counterfactual knowledge: both *first* stipulatively imagining that such-and-such is the case, *and* then engaging in further imagining about what would or could be the case in that scenario (see for instance Weinberg and Meskin 2006: 192). On the view I prefer, strictly speaking we should exclude the latter stage; 'supposition' includes only the former.[13] As soon as a thinker has—for instance—started to imaginatively work out what else would be true, given that starting point, her imagining is no longer stipulative—it is not held fixed on pain of ceasing to be engaged with the scenario in question. Instead, as just indicated, it might well be revised upon reflection.

We see now that Fiocco's correlation earlier, between imagining and stipulation, discussed above, would have been better confined to supposition, at least in my sense. He apparently worries that *generally* imagining is stipulative, on the grounds that in imagining, one can simply stipulate that some given scenario counts as verifying a given proposition. In this way one could, for instance, 'simply stipulate consideration of a possible world in which', for instance, 'transparent iron exists' (2007: 376). However, as discussed, this is somewhat misleading. In the serious pursuit of modal knowledge, what one *can* do is *suppose*, stipulatively, that transparent iron exists, and then try to work out what else would have to be true for that to be true, and whether that scenario as described exhibited any incoherency. However, the latter part of the imaginative scenario would precisely not be stipulative, as I have argued.

This feature of supposing—its stipulative nature—distances it, contra White, from the usages of 'supposing' to denote what one believes or suspects. When one is asked, for instance, 'Who, do you suppose, stole the jewellery?' one is precisely not free to simply stipulate something or someone as the answer. The stipulative nature of imaginative supposing also tells against White's claim that supposing (in this sense) can be 'justified or unjustified'. Note however that, in saying that supposition involves propositionally imagining 'stipulatively', I do not mean that there is no possible causal or rational relation between what one imagines in that case, and reality. At various points, I have mentioned the case of someone who deliberately decides to incorporate into the content of her imagining some propositions which she believes to be true. This is also possible of supposition. One could suppose that *p*, which one believed true, conjoining it with other propositions which one believed. In that case, there would be a non-accidental relation between what one supposed, and what (one believed) was true. Nonetheless, once supposed, it would be fixed; a change in one's belief that *p*, and any subsequent imagining that not-*p*, would mean that one was no longer engaged with the original scenario, where this was a function of one's purposes in engaging in the imagining.

Let's now return to the features which, according to examination of ordinary language, supposition is often judged to exhibit. The first of these concerns the claim that supposition is unconstrained; that the issue of 'imaginative resistance' does not arise for it. In fact, I think this is true of much supposition, but *only contingently, given certain characteristic accompanying purposes.*

---

[13] I still consider supposing to be an action, not a state.

In Chapter 4, I identified one main source of resistance in response to fictive utterances as the case where the reader believes she is being asked to adopt, as a belief, a moral or other evaluation of an actual scenario described identically, yet cannot. That is, I argued, it is not that there is any general constraint on propositional imagining of certain things, but only where the fictive utterance in question is also assumed to be directed towards a particular end: that of changing or adding to one's beliefs about counterfactuals. Equally, then, someone might be instructed to *suppose* that *p*—hold fixed the imagining that *p* with respect to some scenario—but also suspect that they are simultaneously being asked to believe something they cannot believe true of the actual world (*p* or an implication of *p*); in which case, on my view, resistance will also occur. We can see this if we think about the likely reaction, at least from a non-philosopher not already primed to hear the request in a certain way, to being asked to suppose that something morally abhorrent is the case: some racist proposition, for instance. It seems to me that they are likely to balk, perhaps until it is explained what the purpose of the exercise is, and that it is not also intended that they come to believe any such thing.

It seems to me that the tendency for people to think that supposition does not arouse imaginative resistance—e.g. Gendler (2000: 80)—can be explained by the fact that pragmatically, the hearer (and especially the philosophically-trained one) often interprets the request to 'suppose that *p*' as equivalent to 'suppose that *p only for the sake of argument*'; i.e. as, precisely, *not* an invitation to imagine that *p and* to believe it, or to have further beliefs which *p* implies and which one might reject. But that this is so should not mean, at least on the taxonomy I propose, that the instruction to suppose something may never be intended on the part of the speaker as a relatively direct means to the acquisition of beliefs on the part of the hearer; given my account of supposition, it may. Nor does it follow that the hearer may not demur where she finds the beliefs in question objectionable. In that case, as before, resistance will occur.

The second feature listed above that is sometimes claimed for supposition was that, compared to imagining, it tends to be lacking in detail. Again, I take it that this is not a necessary feature of supposition—at least as I am suggesting we characterize it—but rather a contingent one based on its habitual use in the pursuit of counterfactual knowledge. In that case, typically, we want to know what else would be the case, were some event or fact, *described only at a rather general level*, the case. The concrete details of how the event or fact might manifest itself are usually irrelevant to the cognitive goal in question. We see this in many thought experiments. Again, take, for example, the 'violinist' thought experiment by Thomson (1971) quoted above. It would be irrelevant to the cognitive task to which this experiment is put to specify the facial features of the violinist, or any particular element of the individual histories of those characters involved, over and above those pertinent to the conclusion the reader is intended to draw. A related point can be swiftly made for the claim, also noted, that supposition is or tends to be unaccompanied by embellishment 'in arbitrary ways'. Given its purpose-driven nature, it is hardly surprising that supposition tends to avoid what, relative to that purpose, would count as arbitrary.[14] But this is not to say that supposition cannot be detailed. In fact, it can, as we will shortly see.

Finally, I move to the claim that, relatively to imagining, supposition tends to be unaccompanied by emotion. I take it that this is often true, but again that it is a contingent feature of supposition, owing to at least two facts. The first has just been discussed—contingently, owing to the ends to which it tends to be put, what is supposed is often tersely expressed and lacking in detail. This means that in those cases it is unlikely to have sufficient detail to arouse emotion. For most people, emotions do not tend to latch on to general descriptions of situations with which they are not personally connected—even general descriptions of horrific situations—without concrete detail. On the other hand, once sufficient detail is given of a horrific fictional situation, whether or not one is asked to suppose it true or imagine it is likely to make little difference to the reader's or listener's emotional response. The second relevant point is that again, in many familiar contexts, supposition is frequently directed towards a cognitive goal which has nothing to do with scrutinizing directly how one feels or would feel were something else the case. Hence the supposer's attention is likely to be on the cognitive task to which supposition is being put, and not on the possible emotional consequences of what she imagines. For instance, one might comply with the instruction: 'Suppose that your house was on fire; what three things would you save?' Despite the fact that this presents a scenario which would normally arouse strong emotion in real life, no analogous feelings tend to be experienced by the supposer. Arguably this is because the example exhibits both features of supposition just listed: one is given no visceral or emotive details of the fire, to which emotions might have perhaps attached; and secondly, one is commanded only to consider what one would save, and not how one would feel.

I have just argued that failing to give rise to 'resistance', being lacking in detail, and being unaccompanied by emotion are all familiar but contingent features of supposition, based on its characteristic purposes, and not necessary features of it. These points are underlined when we turn to a context in which, I suggest,—though it is rarely acknowledged as such—supposition is standardly present, yet also present may be

---

[14] Perhaps connected to the claim that supposition tends not be detailed is another potential objection to my account of supposition: does 'imagining' not connote a kind of immersion in a particular perspective, or even an association with imagery (Kind 2001), which supposition lacks? If so, how then can supposition be a kind of imagining? (Some—e.g. Gendler 2000: 80—have taken a cue on this matter from Moran's distinction between the 'hypothetical' imagining which is involved in 'counterfactual reasoning' and 'dramatic imagining', which involves 'imaginatively adopting a perspective on something'; although, as the terminology suggests, he himself counts both as forms of imagining (1994: 104–5).) The objection would be ill-founded, however. Readers will recall that in Chapter 1 I argued that propositional imagining need not be associated with imagery; there can be propositional imagining without it. Moreover, to otherwise confine imagining—that is, the whole of it—to that imagining which involves taking a perspective, imagistic or otherwise, seems to do unnecessary violence to ordinary ways of talking, whilst offering few if any simultaneous explanatory benefits; especially given that we are free to characterize as a subtype of imagining perspectival imagining in particular.

great detail in what is to be supposed, emotional response to that content, and 'resistance'. That context is reading fiction.

b) Supposition in relation to fiction

Let us recall a basic feature of my view, defended at length in Chapter 5. A fiction is a set of instructions to a reader to (at least) propositionally imagine certain things, and, usually, to conjoin them (excluding those parts of a fiction which are unreliably narrated, or fictions which contain conflicting narratives, and so on). The author intends the reader to imagine these things, and furthermore intends her to do so partly on the basis of recognizing the former intention (that is, the intention is reflexive). In effect, then, in authoring a work of fiction, the author is stipulating, via her fictive utterances, that certain propositions are to be supposed by the reader: taken as fixed and unrevisable, relative to the scenario she wishes the reader to engage with. That is, in writing a fiction, she is issuing a complex instruction, still analogous to the much more simplified case where a speaker says to a hearer 'Suppose that p'. The fact that the latter instruction is often accompanied by the intent to persuade the hearer of some point, or to get her to work out some counterfactual, whereas in many cases, at least, fictions are not intended for these purposes (though, as we have seen, they may be), does not undermine the basis of the comparison. The important point for current purposes is that in both cases, there is an instruction to hold certain imaginings as fixed and unrevisable 'premises' of the imaginative episode which follows.

In engaging with a fiction, then, the competent reader *supposes* its content true, in my sense: holds it as fixed and unrevisable, on pain of no longer being engaged with the same scenario. This is what I earlier called 'instruction-generated supposition'. That the content of the fiction functions for the competent reader in this way is partly a product of the author's intentions and purposes with respect to that content. The reader's primary intention is to follow the author's instructions, and to imagine what she is intended to imagine, though of course she will likely have further non-competing purposes of her own in doing so. If this is right, then according to the terms laid out above, reading and imaginatively engaging with fiction standardly involve instruction-based supposition. Whatever propositions count as belonging to the fictional content of a given work are there to be supposed.

This is consistent with saying that propositional-imagining-which-is-not-also-supposing may be made appropriate by a fiction; but if so, it will not (normally anyway) count as part of the content, as I have characterized it. For instance, take the violinist thought experiment again. Arguably, relative to her purposes, Thomson intends the reader to imagine various things which do not count strictly speaking as part of this fiction's content. She intends the reader to imagine something concrete about how unpleasant the situation of the protagonist is (so making easier the drawing of the relevant analogy with an unwanted pregnancy), but does not specify anything concrete about what is to be imagined in this respect, *within* the thought experiment's content.

She lets the reader come up with something on her own. (Arguably moreover, she does not *reflexively* intend that the reader imagines some such thing, but merely intends that she does; that is, it is inessential to her aim that the reader imagines such things as a result of realizing she is intended to by the author.) Equally, a fiction may tell us simply that a character satisfies some determinable (e.g. 'pretty'; 'angry-looking'); it may be up to the reader to imagine what she likes about how that determinable is determinately satisfied. In that case, the relevant imagining the reader has will not count as suppositional, in my sense: it may be revised, still within the terms of the fictional scenario in question. Nor, though, will it count as part of the fiction's content, strictly speaking.

One might worry: at various points, I have stressed that for a reader, working out what an author intended her to imagine can sometimes be a *tentative* and *revisable* process. This is most obviously so in the case of implied fictional content. How then can what she imagines in those cases reasonably count as 'fixed'? The answer is that generally, instruction-generated supposition is 'fixed' or 'stipulated' *subject to one caveat*—it is subject to proper understanding of what one is instructed to suppose. What the reader supposes is parasitical on what she believes she is instructed to imagine by the author. The author sets the terms of the fictional scenario. Where her views change on what she is instructed to suppose, what she supposes should change. This is true of all suppositions in response to instructions, even simple ones like 'Suppose that *p*'. Despite a thought's 'revisability' in this sense, it can still count as supposition in the sense I have outlined. For instance, to return to an example discussed in Chapter 2: am I intended to suppose that in *Villette*, Lucy Snowe's 'craving cry', issued whilst sitting on the bench in the garden, is the result of sexual repression, or not? I may first imagine that it is the result of sexual repression. Then, on further reflection about what Brontë must have meant, I may imagine it is not. Even though I have in this way revised the content of my imagining, it still counts as a) a supposition b) engaged with *Villette*/the same fictional scenario. What I may not permissibly do, given Brontë's assumed purposes, upon which my own as reader are parasitical, is understand the instruction to imagine this as given, but nonetheless imagine that her 'craving cry' is the result of some other cause.

There is a marked contrast here between the reader of a fiction and the author who creates that fiction, assuming as I have done that the latter imagines a scenario concurrently with creating it. Her imagining need not count as supposing until a very late stage in the process of writing. In creating a fiction, during that process nearly every proposition which she imagines is potentially up for revision, subject to her further purposes in writing the work. If she is writing a thriller, for instance, she will be aiming to excite the audience and induce suspense in them; and relative to this purpose, she may first imagine one thing, then 'retract' that imagining and imagine something different, all as part of the same scenario. What she supposes, ultimately, holds as fixed for that scenario—may emerge over time. This underlines the earlier contrast I made between 'autonomous' (self-generated) supposition and 'instruction-based' supposition. In the former, what counts as fixed is relative to one's own purposes in imagining; in the latter, it is relative to one's perception of the instructor's purposes. As we have seen extensively throughout this book, working out the content of the instruction is subject to one's understanding of the author's intentions in so issuing it.

It is time, finally, to sum up the explanatory benefits of my account of supposition in relation to others. To treat supposition as completely distinct in kind from imagining (propositional or sensory) would, on my view, be to multiply mental act-kinds rather profligately, whilst failing to explain why supposition apparently exhibits many features of propositional imagining. It also would leave us with no natural umbrella term for both activities, since 'imagining' would now have been taken. At the same time, it is surely not good enough simply to count 'supposition' and 'propositional imagining' as extensionally equivalent, given the differences I have just explored. Arguably, the most important point to note about supposition is its 'fixed' nature, and this is not something true of all propositional imagining. The account I have offered gives us some good resources with which to better understand the practice of supposition where it occurs in counterfactual thinking, but also in other contexts as well. Perhaps surprisingly—returning to a main theme—one of these is the context of reading fiction itself.

6.7 Summary

In this chapter I have explored and extended various themes of the book and their relation to the question of the nature of propositional imagining. On the one hand, I have rejected the thought that generally or 'by default' the trajectory of propositional imagining is constrained only by beliefs about the world and what would be the case, were certain other things the case. Along the way I have detailed further differences between imagining and belief, in terms of their respective relations to truth, in terms of imagining but not belief counting as an action, and in terms of belief but not imagining as being necessarily conjunctive. On the other hand, I have defended the claim that relative to certain particular uses of the imagination—the acquisition of counterfactual knowledge and of modal knowledge—imagining *is* rationally constrained by beliefs about the world, and not wholly stipulative. I have concluded by offering a new account of supposition, according to which it is imagining which is held 'fixed' and unrevisable, relative to the identity of the imaginative episode in question. Perhaps surprisingly, on this basis, it has turned out that much imagining in relation to fiction counts as supposition.

Conclusion

In this book, a central aim has been to defend what many have taken to be the indefensible: extreme actual intentionalism about fictional content. Historically, philosophers working in aesthetics have sometimes been too quick to dismiss the plausibility of the view. Very often, the same allegedly knockdown objections get passed on from survey to survey, quickly rehearsed and taken obviously to be definitive, before discussion moves on to more favoured contenders. With some notable exceptions, too little attention has been paid to the richly relevant literature in cognate fields such as philosophy of language and philosophy of action. In some cases, unfortunate misunderstandings have occurred. I hope that this book has gone some way at least to demonstrating that as a theory of fictional content, extreme intentionalism should be taken seriously.

Meanwhile, if I am right about fictional content, then a number of very interesting consequences follow for other matters. For one thing, a theory of fiction which characterizes it as a set of intentional instructions to imagine certain things is provided with additional motivation. Many philosophers have been attracted to intentionalism about fiction, at least partially, though they have sought to complicate the story needlessly, as I have argued in Chapter 5. But at the same time, some of those very same philosophers (e.g. Currie, D. Davies) have tended to eschew intentionalism about fictional content, without explaining away or even apparently noting the mismatch. On my view there is no mismatch: in making a fiction, the author instructs the reader to imagine certain things, and the intentions which inform those instructions determine fictional content.

Another feature of my discussion has been to connect the lively philosophical literature on David Lewis's account of fictional truth with a discussion of intentionalism and literary interpretation more generally. Though aestheticians often discuss Lewis's view, those working on it from a background of metaphysics or philosophy of language rarely discuss aesthetics. Lewis himself presents his theory with no explicit discussion of the issue of intentionalism and its relation to his topic; meanwhile contemporary critics such as Phillips and Byrne, though (as noted in Chapter 2) presenting strikingly 'intentional-ish' views themselves, do not discuss the matter explicitly or even show themselves to be aware of it. Yet surely those presenting a plausible theory of fictional truth should be at pains to ensure that it intersect with the thoughts of those working specifically on fiction from an aesthetic and psychological point of view. Equally, any discussion of fictional truth should seek to accommodate the practices of competent readers of published works. This, I argued in Chapter 2, is also missing from Lewis's theory, to its detriment.

A further interesting consequence of my theory of fictional content occurs with respect to testimony-in-fiction: for, it turns out, along with other background assumptions about the nature of testimony generally it furnishes a neat explanation of how testimony-in-fiction can provide the reader with justified beliefs. In contrast, I argued in Chapter 3, rivals to actual intentionalism such as hypothetical intentionalism and value-maximizing theory cannot easily do this.

Equally, my account lends itself to a plausible explanation of what has come to be known as 'imaginative resistance'. Focusing on the fact that authors write fictions with a range of intentions, that these intentions have consequences for fictional content, and that competent readers discern these intentions via a grasp of pragmatic context, lends itself to observing that sometimes, authors intend readers to engage in 'counterfactual' imagining: imagining intended to lead to or be accompanied by the acquisition of certain counterfactual beliefs. Imaginative resistance, I argued, occurs where the reader discerns that she is being asked to engage in counterfactual imagining, and specifically, to acquire or reflect upon a belief which in fact she cannot share.

Finally, as we have just seen, my defence of intentionalism and surrounding discussion led us to some evidentially well-grounded and interesting claims about the propositional imagination. In virtue of my central claim that a) what a reader imagines in relation to a fiction should be constrained by the goal of recovering authorial intention, in conjunction with b) an acknowledgement of the multiplicity of intentions—not all of them directed towards counterfactual imagining—with which a fiction may be created, we arrived at c) a rejection of a popular view of imagining according to which it is normally or 'by default' inferentially constrained as belief with the same content would be. (As we saw, this is not to say that it is unconstrained.) Equally, partly in the light of those cases where fictions clearly *are* directed towards counterfactual imagining constrained in belief-like ways, I rejected a view of propositional imagining as wholly stipulative and unconstrained. In this way, room is left for views according to which imagining can be a good guide to counterfactuals and/or possibilities. In all cases, I have suggested, the presence and nature of constraints upon a given episode of imagining depend on its aim. Indeed, this is one of the central messages of the book: imagining is a flexible action which can be directed at a variety of useful and pleasurable ends, both cognitive and non-cognitive. This may seem obvious to anyone who has ever read much published fiction; but nonetheless it still needed to be spelled out in a theoretically respectable way in order to do explanatory work. I hope to have done this here.

Bibliography

Alward, Peter (2010) That's the fictional truth, Ruth. *Acta Analytica* 25(3): 347–63.
Anscombe, G.E.M. (1957) *Intention*. Oxford: Basil Blackwell.
Atwood, Margaret (1994) Running with the tigers. In L. Sage (ed.) *Flesh and the Mirror: Essays on the Art of Angela Carter*. London: Virago Press, pp. 117–35.
Audi, R. (1973) Intending. *Journal of Philosophy* 70: 387–403.
Aune, Bruce (1977) *Reason and Action*. Dordrecht: D. Reidel Publishing Company.
Austen, Jane (1990) *Emma*. Oxford: Oxford University Press. First published 1816.
Bach, Kent (1994) Conversational implicature. *Mind and Language* 9: 124–62.
Bach, Kent (2012) Saying, meaning and implicating. In K. Allan and K. Jaszczolt (eds.) *The Cambridge Handbook of Pragmatics*. Cambridge: Cambridge University Press, pp. 47–68.
Barrie, J.M. (2008) *Peter Pan*. London: Puffin. First published 1911.
Beardsley, Monroe (1992) The authority of the text. In G. Iseminger (ed.) *Intention and Interpretation*. Philadelphia, PA: Temple University, pp. 24–40.
Beecher Stowe, Harriet (2014) *Uncle Tom's Cabin*. Amazon CreateSpace independent publishing platform. First published 1852.
Bond, Christopher (2016) Gnosis and the sexual transgressive in Pat Barker's *Regeneration* Trilogy. *Critique: Studies in Contemporary Fiction* 57: 1–15.
Borges, Jorge Luis (transl James E. Irby) (1970) *Labyrinths*. London: Penguin. First published 1962.
Boyd, Brian (1997) Shade and shape in *Pale Fire*. *Nabokov Studies* 4: 173–224.
Braddon-Mitchell, D. and Nola, R. (2009) *Conceptual Analysis and Philosophical Naturalism* (Introduction). Cambridge, MA: MIT Press.
Bratman, Michael (1987) *Intention, Plans, and Practical Reason*. Cambridge, MA: Harvard University Press.
Brontë, Charlotte (1844) Letter to Constantin Heger. Held in British Library (Add MS 38732).
Brontë, Charlotte (1966) *Jane Eyre*. London: Penguin. First published 1847.
Bronte, Charlotte (1985) *Villette*. London: Penguin. First published 1853.
Burge, Tyler (1993) Content preservation. *Philosophical Review* 102: 457–88.
Burgess, Anthony (1972) *A Clockwork Orange*. London: Penguin. First published 1962.
Byrne, Alex (1993) Truth in fiction: the story continued. *Australasian Journal of Philosophy*. 71(1): 24–35.
Carroll, Lewis (1928) *Alice in Wonderland*. London: Macmillan. First published 1865.
Carroll, Lewis (2009) *Through the Looking Glass and What Alice Found There*. Westport, Co. Mayo: Evertype. First published 1897.
Carroll, Noel (1992) Art, intention and conversation. In Gary Iseminger (ed.) *Intention and Interpretation*. Philadelphia, PA: Temple University Press, pp. 97–131.
Carroll, Noel (2000) Intentionalism and interpretation: the debate between actual and hypothetical intentionalism. *Metaphilosophy* 31(1/2): 75–95.
Carroll, Noel (2007) Narrative closure. *Philosophical Studies* 135(1): 1–15.
Carter, Angela (1996) *Burning your Boats: Collected Short Stories*. London: Vintage. First published 1995.

Casey, E. (2000) *Imagining: A Phenomenological Study*. Bloomington, IN: Indiana University Press. First published 1976.

Chalmers, David (2002) Does conceivability entail possibility? In T. Gendler and J. Hawthorne (eds.) *Conceivability and Possibility*. Oxford: Oxford University Press, pp. 145–200.

Churchwell, Sarah (2014) Marilynne Robinson's *Lila*: a great achievement in US fiction. *The Guardian*, 7 November, 2014. [Online] http://www.theguardian.com/books/2014/nov/07/marilynne-robinson-lila-great-achievement-contemporary-us-fiction-gilead Accessed 31 March, 2015.

Coady, C.J. (1994) *Testimony: A Philosophical Study*. Oxford: Clarendon Press.

Conan Doyle, Arthur (1960) *The Complete Sherlock Holmes*. New York, NY: Doubleday.

Conrad, Joseph (1961) *The Secret Agent*. London: Everyman. First published 1907.

Crompton, Sarah (2016) J.K. Rowling: 'Harry Potter's world is always in my head'. *The Guardian/Observer*, 5 June, 2016. [Online] https://www.theguardian.com/stage/2016/jun/05/jk-rowling-harry-potter-cursed-child-jack-thorne-john-tiffany-interview Accessed 23 August, 2016.

Culler, J. (1974) *Flaubert: The Uses of Uncertainty*. Ithaca, NY: Cornell University Press.

Culler, J. (2008) The realism of Madame Bovary. *MLN* 122(4): 683–96.

Currie, Gregory (1990) *The Nature of Fiction*. Cambridge: Cambridge University Press.

Currie, Gregory (1993) Interpretation and objectivity. *Mind*, New Series 102(407): 413–28.

Currie, Gregory (1995a) The moral psychology of fiction. *Australasian Journal of Philosophy* 73(2): 250–9.

Currie, Gregory (1995b) Imagination and simulation: aesthetics meets cognitive science. In M. Davies and T. Stone (eds.) *Mental Simulation*. Oxford: Basil Blackwell, pp. 151–69.

Currie, Gregory (2004) Interpretation and pragmatics. In *Arts and Minds*. Oxford: Oxford University Press, pp. 107–33.

Currie, Gregory and Ravenscroft, Ian (2002) *Recreative Minds: Imagination in Philosophy and Psychology*. Oxford: Oxford University Press.

Daniels, Norman (2013) Reflective equilibrium. In Edward N. Zalta (ed.) *The Stanford Encyclopedia of Philosophy* (Winter). [Online] http://plato.stanford.edu/archives/win2013/entries/reflective-equilibrium/.Stanford, CA: Stanford University. Accessed 15 March, 2017.

Davidson, Donald (1980) Intending. In *Essays on Actions and Events*. Oxford: Oxford University Press, pp. 83–102. First published 1978.

Davidson, Donald (2006) A nice derangement of epitaphs. In *The Essential Davidson*. Oxford: Oxford University Press, pp. 251–66. First published 1986.

Davies, David (2004) *Art as Performance*. Oxford: Wiley Blackwell.

Davies, David (2007) *Aesthetics and Literature*. London: Continuum.

Davies, David (2015) Fictive utterance and the fictionality of narratives and works. *British Journal of Aesthetics* 55(1): 39–55.

Davies, Stephen (2006) Authors' intentions, literary interpretations and literary value. *British Journal of Aesthetics* 46(3): 223–47.

Davis, Wayne (1992) Speaker meaning. *Linguistics and Philosophy* 15(3): 223–53.

Denham, Alison (2000) *Metaphor and Moral Experience*. Oxford: Oxford University Press.

Deutsch, Harry (2000) Making up Stories. In A. Everett and T. Hofweber (eds.) *Empty Names, Fiction, and the Puzzles of Non-Existence*. Stanford, CA: CSLI Publications, pp. 149–82.

Dickens, Charles (1994) *Great Expectations*. London: Penguin. First published 1861.

Dickie, George (1983) The new institutional theory of art. *Proceedings of the 8th Wittgenstein Symposium* 10, 57–64.

Dickie, George and Wilson, Kent (1995) The intentional fallacy: defending Beardsley. *Journal of Aesthetics and Art Criticism* 53: 233–50.
Donnellan, Keith (1968) Putting Humpty Dumpty together again. *The Philosophical Review* 77: 203–15.
Dorsch, Fabian (2012) *The Unity of the Imagination*. Heusenstamm: Ontos-Verlag.
Doyle, Charlotte L. (1998) The writer tells: the creative process in the writing of literary fiction. *Creativity Research Journal* 11(1): 29–37.
Driver, Julia (2008) Imaginative resistance and ontological necessity. *Social Philosophy and Policy* 25(1): 301–13.
Dubrow, Heather (1982) *Genre*. London: Routledge.
Eagleton, Terry (1988) *Myths of Power: A Marxist Study of the Brontës*. London: Macmillan.
Easton Ellis, Brett (2015) *American Psycho*. London: Picador. First published 1991.
Eigner, Edwin M. (1970) Bulwer-Lytton and the changed ending of *Great Expectations*. *Nineteenth-Century Fiction* 25(1): 104–8.
Eliot, George (1986) *Daniel Deronda*, London: Penguin. First published 1876.
Ericsson, Anders (2003) Valid and non-reactive verbalization of thoughts during performance of tasks: towards a solution to the central problems of introspection as a source of scientific data. *Journal of Consciousness Studies* 10(9–10): 1–18.
Evnine, Simon (1999) Believing conjunctions. *Synthese* 118: 201–27.
Ezard, John (2002) Narnia books attacked as racist and sexist. *The Guardian*, 3 June. [Online] https://www.theguardian.com/uk/2002/jun/03/gender.hayfestival2002 Accessed 10 August, 2015.
Farnell, G. (2014) The Gothic, the Death Drive and Angela Carter. *Women: A Cultural Review* 25(3): 270–86.
Farrell, J.G. (1992) *The Singapore Grip*. London: Phoenix. First published 1978.
Faulkner, Paul (2007) On telling and trusting. *Mind* 116(464): 875–902.
Fay, Sarah (2008) Marilynne Robinson. The Art of Fiction No. 198. *Paris Review* 186.
Fiocco, Marcello Oreste (2007) Conceivability, imagination and modal knowledge. *Philosophy and Phenomenological Research* 74(2): 364–80.
Fowler, Karen Joy (2013) *We Are All Completely Beside Ourselves*. London: Serpent's Tail.
Fricker, Elizabeth (1995) Telling and trusting: reductionism and anti-reductionism in the epistemology of testimony. *Mind* 104(414): 393–411.
Friend, Stacie (2008) Imagining fact and fiction. In K. Stock and K. Thomson-Jones (eds.) *New Waves in Aesthetics.*, London: Palgrave Macmillan, pp. 150–69.
Friend, Stacie (2011) Fictive utterance and imagining II. *Proceedings of the Aristotelian Society, Supplementary Volume* 85: 163–80.
Friend, Stacie (2012) Fiction as a genre. *Proceedings of the Aristotelian Society* 112(2): 179–209.
Friend, Stacie (2014) Believing in Stories. In Greg Currie, Matthew Kieran, Aaron Meskin, and Jon Robson (eds.) *Aesthetics and the Sciences of Mind*. Oxford: Oxford University Press, pp. 227–48.
Frye, Northrop (1957) *Anatomy of Criticism: Four Essays*. Princeton, NJ: Princeton University Press.
Frye, Northrop (1963) Literature as context: Milton's *Lycidas*. In *Fables of Identity: Studies in Poetic Mythology*. New York, NY: Harcourt, pp. 119–29.
Funke Butler, Sarah (2011) The symbolism survey. *Paris Review*, 5 December. [Online] http://www.theparisreview.org/blog/2011/12/05/document-the-symbolism-survey/ Accessed 15 April, 2015.

Furbank P.N. and Haskell F.J.H (1953) E.M. Forster. The Art of Fiction No. 1. *Paris Review* 1 (Spring).

Furneaux, Holly (2009) *Queer Dickens: Erotics, Families, Masculinities*. Oxford: Oxford University Press.

Gaiman, Neil and Ishiguro, Kazuo (2015) "Let's talk about genre": Neil Gaiman and Kazuo Ishiguro in conversation. *New Statesman*, 4 June. [Online] http://www.newstatesman.com/2015/05/neil-gaiman-kazuo-ishiguro-interview-literature-genre-machines-can-toil-they-can-t-imagine. Accessed 22 June, 2016.

Garcia-Carpintero, Manuel (2013) Norms of fiction-making. *British Journal of Aesthetics* 53(3): 339–57.

Gardner, Martin (2000) *The Annotated Alice*. 2nd edition. London: Penguin. First published 1970.

Gaskin, Richard (2013) *Language, Truth and Literature: A Defence of Literary Humanism*. Oxford: Oxford University Press.

Gaut, Berys (2000) 'Art' as a cluster concept. In N. Carroll (ed.) *Theories of Art Today*. Madison, WI: University of Wisconsin Press, pp. 25–44.

Gaut, Berys (2003) Creativity and imagination. In B. Gaut and P. Livingston (eds.) *The Creation of Art*. Cambridge: Cambridge University Press, pp. 148–73.

Gendler, Tamar (2000) The puzzle of imaginative resistance. *Journal of Philosophy* 97(2): 55–81.

Gendler, Tamar (2006) Imaginative resistance revisited. In Shaun Nichols (ed.) *The Architecture of the Imagination*. Oxford: Oxford University Press, pp. 149–73.

Gendler, Tamar (2008) Alief and belief. *Journal of Philosophy* 105(10): 634–63.

Gibson, John (2007) *Fiction and the Weave of Life*. Oxford: Oxford University Press.

Goldman, A. (1976) Discrimination and Perceptual Knowledge. *Journal of Philosophy* 73(20): 771–91.

Goodman, Nelson (1982) Fiction for five fingers. *Philosophy and Literature* 6(1): 162–4.

Gordon, Robert M. (1992) The simulation theory: objections and misconceptions. *Mind and Language* 7(1): 11–34.

Gould, Stephen J. and Lewontin, Richard C. (1997) The spandrels of San Marco and the Panglossian paradigm: a critique of the adaptionist programme. *Proceedings of the Royal Society of London* Series B 205(1161): 581–98.

Grant, Annette (1976) John Cheever. The Art of Fiction No. 62. *Paris Review*. Fall (67).

Green, Anne (1982) *Flaubert and the Historical Novel: 'Salammbô' Reassessed*. Cambridge: Cambridge University Press.

Green, Mitchell (2010) How and what we can learn from fiction. In Garry Hagberg and Walter Jost (eds.) *A Companion to the Philosophy of Literature*. Oxford: Wiley-Blackwell, pp. 350–66.

Greene, Graham (1971) *The Power and the Glory*. London: Penguin. First published 1940.

Greene, Graham (1974) *The Heart of the Matter*. London: Penguin. First published 1948.

Grice, H.P. (1957) Meaning. *The Philosophical Review* 66(3): 377–88.

Grice, H.P. (1969) Utterer's meaning and intention. *The Philosophical Review* 78(2): 147–77.

Grice, H.P. (1975) Logic and conversation. In P. Cole and J.L. Morgan (eds.) *Syntax and Semantics, Volume 3: Speech Acts*. New York, NY: Academic Press, pp. 41–58.

Grice, H.P. (1989) Retrospective epilogue. In *Studies in the Way of Words*. Cambridge, MA: Harvard University Press, pp. 339–85.

Guppy, Shusha (1984) Edna O'Brien, The Art of Fiction No. 82. *Paris Review.* Summer 92.
Hanley, Richard (2004) As good as it gets: Lewis on truth in fiction. *Australasian Journal of Philosophy* 82(1): 112–28.
Harman, G. (1976) Practical reasoning. *The Review of Metaphysics* 29: 431–63. Reprinted 1997 in A. Mele (ed.) *The Philosophy of Action.* Oxford: Oxford University Press, pp. 149–77.
Hartner, D. (2013) Conceptual analysis as armchair psychology: in defence of methodological naturalism. *Philosophical Studies* 165: 921–37.
Hartner, D. (2014) From desire to subjective value: what neuroeconomics reveals about naturalism. *Erasmus Journal for Philosophy and Economics* 7(1): 1–26.
Hawthorne, Nathaniel (1999) *The House of the Seven Gables.* Mineola, NY: Dover Thrift. First published 1851.
Housman, A.E. (1933) *The Name and Nature of Poetry.* Cambridge: Cambridge University Press.
Huddleston, Andrew (2012) The conversation argument for actual intentionalism. *British Journal of Aesthetics* 52(3): 241–56.
Ichikawa, Jonathan and Jarvis, Benjamin (2012) Rational imagination and modal knowledge. *Noûs* 46(1): 127–58.
Irvin, Sherri (2006) Authors, intentions and literary meanings. *Philosophy Compass* 1(2): 114–28.
Irwin, William (2015) Authorial declaration and extreme intentionalism: is Dumbledore gay? *Journal of Aesthetics and Art Criticism* 73(2): 141–7.
Jackson, F. (2000) *From Metaphysics to Ethics: A Defence of Conceptual Analysis.* Oxford: Oxford University Press.
Jackson, Frank and Pettit, Philip (1993) Folk belief and commonplace belief. *Mind and Language* 8(2): 298–305.
James, E.L. (2012) *Fifty Shades Darker.* London: Arrow Books.
Jones, Ernest (1910) The Oedipus-complex as an explanation of Hamlet's mystery: a study in motive. *The American Journal of Psychology* 21(1): 72–113.
Kieran, Matthew (1996) In defence of critical pluralism. *British Journal of Aesthetics* 36(3): 239–51.
Kind, Amy (2001) Putting the image back into the imagination. *Philosophy and Phenomenological Research* 62(1): 85–109.
Kind, Amy (2013) The heterogeneity of the imagination. *Erkenntnis* 78 (1): 141–59.
Knapp, Steven and Michaels, Walter Benn (1987) Against theory 2: hermeneutics and deconstruction. *Critical Inquiry* 14: 49–68.
Korsmeyer, Carolyn (2011) *Savoring Disgust: the Foul and the Fair in Aesthetics.* Oxford: Oxford University Press.
Kripke, Saul (1980) *Naming and Necessity.* Cambridge, MA: Harvard University Press.
Kung, Peter (2010) Imagining as a guide to possibility. *Philosophy and Phenomenological Research* 81(3): 620–63.
Kung, Peter (2014) You really do imagine it: against error theories of the imagination. *Noûs* 50(1): 90–120.
Lamarque, Peter (1990a) Reasoning to what is true in fiction. *Argumentation* 4: 333–46.
Lamarque, Peter (1990b) The death of the author: an analytical autopsy. *British Journal of Aesthetics* 30(4): 319–33.
Lamarque, Peter and Olsen, Stein H. (1994) *Truth, Fiction and Literature.* Oxford: Oxford University Press.

Langland-Hassan, Peter (2012) Pretense, imagination, and belief: the Single Attitude Theory. *Philosophical Studies* 159: 155–79.

Langland-Hassan, Peter (2016) On choosing what to imagine. In A. Kind (ed.) *Knowledge through Imagination*. Oxford: Oxford University Press, pp. 61–82.

Lebbon, Tim (2006) *Dusk*. New York, NY: Bantam Spectra.

Le Marchand, Jean (1953) Francois Mauriac. The Art of Fiction No. 2. *Paris Review*, Summer (2).

Le Poidevin, Robin (2001) Fate, fiction and the future. *Philosophical Papers* 30(1): 69–92.

Leslie, Alan (1994) Pretending and believing: issues in the theory of ToMM. *Cognition* 50: 211–38.

Levin, J. (2011) Imaginability, possibility, and the puzzle of imaginative resistance. *Canadian Journal of Philosophy* 41(3): 391–421.

Levin, J. (2013) Functionalism. In Edward N. Zalta (ed.) *The Stanford Encyclopedia of Philosophy* (Fall). [Online] Stanford, CA: Stanford University. http://plato.stanford.edu/archives/fall2013/entries/functionalism/. Accessed 15 March, 2017.

Levinson, Jerrold (1992) Intention and interpretation: a last look. In Gary Iseminger (ed.) *Intention and Interpretation*. Philadelphia, PA: Temple University Press. pp. 221–56.

Levinson, Jerrold (2002) Hume's standard of taste: the real problem. *Journal of Aesthetics and Art Criticism* 60(3): 227–38.

Levinson, Jerrold (2006) Hypothetical intentionalism: statement, objections, and replies. In *Contemplating Art*. Oxford: Oxford University Press, 302–15.

Levinson, Jerrold (2010) Defending hypothetical intentionalism. *British Journal of Aesthetics* 50(2): 139–50.

Levinstein, Ben (2007) Facts, interpretation and truth in fiction. *British Journal of Aesthetics* 47(1): 64–75.

Levy, Neil (2005) Imaginative resistance and the moral/conventional distinction. *Philosophical Psychology* 18(2): 231–41.

Lewis, C.S. (1959) *The Lion, the Witch and the Wardrobe*. London: Penguin.

Lewis, David (1972) Psychophysical and theoretical identifications. *Australasian Journal of Philosophy* 50(3): 249–58.

Lewis, David (1983) Truth in Fiction. Reprinted in his *Philosophical Papers, Vol. 1*. Oxford: Oxford University Press, pp. 261–80.

Liao, Shen-yi, Strohminger, Nina, and Sekhar Sripada Chandra (2014) Empirically investigating imaginative resistance. *British Journal of Aesthetics* 54(3): 339–55.

Livingston, Paisley (2005) *Art and Intention: A Philosophical Study*. Oxford: Oxford University Press.

Lorand, Ruth (2001) Telling a story or telling a world? *British Journal of Aesthetics* 41(4): 425–43.

Ludwig, Kirk (1992) Impossible doings. *Philosophical Studies* 65(3): 257–81.

Mahtani, Anna (2012) Imaginative resistance without conflict. *Philosophical Studies* 158: 415–29.

Mantel, Hilary (2012) *Bring Up the Bodies*. London: Fourth Estate.

Matravers, Derek (2014) *Fiction and Narrative*. Oxford: Oxford University Press.

McCann, Hugh (1987) Rationality and the range of intention. *Midwest Studies in Philosophy* 10(1): 191–211.

Mitford, Nancy (1949) *The Pursuit of Love*. London: Penguin. First published 1945.

Moran, Richard (1994) The expression of feeling in imagination. *Philosophical Review* 103(1): 75–106.

Moran, Richard (2001) *Authority and Estrangement: An Essay on Self-Knowledge*. Princeton, NJ: Princeton University Press.
Moran, Richard (2005) Getting told and being believed. *Philosophers' Imprint* 5(5).
Munro, Alice (1991) *The Beggar Maid*. New York, NY: Vintage.
Murakami, Haruki (2002) Super-Frog saves Tokyo. GQ magazine, June. [Online] http://www.gq.com/entertainment/books/200206/haruki-murakami-super-frog-saves-tokyo-full-story Accessed 24 March, 2015.
Murakami, Haruki (2003) *South of the Border, West of the Sun*. London: Vintage. First published 1992.
Nabokov, Vladimir (2001) *Collected Stories*. London: Penguin. First published 1995.
Nanay, Bence (2010) Imaginative resistance and conversational implicature. *Philosophical Quarterly* 64(240): 586–600.
Neale, Stephen (1992) Paul Grice and the philosophy of language. *Linguistics and Philosophy* 15: 509–59.
Newton, Judith (1985) Villette. In J. Newton and D. Rosenfeld (eds.) *Feminist Criticism and Social Change, Vol. 10*. London: Routledge, pp. 105–33.
Nichols, Shaun (2004) Imagining and believing: the promise of a single code. *Journal of Aesthetics and Art Criticism* 62(2): 129–39.
Nichols, Shaun ed. (2006) *The Architecture of the Imagination*. [Introduction]. Oxford: Oxford University Press.
Nolan, Daniel (2009) Platitudes and metaphysics. In David Braddon-Mitchell and Robert Nola (eds.) *Conceptual Analysis and Philosophical Naturalism*. Cambridge, MA: MIT Press, pp. 267–300.
Noordhof, Paul (2002) Imagining objects and imagining experiences. *Mind and Language* 17(4): 426–55.
Northover, A. (2009) Animal ethics and human identity in JM Coetzee's *The Lives of Animals*. *Scrutiny 2* 14(2): 28–39.
O'Brien, Lucy (2005) Imagination and the motivational view of belief. *Analysis* 65(1): 55–62.
O'Shaughnessy, Brian (2003) *Consciousness and the World*. Oxford: Clarendon Press.
Owens, David (2003) Does belief have an aim? *Philosophical Studies* 115(3): 283–305.
Oxindine, Annette (1997) Rhoda submerged: lesbian suicide in *The Waves*. In Eileen Barrett and Patricia Cramer (eds.) *Virginia Woolf: Lesbian Readings*. New York, NY: New York University Press, pp. 203–21.
Paley, Grace (1998) *The Collected Stories*. London: Virago. First published 1994.
Peacocke, Christopher (1985) Imagination, experience and possibility. In J. Foster and H. Robinson (eds.) *Essays on Berkeley*. Oxford: Clarendon Press, pp. 19–35.
Phillips, John (1999) Truth and inference in fiction. *Philosophical Studies* 94: 273–93.
Predelli, Stefano (2010) Malapropisms and the simple picture of communication. *Mind & Language* 25(3): 329–45.
Pritchard, Duncan (2004) The epistemology of testimony. *Philosophical Issues* 14: 326–48.
Pritchard, Duncan (2008) Sensitivity, safety and anti-luck epistemology. In J. Greco (ed.) *The Oxford Handbook of Skepticism*. Oxford: Oxford University Press, pp. 437–55.
Pyrhönen, H. (2007) Imagining the impossible: the erotic poetics of Angela Carter's 'Bluebeard' stories. *Textual Practice* 21(1): 93–111.
Railton, Peter (2014) Reliance, trust and belief. *Inquiry* 57(1): 122–50.

Recanati, Francois (1986) On defining communicative intentions. *Mind and Language* 1(3): 213–42.
Recanati, Francois (2003) *Literal Meaning*. Cambridge: Cambridge University Press.
Rhys, Jean (2001) *Wide Sargasso Sea*. London: Penguin Student Editions. First published 1966.
Rich, Adrienne (1973) Jane Eyre: the temptations of a motherless woman. In A. Rich *Lies, Secrets and Silence: Collected Prose 1966-1978*. New York, NY: W.W. Norton, pp. 89–106.
Rich, Nathaniel (2009) James Ellroy. The Art of Fiction No. 201. *Paris Review*. Fall 190.
Robinson, Marilynne (2005) *Gilead*. London: Virago Press. First published 2004.
Roeser, S. (2012) Emotional engineers: toward morally responsible design. *Science and Engineering Ethics* 18(1): 103–15.
Ryan, Marie-Laure (1980) Fiction, non-factuals and the principle of minimal departure. *Poetics* 9: 403–22.
Safran Foer, Jonathan (2002) *Everything is Illuminated*. Boston, MA: Houghton Mifflin.
Sainsbury, R.M. (2014) Fictional worlds and fictional operators. In M. Garcia-Carpintero and G. Martinez (eds.) *Empty Representations*. Oxford: Oxford University Press, pp. 277–89.
Sceats, Sarah (2001) Oral sex: vampiric transgression and the writing of Angela Carter. *Tulsa Studies in Women's Literature* 20(1): 107–21.
Schlicke, Paul (2011) *The Oxford Companion to Charles Dickens*. Oxford: Oxford University Press.
Schor, N. (1980) Details and decadence: end-troping in *Madame Bovary*. *SubStance* 9(1): 27–35.
Schuyler, George (2013) *Black No More*. Rockville, MD: Disruptive Publishing. First published 1931.
Schwitzgebel, Eric (2002) A dispositionalist, phenomenal account of belief. *Noûs* 36: 249–75.
Scruton, Roger (1974) *Art and Imagination*. London: Methuen.
Searle, John (1969) *Speech Acts: An Essay in the Philosophy of Language*. Cambridge: Cambridge University Press.
Searle, John (1975) The logical status of fictional discourse. *New Literary History* 6(2): 319–32.
Setiya, Kieran (2014) Intention. In Edward N. Zalta (ed.) *The Stanford Encyclopedia of Philosophy* (Spring). [Online] Stanford, CA: Stanford University. http://plato.stanford.edu/archives/spr2014/entries/intention/. Accessed 21 April, 2017.
Sheets, R. (1991) Pornography, fairy tales, and feminism: Angela Carter's "The Bloody Chamber". *Journal of the History of Sexuality* 1(4): 633–57.
Shipley, Diane (2008) The great chick-lit cover up. *The Guardian*, 29 July 2008. [Online] https://www.theguardian.com/books/booksblog/2008/jul/29/thegreatchicklitcoverup Accessed 7 July, 2016.
Shriver, Lionel (2007) *The Post-Birthday World*. New York, NY: Harper Collins.
Simpson, Mona and Buzbee, Lewis (1983) Raymond Carver. The Art of Fiction No. 76. *Paris Review*. Summer. 88.
Sinhababu, Neil (2013) The desire-belief account of intention explains everything. *Noûs* 47(4): 680–96.
Smith, Monika (1996) Trollope's dark vision: domestic violence and *The Way We Live Now*. *Victorian Review* 22(1): 13–31.
Sorenson, Roy (2011) What lies behind misspeaking. *American Philosophical Quarterly* 48(4): 399–409.
Spark, Muriel (2001) The Ormolu Clock. In M. Spark *The Complete Short Stories*. London: Penguin, pp. 341–50.
Stannard, Martin (2009) *Muriel Spark: The Biography*. London: Phoenix.

Stecker, Robert (1994) Art interpretation. *Journal of Aesthetics and Art Criticism* 52(2): 193–206.
Stecker, Robert (2006) Moderate actual intentionalism defended. *Journal of Aesthetics and Art Criticism* 64(4): 429–38.
Stich, Stephen P. and Nichols, Shaun (2000) A cognitive theory of pretense. *Cognition* 74(2): 115–47.
Stock, Kathleen (2003) The tower of Goldbach and other impossible tales. In M. Kieran and D. Lopes *Imagination, Philosophy and the Arts*. London: Routledge, pp. 107–24.
Stock, Kathleen (2005) Resisting imaginative resistance. *Philosophical Quarterly* 55(221): 607–24.
Stock, Kathleen (2007a) Fiction and psychological insight. In M. Kieran and D. Lopes *Knowing Art: Essays in Aesthetics and Epistemology*. Philosophical Studies series 10. Dordrecht: Springer, pp. 51–66.
Stock, Kathleen (2007b) Sartre, Wittgenstein and learning from imagination. In Peter Goldie and Elisabeth Schellekens (eds.) *Philosophy and Conceptual Art*. Oxford: Oxford University Press, pp. 171–94.
Stock, Kathleen (2008) Imagining and seeing-in. *Journal of Aesthetics and Art Criticism* 66(4): 365–80.
Stock, Kathleen (2009) Fantasy, imagination and film. *British Journal of Aesthetics* 49(4): 357–69.
Stock, Kathleen (2011) Fictive utterance and imagining. *Aristotelian Society Supplementary Volume* 85(1): 145–61.
Stock, Kathleen (2016a) Imagination and fiction. In A. Kind (ed.) *The Routledge Handbook of Philosophy of Imagination*. London: Routledge, pp. 204–16.
Stock, Kathleen (2016b) Learning from fiction and theories of fictional content. *Teorema* 35(3): 69–83.
Stock, Kathleen (2017a) Fiction, testimony, belief and history. In H. Bradley, E. Sullivan-Bissett, and P. Noordhof (eds.) *Art and the Nature of Belief*. Oxford: Oxford University Press.
Stock, Kathleen (2017b) Imaginative resistance. In H. Maibom (ed.) *The Routledge Handbook to the Philosophy of Empathy*, London: Routledge, pp. 327–38.
Strawson, P.F. (1964) Intention and convention in speech acts. *The Philosophical Review* 73(4): 439–60.
Strawson, P.F. (1970) Imagination and perception. In L. Foster and J.W. Swanson (eds.) *Experience and Theory*. Amherst, MA: University of Massachusetts Press, pp. 31–54.
Sutherland, John (1996) *Is Heathcliff A Murderer? Puzzles in 19th-Century Fiction*. Oxford: Oxford University Press.
Taylor, Marjorie (2013) *The Oxford Handbook of the Development of the Imagination*. Oxford: Oxford University Press.
Taylor, Marjorie, Hodges, Sara D., and Kohányi, Adèle (2003) The illusion of independent agency: do adult fiction writers experience their characters as having minds of their own? *Imagination, Cognition and Personality* 22: 361–80.
Taylor, Paul (1981) Misconstrued wants and unconscious intentions. *Philosophical Papers* 10(2): 66–76.
Taylor, Paul (2014) Meaning, expression and the interpretation of literature. *Journal of Aesthetics and Art Criticism* 72(4): 379–91.
Thackeray, W.M. (2003) *Vanity Fair*. Cambridge, MA: Spark Educational Publishing. First published 1847.
Thagard, P. (2006) Desires are not propositional attitudes. *Dialogue* 45: 151–6.

Thomson, J.J. (1971) A defense of abortion. *Philosophy and Public Affairs* 1: 47–66.
Toibin, Colm (2002) *Love in A Dark Time*. London: Picador.
Tolkien. J.R.R. (1955) *The Return of the King*. Boston, MA: Houghton Mifflin.
Tolkien, J.R.R. (2013) *The Hobbit, or There and Back Again*. New York, NY: Harper Collins. First published 1937.
Tolstoy, Leo (1995) *Anna Karenina*. Oxford: Oxford World Classics. First published 1873.
Van Inwagen, Peter (1998) Modal epistemology. *Philosophical Studies* 92(1/2): 67–84.
Van Leeuwen, Neil (2011) Imagination is where the action is. *Journal of Philosophy* 108(2): 55–77.
Van Leeuwen, Neil (2013) The meanings of 'imagine' Part One: constructive imagination. *Philosophy Compass* 8(3): 220–30.
Velleman, J. David (2000) *The Possibility of Practical Reason*. Oxford: Oxford University Press.
Velleman, J. David (2003) Narrative explanation. *Philosophical Review* 112(1): 1–25.
Vlach, Frank (1981) Speaker meaning. *Linguistics and Philosophy* 4: 359–92. http://www.theguardian.com/film/2009/feb/25/u-571-reel-history. Accessed 7 January, 2015.
Walton, Kendall (1970) Categories of Art. *Philosophical Review* 79(3): 334–67.
Walton, Kendall (1990) *Mimesis as Make-Believe*. Cambridge, MA: Harvard University Press.
Walton, Kendall (1994) Morals in fiction and fictional morality/I. *Aristotelian Society* Supp. Vol. 68: 27–50.
Waters, Sarah (2009) *The Little Stranger*. London: Virago.
Waugh, Evelyn (1942) *Put Out More Flags*. London: Penguin.
Weatherson, Brian (2004) Morality, fiction and possibility. *Philosophers' Imprint* 4(3).
Weinberg, Jonathan (2008) Configuring the cognitive imagination. In K. Stock and K. Thomson-Jones (eds.) *New Waves in Aesthetics*. London: Palgrave-Macmillan. pp. 203–23.
Weinberg, Jonathan and Meskin, Aaron (2006) Puzzling over the imagination: philosophical problems, architectural solutions. In Shaun Nichols (ed.) *The Architecture of Imagination: New Essays on Pretence, Possibility, and Fiction*. Oxford: Oxford University Press, pp. 175–202.
Weisberg, D.S. and Goodstein, J. (2009) What belongs in a fictional world? *Journal of Cognition and Culture* 9: 69–78.
White, Alan (1990) *The Language of Imagination*. Oxford: Blackwell.
Williamson, Timothy (2007) Philosophical knowledge and knowledge of counterfactuals. *Grazer Philosophische Studien* 74(1): 89–123.
Wilson, Deirdre and Sperber, Dan (2004) Relevance theory. In L.R. Horn and G. Ward (eds.) *The Handbook of Pragmatics*. Oxford: Blackwell, pp. 607–63.
Wimsatt, W. and Beardsley, M. (1946) The intentional fallacy. *The Sewanee Review* 54(3): 468–88.
Woods, Gregory (1998) *A History of Gay Literature: The Male Tradition*. New Haven, CT: Yale University Press.
Woodward, Richard (2011) Truth in fiction. *Philosophy Compass* 6(3): 158–67.
Woolf, Virginia (1951) *The Waves*. London: Penguin. First published 1931.
Woolf, Virginia (1964) *Mrs Dalloway*. London: Penguin. First published 1925.
Wright, Larry (1973) Functions. *Philosophical Review* 82(2): 139–68.
Yablo, Stephen (1993) Is conceivability a guide to possibility? *Philosophy and Phenomenological Research* 53(1): 1–42.
Yablo, Stephen (2008) Coulda, woulda, shoulda. Reprinted in S. Yablo *Thoughts: Papers on Mind, Meaning and Modality*. Oxford: Oxford University Press, pp. 103–49.

Index

Alward, Peter 68n15
anti-intentionalism 14, 52, 83

Carroll, Noel 4, 34–5, 37, 38, 83, 84, 85, 86, 90, 93, 95, 99
catastrophizing 181
conversational utterance 30–5, 38–40, 47–9
critical monism 104–6
critical pluralism 104–6
Currie, Gregory 15, 66–8, 85, 92–5, 105, 153–5, 157, 167, 177–8
Currie, Gregory and Ravenscroft, Ian 176

Davies, David 15, 61, 155–6, 157
Davies, Stephen 95, 96–7, 99–100
Deutsch, Harry 156–7, 160

experiential imagining, *see* imagining, sensory
explanatory theory, an 6–7, 13
extreme intentionalism
 four challenges to 37
 and implied fictional truths 58–63
 and intended readership 29–30
 introduced 1, 13–15
 and 'layers' of meaning 104–6
 and miswriting 43–4, 85–6, 90–2, 94–5
 and post hoc meanings 101–4
 specified 30, 66, 172
 and 'unsuccessful' intentions 82–6, 88–95
 versus value-maximizing approaches 96–101

F-imagining, *see* imagining
fantasizing 60, 181
fiction
 concept of 5
 contrasted with fictional work 150
 and counterfactuals 49–58, 123–36, 159–60
 fiction within 170–1, 173–4
 images which are 150–2
 and its relation to truth and belief 153–8
 'multiple' 169–74
 nature of 145–74
 reliability of facts in 114–21
 specified 149
 as subject to genre conventions 68–74
 treated as a fictional conversation 66–8
 treated as genre 163–7
 treated as indistinguishable from non-fiction 167–9
 treated as normatively constituted 161–3

fictional content, *see* fictional truth
fictional truth
 and authorial purposes 76–81
 differentiated from other phenomena 3
 and hidden meaning 74–81
 implied 46–74
 introduced 1, 14, 40–3
 and its relation to sentence meaning 40–3, 45–6
 and ontology 61–3
 and ordinary conversation 47–9, 67–8
 the role of imagining in understanding 35–7
 and 'silly questions' 54–5, 58
 and symbols 53–4, 60, 78–9
 treated as a counterfactual 49–8, 59–61
Fiocco, Marcello 192–8, 202
Friend, Stacie 115–21, 149, 154, 158, 159–60, 163–7

Garcia-Carpintero, Manuel 158, 161–3
Gaskin, Richard 46n1
Gendler, Tamar Szabó 122, 125, 126, 133, 134, 137–40, 198, 203
genre 68–74
Grice, H.P. 19, 30–4, 38–9, 136–7, 150

Huddleston, Andrew 35
hypothetical intentionalism 92–6, 106–12

imagination
 the concept of 4–5, 8
imagining
 F-imagining 20–9, 35–7
 objectual 24–7
 phenomenal 24
 propositional, *see* propositional imagining
 sensory 23–4, 26
imaginative resistance 121–44
intention 15–18, 39
 reflexive 18–20

Kung, Peter 141, 142, 143, 192–8

Lamarque, Peter 53, 106
Lamarque, Peter and Olsen, Stein 59–60, 155–6, 157
Langland-Hassan, Peter 182–7
Levinson, Jerrold 79, 85, 92–4, 95, 97, 105
Lewis, David 50–8, 177–8
Livingston, Paisley 14, 83, 84

Mahtani, Anna 124
Matravers, Derek 27, 148, 159, 167–9
moderate actual intentionalism, *see* modest actual intentionalism
modest actual intentionalism 14, 83–5

Nanay, Bence 136–7
Nichols, Shaun 176
non-fiction 158–61

objectual imagining, *see* imagining

partial actual intentionalism, *see* modest actual intentionalism
Phillips, John 58, 67
propositional imagining 21–4
   and belief 20–1, 187–91
   and one's belief set 145–8
   and cognitive architecture 182–7
   contrasted with phenomenal imagining 24–7
   contrasted with sensory imagining 23–7
   and counterfactuals 127–36, 175–82, 184–7, 191–8
   and intention 182–7
   is potentially conjunctive 27–8, 190–1
   is 'quasi-factual' 22–3
   need have no rich phenomenology 26–7
   and possibility 140–4, 191–8
   and supposition 198–207
   whether is 'belief-like' 176–91
   whether is unconstrained 191–8

Schwitzgebel, Eric 147–8, 189
Shakespeare's *Hamlet* 102–4
Stecker, Robert 14, 40, 43, 80, 83, 84, 86, 104
Stich, Stephen and Nichols, Shaun 177, 182
stock characters 72–3
Strawson, P.F. 8, 40, 43
supposition, *see* propositional imagining, and supposition

testimony
   in fiction 107–8, 109–12, 114–21
   and hypothetical intentionalism 106–12
   theories of 108–9
   and value-maximizing theory 106–12

unreliable narration 63–6, 171–3

value-maximizing theory 96–101, 106–12
Van Leeuwen, Neil 62–3, 68–70, 176, 179, 185
Velleman, David 23, 188

Walton, Kendall 51, 53, 54, 62, 63, 70, 73, 124, 135, 148–9, 152–3
Weatherson, Brian 121, 122, 123, 124, 131, 133, 139, 198
Weinberg, Jonathan and Meskin, Aaron 176, 178, 182, 198, 202
White, Alan 199–200, 202

Yablo, Stephen 24–5, 124, 133, 140, 142, 191–2

The manufacturer's authorised representative in the EU for product safety is
Oxford University Press España S.A. of el Parque Empresarial San Fernando de
Henares, Avenida de Castilla, 2 – 28830 Madrid (www.oup.es/en or product.
safety@oup.com). OUP España S.A. also acts as importer into Spain of products
made by the manufacturer.

www.ingramcontent.com/pod-product-compliance
Lightning Source LLC
LaVergne TN
LVHW010340260326
834688LV00036B/802